BOY DADS ONLY!

BECOMING EMOTIONALLY INTELLIGENT, STRONG, AND SECURE THROUGH FATHER-SON RELATIONSHIPS FOR NEW DADS AND THE EXPECTANT FATHERS

ALEX GRACE

INFINITE PUBLISHING

Copyright © 2024 by Alex Grace

All rights reserved.

No part of this book may be reproduced in any form or by any electronic or mechanical means, including information storage and retrieval systems, without written permission from the author, except for the use of brief quotations in a book review.

The content contained within this book may not be reproduced, duplicated, or transmitted without direct written permission from the author or the publisher.

Under no circumstances will any blame or legal responsibility be held against the publisher, or author, for any damages, reparation, or monetary loss due to the information contained within this book, either directly or indirectly.

Legal Notice:

This book is copyright protected. It is only for personal use. You cannot amend, distribute, sell, use, quote, or paraphrase any part, or the content within this book, without the consent of the author or publisher.

Disclaimer Notice:

Please note the information contained within this document is for educational and entertainment purposes only. All effort has been executed to present accurate, up-todate, reliable, complete information. No warranties of any kind are declared or implied. Readers acknowledge that the author is not engaged in the rendering of legal, financial, medical, or professional advice. The content within this book has been derived from various sources. Please consult a licensed professional before attempting any techniques outlined in this book.

By reading this document, the reader agrees that under no circumstances is the author responsible for any losses, direct or indirect, that are incurred as a result of the use of the information contained within this document, including, but not limited to, errors, omissions, or inaccuracies.

CONTENTS

Introduction   v

Chapter 1   1
Laying The Pavement of Fatherhood

Chapter 2   19
The Swiss Army Knife for All Things Feelings

Chapter 3   35
Healthy Masculinity And Why Real Men Do Cry

Chapter 4   47
Practical Parenting Strategies

Chapter 5   68
Navigating the Digital Age

Chapter 6   87
Maximizing Health and Wellness For Dads and Sons

Chapter 7   106
Fostering Lifelong Learning and Growth

Chapter 8   124
Planning Father-Son Escapades

Conclusion   143

References   149

INTRODUCTION

"My father gave me the greatest gift anyone could give another person, he believed in me." - Jim Valvano

Picture this: It's a crisp autumn afternoon, the kind where the leaves crunch under your feet, and I'm in our backyard in Portland, Oregon, tossing a football with my son. Nothing extraordinary, just a dad and his boy playing catch. Then it happens—he makes a perfect catch, and his face lights up like a Christmas tree. It hit me like a ton of bricks at that moment: these simple interactions are the building blocks of our kids' futures.

Welcome to "For The Boy Dads!" This isn't just another parenting book; it's more like a playbook for the greatest game you'll ever play —fatherhood. Think of it as your guide to being the MVP in your son's life, whether you're a dad, grandpa, or just about to become one.

Now, let me tell you a bit about myself. I'm a DADpreneur. Yeah, you heard that right—part dad, part entrepreneur, all heart. My journey from being just a guy tossing a football to writing this book is filled with moments that are funny, challenging, and downright heartwarming. And trust me, I've learned a thing or two along the way that I can't wait to share with you.

In this book, we'll dive into stories that are a lot like those late-night chats over a cold beer. We'll cover everything from decoding the mystery of teenage grunts to navigating the wild world of social media. Each chapter is packed with tips you can use right away, kind of like that friend who always has the best life hacks.

Remember the first time you tried to assemble a piece of furniture without instructions? Yeah, parenting can feel like that. But don't worry, this book is your instruction manual, written in a language we all understand—no confusing diagrams, just straightforward advice.

The father-son bond is one of the most amazing and, let's be honest, sometimes baffling relationships out there. We're expected to be involved in ways our own dads probably never were, and that's a good thing. But it also means we need a new set of tools to get the job done. This book is here to load up your toolbox with practical advice, fun exercises, and expert insights to help you build a rock-solid relationship with your son.

So, get ready. We're going to share laughs, face challenges, and celebrate victories together. Whether you're patching up a rocky relationship or starting fresh, the stories and strategies here are designed to make a real difference.

Let's embark on this adventure with the excitement of a kid on the first day of summer. The reward? A deeper, more meaningful connection with your son that will last a lifetime. So, grab your coffee (or your Kombucha if you're into that), sit back, and let's dive in. We're going to rock this dad thing together!

INTRODUCTION

BONUS

Hi there new Boy Dad! As you begin this exciting adventure, I understand that there are many questions and uncertainties that will arise, especially when it comes to conversations and building rapport with your son.

So before we get started on this journey together, I wanted to make you something as a "thank you" for purchasing this book. You might notice that this is a theme in all of my books, so don't be surprised if you find more gems sprinkled throughout the chapters ahead.

This 5 step guide is completely free and I created it just for you.

In this comprehensive guide you'll find practical advice and valuable tips that will be here to help you open up essential conversations, strengthen your bond, and support your son's emotional growth.

Here's a sneak peak into what you'll discover in this guide:

Expressing Emotions: Learn to talk about feelings

Handling Disappointment: Strategies for dealing with setbacks

Celebrating Success: Acknowledging and sharing joy

Dealing with Peer Pressure: Staying true to oneself

The Importance of Empathy: Understanding others' feelings

Simply **scan the QR code below** to unlock your free copy of **"The 5 Essential Conversations for Boy Dads"** and start embracing boy dad fatherhood.

Now, you ready to dive in?

CHAPTER 1
LAYING THE PAVEMENT OF FATHERHOOD

A h, fatherhood! Remember when your biggest worry was whether to binge-watch your favorite series or head out for a night on the town? Those carefree days might take a backseat, or perhaps more suitably put, a "baby seat," but for an incredible reason. Becoming a dad isn't just about changing diapers or mastering the perfect swaddle—it's about transforming into a guide, protector, and the main guy a new little human being looks up to.

1.1 EMBRACING YOUR ROLE WITH CONFIDENCE: TRANSITIONING INTO FATHERHOOD

Let's talk about the seismic shift that happens when you go from being 'just you' to being someone's dad. It's like being handed the keys to the world's most unpredictable theme park. And just like any first-time visitor, it's natural to feel a bit, well, lost.

The psychological transition from man to father is profound. Suddenly, you're not just responsible for yourself but for a tiny human who thinks you're their superhero. This change can rattle your identity more than you might expect.

Before I became a dad and before I met my beautiful wifey, my weekends were all about motorcycle trips, spontaneous rock concerts, and enjoying the feeling of the wind blowing through my hair. I lived for the thrill of the open road and the electric buzz of live music. But then, I met my now-life partner, and one thing led to another: fatherhood hit, and I found myself trading in my favorite leather jacket for a baby carrier and concert tickets for bedtime stories. I remember the first time I successfully changed a diaper without creating a disaster—trust me, it felt like winning a championship game. And let's not even talk about the first time I got our baby to sleep through the night; it was like finding the Holy Grail.

These days, my adventures are different. I used to spend my weekends watching soccer with the guys, chowing down a couple of large pizzas, and sinking some beers. Now, they tend to involve building pillow forts, playing peekaboo, and trying to convince a toddler that broccoli is, in fact, delicious. It's a whole new kind of thrill, and it's brought a sense of purpose and satisfaction I never knew was possible. I wouldn't trade it for the world.

Setting realistic expectations is crucial. TV and movies portray parenting as a series of heartwarming moments with perfectly behaved children. Let's bust that myth right now. Real fatherhood involves messy mistakes and learning on the go. It's okay not to have all the answers. What's important is showing up and doing your best. Expect the following:

- Sleepless nights
- Inexplicable baby meltdowns
- The chaos of toddler life
- The whirlwind of school days

Though these challenges sound scary and uncomfortable, each phase also comes with its own set of joys.

No dad is an island, and building a support network is essential. Connect with other fathers—trust me, they're going through or have gone through what you're experiencing, and they can offer invaluable support and advice. Whether it's through community groups or online forums, sharing your fears, successes, and dad hacks can make the journey smoother. Remember, vulnerability among fellow dads isn't a sign of weakness; it's a badge of strength.

Maintaining self-care isn't just a nice-to-have; it's a must-have. Fatherhood is a marathon, not a sprint; you must keep your tank full to be there for the long haul. Find time for the gym, grab that coffee with a friend, dive into a new book, or meditate for a few minutes each day. These little breaks aren't selfish—they're essential. They help you recharge and give you the space to be a more present and patient father.

Reflective Pause

Take a moment now to jot down some personal goals that aren't about being a dad. How can you integrate these into your weekly routine to ensure you're caring for yourself as you care for your little one?

Fatherhood transforms you. It challenges you. But most of all, it can fulfill you in ways you've never imagined. As you step into this role, remember that while the days are long, the years are short. Make them count.

1.2: UNDERSTANDING YOUR SON'S WORLD: INSIGHTS INTO MODERN BOYHOOD

Alright, dads, let's dive into the wild world of modern boyhood. It's a whole new ball game from when we were kids. Today's boys are growing up in a world where digital landscapes are as familiar as playgrounds are to us. Back in the day, we rode bikes until the streetlights came on, and our social interactions happened face-to-face. Today, our sons might be more inclined to engage in epic online battles than dodgeball in the backyard.

From gaming to social media, these digital arenas hold sway over our sons' lives. The key is not to shun technology but to guide our sons through this digital maze with wisdom and responsibility. For instance, while gaming often gets a bad rap, it's not all doom and gloom. Games can enhance problem-solving skills and strategic thinking. However, they also require us to set boundaries and ensure that our sons are consuming content that is age-appropriate and enriching rather than mind-numbing or, worse, toxic.

Now, tackling the beast of peer pressure, which has only intensified with the advent of social media, is another battlefield for modern dads. Our sons are exposed to the world's scrutiny 24/7, which can lead to unrealistic comparisons and expectations. Here's where instilling self-confidence comes into play. It's about reinforcing their ability to make decisions that are right for them, even when faced with a tide of opposing voices. A practical approach involves role-playing scenarios where you and your son walk through various peer pressure situations, discussing the 'what' and the 'why' behind confident choices. It's important not to simply demonize vices or habits that could be considered harmful but to gently prompt your son to consider the potential harm himself.

Here are five different role-playing scenarios to try with your son:

- **Peer Pressure to Try Smoking or Vaping:** You play the friend offering a cigarette or vape, and he practices saying no and explaining why it's not a good idea.
- **Handling Cyberbullying:** You act as an online bully sending mean messages, and he practices responding appropriately or seeking help from an adult.
- **Dealing with Academic Dishonesty:** You pretend to be a classmate asking him to cheat on a test or homework, and

he practices refusing and explaining the importance of honesty.
- **Resisting the Pressure to Engage in Pranks or Vandalism:** You take on the role of a friend, encouraging him to participate in a harmful prank or an act of vandalism, and he practices refusing and discussing better alternatives.
- **Managing Conflict with Friends:** You act as a friend who's upset and starting an argument, and he practices using calm communication and problem-solving to resolve the conflict.

Encouraging healthy hobbies and interests forms the cornerstone of well-rounded development. Whether your son is drawn to the soccer field, the science lab, or the art studio, active participation is key. There is profound value and insight to be discovered through the struggle of learning a new skill, and the lessons learned here will be valuable in other areas of your son's life. It's not just about signing them up and cheering from the sidelines; it's about engagement. If he's into painting, grab a brush and join him. If coding is his passion, take a basic programming class together. This shared journey doesn't just bolster his skills; it strengthens your bond. Plus, it shows him that his interests are valuable and worth investing in, setting a foundation for lifelong learning and curiosity.

Navigating modern boyhood as a dad today means being both a guide and a fellow explorer in the evolving landscape of childhood. By understanding the generational shifts, responsibly integrating technology, teaching resilience against peer pressure, and nurturing diverse interests, we lay down the tracks for our sons to thrive in a world that looks very different from the one we knew. Let's ensure these tracks are solid and well-fortified, leading them confidently into the future.

Story Time: Bridging the Digital Divide

One Saturday morning, I found myself in the unfamiliar territory of a Fortnite battleground. My son had been raving about this game for weeks, and his enthusiasm was contagious. So, I decided to dive in. Little did I know, I was about to get schooled by a ten-year-old.

The first few rounds were a disaster. I was more of a liability than a teammate. But my son, with the patience of a seasoned gamer, guided me through the basics. He explained the importance of strategy, the thrill of victory, and even the disappointment of defeat. This wasn't just a game to him—it was a world where he could showcase his skills and creativity.

As we played, I realized something profound: this digital playground was just as valid and vital as the physical ones of my childhood. My son's world wasn't less meaningful than mine just because it was different; it was simply evolving with the times. We spent the afternoon strategizing, laughing at my mistakes, and celebrating our small victories. It was a bonding experience that went beyond the screen.

This shared experience taught me to appreciate and understand his digital interests better. I saw the potential for critical thinking, teamwork, and resilience. More importantly, I saw an opportunity to connect with him on his terms and in his world. By embracing and participating in his interests, I was able to bridge the gap between our generations, fostering a deeper connection and a newfound respect for the digital landscape he inhabits.

So, dive in, whether it's Fortnite, coding, or any other modern interest your son may have. Engage with him. It's not about mastering the game; it's about mastering the art of connection. And trust me, even if you're terrible at the game, the effort will score you major dad points.

1.3 THE ART OF COMMUNICATION: YOUR OWN FRIDAY NIGHT CATCH-UP

Navigating the waves of fatherhood inevitably brings us to the shores of communication—a skill that, believe it or not, does more than just get us through dinner without a food fight. Mastering age-appropriate communication is like picking the right tool for the job. You wouldn't use a sledgehammer to crack a nut, right? Similarly, chatting with a toddler about his day requires a different approach than discussing school with your teenager. For the little ones, it's all about simplicity and patience. Open-ended questions are your best friends here. Instead of asking yes-or-no questions like "Did you have fun today?" try "What was the best part of your day?" It's like magic; suddenly, you have a chatterbox on your hands, spilling all the beans about his day.

I remember when my son was just a little tyke, about four years old. Every evening, I'd ask, "What was the best part of your day?" And boy, the stories he'd come up with! From imaginary dragon battles to discovering a shiny rock in the playground, it was like opening a treasure chest in his mind. Each answer was a glimpse into his world, filled with wonder and excitement.

As your son grows, your communication style needs to evolve. For teens, it's more about reading between the lines and understanding that sometimes, "I'm fine" might not mean they're fine. This is where active listening comes into play. It's about giving your full attention, nodding along, and throwing in an occasional "Tell me more about that" to show you're engaged. It's not just about the words; it's the silence between the pauses where they're gathering their thoughts or mustering the courage to share more. This skill helps in decoding those heavy sighs at the dinner table or the eye rolls that could rival any world-class performance.

When my son hit his teenage years, "I'm fine" became his favorite phrase. It was like pulling teeth, trying to get more out of him. So, I started paying attention to the little things—his body language, the way he slumped in his chair, or the frustrated way he tossed his backpack. One evening, after a particularly heavy sigh, I just said, "Looks like something's on your mind. Want to talk about it?" That simple prompt opened the floodgates to a conversation about his struggles with a school project.

Now, let's touch on those tough topics—bullying, failure, emotional distress. These are not your run-of-the-mill conversations where advice like "Just shake it off, buddy!" will do. Here, empathy and tactfulness take center stage. Imagine your son comes home, shoulders slumped, more silent than usual. You find out he's been bullied. Knee-jerk reactions might range from outrage to plotting a parent-teacher conference showdown. But first, get down to his level and say, "That sounds really tough; I'm here for you. Want to talk about what happened?" It's about creating a safe space where vulnerability is not just accepted but welcomed.

When my son faced bullying, my first instinct was to march into the school and raise hell. But I knew he needed to feel safe and heard first. So, I sat with him, put my arm around his shoulders, and listened. No judgment, no interruptions. I just listened. It was one of the hardest but most rewarding conversations we ever had.

Role-playing can be a fantastic way to prepare for these discussions. Practice different scenarios where you respond to his concerns, which can make the actual conversation more intuitive and less daunting. Here are a few examples:

- **Peer Pressure:** Pretend to be a friend offering him something he knows he shouldn't try. Help him practice saying no and explaining why it's not for him.
- **Cyberbullying:** Act out a scenario where someone is sending him mean messages online. Discuss how to respond and how to seek help from an adult.

- **School Stress:** Role-play a situation where he's overwhelmed by homework or a project. Help him think through how to tackle it step-by-step.
- **Conflict Resolution:** Simulate a disagreement with a friend—practice using calm communication to resolve it.
- **Failure and Resilience:** Discuss a scenario where he didn't make the team or got a bad grade. Talk about how to handle disappointment and keep trying.

Creating an open environment ties all these threads together. It's about fostering a space where no topic is off-limits and no question is too trivial. Regular check-ins can help immensely. Maybe establish a ritual, like a weekly walk or a special dinner, where the focus is on catching up on each other's lives. These moments can lay the groundwork for tough conversations, making them less about confrontational sit-downs and more about regular chat sessions.

I started a tradition with my son called "Friday Night Catch-Up." Every Friday, we'd grab some snacks and just talk—no agenda, no pressure. Sometimes, we'd laugh about funny things that happened during the week, and other times, we'd dive into deeper issues. It became our sacred time, a ritual that kept us connected through all the ups and downs.

Remember, effective communication isn't about having the perfect response or solving every problem. It's about showing up, being present, and opening up the channels that let your son know, "Hey, I'm here, and I'm listening." Whether it's pondering over dinosaurs or dealing with heartbreaks, how you communicate can shape your relationship more than anything else. So, keep those lines open, stay flexible in your approach, and watch conversations with your son deepen into dialogues that enrich your father-son bond for years to come.

1.4 SETTING THE EMOTIONAL TONE: HOW TO BE AN APPROACHABLE DAD

Have you ever watched a movie where the dad character is so stoic that you wonder if he's auditioning for a spot as a royal guard? Well, let's toss that script out. Being an approachable dad starts with showing your emotions and and letting your son know it's perfectly fine for guys to express how they feel. It's about breaking down those tough-guy stereotypes and showing up as human—laughs, tears, frustrations, and all. It's letting your son know that while many boys and men like to joke around with their pals, watch the football, and goof about, we all have a side to us which is more tender and vulnerable and that this side of us requires our acknowledgement and consideration if we are to be happy. Remember, emotional intelligence isn't just about handling your emotions; it's about understanding and managing them in ways that teach your son to do the same.

I remember a time when I came home from a particularly rough day at work. Instead of bottling it up, I said to my son, "Dad's had a tough day and feels a bit on edge. Let's chill with a funny movie to lighten things up." We ended up watching one of his favorite comedies, and by the end, we were laughing and feeling much better. It's simple but powerful, showing him that acknowledging feelings is the first step to dealing with them effectively.

Building trust through consistency is like setting the tempo in music; it creates a rhythm that your son can rely on. It's about being the dad who says he'll be at the soccer game and is there, cheering from the sidelines, come rain or shine. This reliability in your actions and emotions lays a foundation of trust that teaches your son security and stability. It tells him, "You can count on me," which, is a priceless reassurance in a world full of uncertainties. It's about the small promises—like being there for dinner or keeping to weekend plans—that accumulate into a trust fund of sorts, one that supports him in feeling secure, not just physically but emotionally too.

Now, let's talk about respect. It's a two-way street that is crucial in any relationship, especially between you and your son. Respecting your son means listening to his opinions, giving him space to grow, and acknowledging his boundaries. This could mean understanding his need for privacy as he grows older or appreciating his views even when they differ from yours. It's about affirming his right to his own feelings, thoughts, and experiences. For example, if he's not into football like you were at his age, that's okay. Maybe he's more of a chess enthusiast or a budding artist. Encouraging his interests, even when they're not what you expected, shows respect for the person he's becoming, not just the son you imagined.

Positive reinforcement over criticism is about focusing on what your son is doing right, not just correcting what he's doing wrong. It's the high fives after he clears his plates from the table, the proud nod when he shares his toys during playdates, or the encouragement when he tries something new, even if he doesn't quite succeed. This approach boosts his self-esteem and makes him more likely to repeat those good behaviors. It's like watering the plants in your garden; give them enough sunlight, water, and love, and they'll thrive. Every positive word is a sunbeam, encouraging your son to grow strong and confident.

Here are some practical ways to set a positive emotional tone:

- **Show Vulnerability:** Share your own feelings and challenges with your son. It helps him understand that it's okay to express emotions.
- **Be Consistent:** Keep promises, show up when you say you will, and be a steady presence in his life.
- **Respect His Individuality:** Support his interests, even if they're different from your own. Show him that you value his unique personality.

- **Use Positive Reinforcement:** Focus on what he does well and celebrate his successes, no matter how small.

In embracing these approaches, you set an emotional tone in your home that is warm, secure, and nurturing. It creates an environment where your son knows that home is not just where he lives but where he is understood and accepted. By being open-minded with your emotions, consistent in your actions, respectful of his individuality, and generous with your encouragement, you're not just raising a son; you're nurturing a future man who values emotional intelligence, trusts deeply, respects others, and understands the power of positivity. And in the grand scheme of things, that's a legacy worth leaving.

One of our family traditions is the "Sunday Check-In." Every Sunday evening, we sit down as a family and share one thing that made us happy, one that was challenging, and one that we're looking forward to in the week ahead. It's a simple routine, but it opens up a line of communication and keeps us connected. It's amazing how this small practice has brought us closer and helped us understand each other better.

Setting the emotional tone isn't a one-time task—it's an ongoing effort. But the rewards are immense. You'll see your child grow into a young man who is comfortable with his emotions, confident in his relationships, and equipped to handle life's ups and downs with grace and resilience. And that, my friends, is worth every moment of effort.

1.5 YOUR SECRET WEAPON: LOVE, LAUGHTER, AND LOTS OF DAD HUGS

Let's face it: the days of the stoic, unemotional dad are as outdated as dial-up internet. Today's dads know the power of a hug, the magic of a high-five, and the strength found in those three little words: "I love you." Understanding the profound impact of physical touch is crucial for developing a strong, emotionally secure relationship with your son. A simple pat on the back, a comforting hug, or a playful tousle of the hair can often convey your love and support more than words ever could.t. These gestures, small as they may seem, help build a foundation of trust and safety, which are crucial elements in a healthily developing mind.

I remember when my son had a particularly rough day at school. He came home looking dejected, his backpack slung over one shoulder like a sack of worries. Without saying a word, I pulled him into a firm, reassuring hug. It was like flipping a switch. That physical reassurance helped melt away the stress and anxiety, letting him know, without words, that he wasn't alone.

But let's remember the power of words in showing affection. Verbal affirmations are your verbal high-fives; they boost self-esteem and reinforce the security your physical presence brings. It's about catching your son doing something right and celebrating it. "Hey buddy, I noticed you shared your toys with your friend today—that was really cool of you!" or "I love how you helped set the table without being asked, that's being a great team player!" These phrases do more than acknowledge good behavior; they celebrate character traits you want to encourage—generosity, initiative, and teamwork. This kind of language nurtures an environment where your son knows his actions are noticed and appreciated, which is incredibly empowering for a child. It's about giving him the verbal tools to understand his worth and build a strong sense of self.

Practical Ways to Show Verbal Affection:

- **Positive Reinforcement:** "Great job on your homework tonight; I'm proud of you!"
- **Acknowledging Effort:** "I saw how hard you worked on that project; it's amazing!"
- **Expressing Love:** "I love you to the moon and back, buddy."

If affection is a language, then quality time is the conversation. It's about those moments when the world slows down just enough for you to explore it together. Whether it's building a model airplane, cooking a meal, or just walking the dog, it's the togetherness that counts. These activities become shared adventures and stories in the great book of 'Us'. During these times, your son learns more than just how to mix ingredients or throw a ball; he learns about who you are and in turn, who he is becoming. He sees how you handle challenges, how you celebrate successes, and how you navigate the world. Each activity, each shared moment, is an investment in his future, showing him that he is valued and loved, not for what he achieves, but for who he is.

One of our favorite traditions is "Saturday Morning Pancakes." Every Saturday, my son and I whip up a batch of pancakes, experimenting with different recipes and toppings. It's our special time to bond, laugh at our kitchen mishaps, and talk about anything and everything. Those Saturday mornings have become a cornerstone of our relationship, a time when we both look forward to connecting and creating memories.

Ideas for Quality Time Activities:

- **Cooking Together:** Try new recipes and let your son take the lead on some steps.
- **Outdoor Adventures:** Go for hikes, bike rides, or simple walks around the neighborhood.
- **Game Nights:** Board games, video games, or even card games can be great fun and a way to bond.

Understanding and adapting to your son's individual need for affection completes this circle of support. Each child is unique—some may relish long bear hugs, while others might prefer a quick pat on the back or a thumbs-up. As fathers, it's our job to read these cues and respond in ways that resonate with their personality. As they grow, their needs change, and staying attuned to these shifts is crucial. It's like being a detective in your own home, always on the lookout for clues on how best to support your son's emotional language. Maybe your teenage son isn't into bear hugs anymore, but that fist bump as he heads to school might make his day.

Tips for Reading Your Son's Cues:

- **Observe Body Language:** Notice how he responds to different types of physical affection.
- **Ask Directly:** Sometimes, simply asking what he prefers can give you the insight you need.
- **Be Flexible:** Adapt your approach as he grows and his preferences change.

The art of fatherly affection, through touch, through words, and through quality time, is about building a bridge to your son's heart. It's about creating a bond that holds firm through the storms of life, a bond that supports and empowers. It's about being there, physically and emotionally, in ways that tell your son, "No matter what happens, you've got me, and I've got you."

1.6 CHEF DAD: SEASONING DISCIPLINE JUST RIGHT

Navigating the tightrope of discipline and understanding with your son is like being a skilled chef—too little salt and your dish is bland; too much and it's inedible. Striking that perfect balance is key, and it starts with setting clear, fair, and age-appropriate rules. Think of these rules not as restrictions but as clear guidelines that help your son understand the world around him. For instance, a rule as simple as "toys need to be put away after play" teaches organization and respect for belongings. Consistency in enforcing these rules does the magic of creating a secure and predictable environment. It's about being the same dad who praises the effort of tidying up, whether it's a Monday evening or Saturday morning. This consistency isn't just about discipline; it's about creating a reliable framework within which your son can explore, learn, and mess up, knowing that the safety net (that's you!) is always there, firm, and steady.

I remember when my son left his bike out in the rain one too many times. Instead of giving him a lecture, I set a simple rule: "Bikes need to be stored in the garage every night." The first few nights, he forgot, and I gently reminded him. By the end of the week, it became second nature. Now, our bike stays dry, and he's learned a little bit about responsibility.

Now, let's dial up the empathy in discipline. It's easy to cross arms and declare a rule, but understanding why a rule is broken is where true parenting prowess shines. Let's say your son has broken a curfew. Instead of the usual suspects—grounding or losing privileges—a sit-down to unearth the 'why' can be more enlightening. Maybe he lost track of time or felt peer pressure to stay out late. This is where empathetic listening comes into play. It's about hearing his side of the story, validating his feelings, and then guiding him back to the why behind the rule. It turns a moment of discipline into a teachable moment about responsibility and the importance of making safe and effective choices. This approach doesn't just solve the immediate problem; it builds a toolkit for your son to use in future decision-making scenarios.

One evening, my son came home late, well past his curfew. Instead of launching into a tirade, I asked him to sit with me. Over a cup of hot cocoa, he shared that he lost track of time while helping a friend. We talked about the importance of communication and keeping track of time. That night, instead of a punishment, he got a lesson in responsibility and trust.

Exploring alternative discipline techniques can transform your home dynamics in ways that traditional 'time-out' methods may not. Natural consequences are a fantastic teacher. Say your son forgets his lunch in his rush to beat the school bus; rushing it to school might seem like the immediate fix, but letting him handle the natural consequence of skipping a meal or borrowing from a friend can be a more enduring lesson in responsibility. Then there are problem-solving discussions—these are golden. They shift the focus from what he's done wrong to how he can make it right, creating a more constructive narrative rather than one of punishment. It's collaborative instead of confrontational. For example, if he's spilled paint on the carpet, discuss ideas on how to clean it up and how to prevent future accidents from occurring. This method solves the issue and empowers him with problem-solving skills and the understanding that mistakes are fixable, not fatal. In reality, life is full of mistakes and it's all about how you respond to them.

Alternative Discipline Techniques:

- **Natural Consequences:** If he forgets his lunch, let him find a solution.
- **Problem-Solving Discussions:** Work together to clean up messes and prevent future ones.
- **Collaborative Rule-Making:** Involve him in setting rules so he understands their importance.

Maintaining a positive focus is like watering the plants—you nurture the good and watch it grow. Focusing on positive behaviors means catching your son doing something right and shining a spotlight on it. It could be as simple as acknowledging when he shares with his sibling or when he does his homework without being reminded. This positive reinforcement makes him more likely to repeat those behaviors, knowing they are appreciated. It's about building an environment where positive actions are recognized and celebrated, making them more desirable than negative ones. This doesn't mean ignoring wrong actions but balancing corrections with a heavy dose of affirmation, ensuring that your son knows he is loved and valued, not for his perfection, but his effort and willingness to learn from mistakes. While you might gently let your son know that it's not healthy to play his favorite video game for several hours without stopping (even if you want to join him) it's equally important to show encouragement by celebrating his adventurism when he decides to try a new class at school, or attempts to learn how to ride a skateboard.

I started a "Caught You Being Good" jar. Whenever I noticed my son doing something positive, I'd write it down and put it in the jar. We'd read through them at the end of the week and celebrate with a small treat. It became a fun and effective way to encourage good behavior. One week, he was particularly helpful around the house, so on Sunday evening, we sat down and pulled out all the notes. "You helped set the table without being asked," I read one. "You shared your toys with your sister," said another. Each note brought a big smile to his face. We made it a tradition to choose a special activity as a reward—sometimes it was a trip to the ice cream parlor, other times a movie night with his favorite film. It was amazing to see how much this little jar motivated him to keep up the good work. Plus, it gave us a reason to celebrate the positive things he did, reinforcing the behaviors I wanted to see more of.

Practical Ways to Show Verbal Affection:

- **Positive Reinforcement:** "Great job on your homework tonight; I'm proud of you!"
- **Acknowledging Effort:** "I saw how hard you worked on that project; it's amazing!"
- **Expressing Love:** "I love you to the moon and back, buddy."

As corny as this might feel at first, think about how you best function when someone is giving you positive feedback.

CHAPTER 2
THE SWISS ARMY KNIFE FOR ALL THINGS FEELINGS

You're knee-deep in what can only be described as a toy apocalypse, and your son is on the brink of a meltdown, and you? You're about to lose your cool because, let's face it, stepping on a Lego piece is the adult version of a booby trap. But then, you remember, this moment isn't just about surviving the chaos; it's a golden opportunity to teach, learn, and grow together. Welcome to the wild world of Emotional Intelligence (EI), where navigating feelings isn't just for superheroes in capes – it's dad territory, too.

2.1 EMOTIONAL IQ: WHAT THE HECK IS IT AND HOW TO TURN IT INTO DAD'S SECRET WEAPON"

Defining Emotional Intelligence (EI)

So, what exactly is Emotional Intelligence? Think of it as the Swiss Army knife for handling all things emotional. It's your go-to tool for understanding, using, and managing not just your emotions but those of others around you – especially your mini-me. EI is composed of five powerful skills that can turn you from a good dad into a great one: self-awareness, self-regulation, motivation, empathy, and social skills.

- **Self-awareness:** This is about knowing your own emotional state. Are you angry? Stressed? Overjoyed? Recognizing these emotions is step one in handling them like a pro.
- **Self-regulation:** It involves controlling your emotions. It's the difference between snapping when you step on that Lego and taking a deep breath to model calm behavior.
- **Motivation:** This is your drive to achieve goals, not just for personal gains but for the well-being of your family.
- **Empathy:** Understanding your son's feelings. It's seeing the world through his eyes and letting him know it's okay to have big feelings.
- **Social skills:** These help you navigate interactions effectively. From playdates to parent-teacher meetings, these skills ensure you're both heard and understood.

Importance of EI in Fatherhood

Now, why should you, as a dad, care about beefing up your EI? Because it's a game changer in how you connect with your son. Don't skip this part. Emotional intelligence allows you to understand what your son is feeling, which bridges communication gaps and deepens your relationship. It helps you lead by example; showing your son how to handle emotions effectively teaches him to do the same. And let's be honest, parenting throws curveballs. High EI equips you to catch them without losing your cool. It's about being the dad who can navigate both his toddler's tantrums and his teenager's mood swings with grace.

I remember a day my son came home from school, clearly upset. Instead of diving straight into "What happened?" I tried a different approach. I sat beside him, offered a snack, and simply said, "I'm here when you're ready to talk." After a few minutes, he opened up about a rough day with a friend. That small act of patience and empathy turned what could have been a grumpy evening into a bonding moment.

EI as a Learned Skill

If you're sitting there thinking, "But Alex, I'm not an emotional guru," here's some good news – emotional intelligence isn't a 'you have it or you don't' kind of deal. It's a skill, and like all skills, it can be honed. Think of it like leveling up in a video game. The more you practice, the better you get. Whether you're starting with a solid base or from scratch, every dad can improve his EI with effort and intention.

Assessing Personal EI

So, how do you start this journey? First, assess where you stand. Take a moment to reflect on each of the five EI skills. Maybe you're a champ at motivation but could use a boost in empathy. Recognizing your strengths and areas for improvement is like setting the GPS before you hit the road—it gives you a clear direction.

Reflection Exercise

Grab a journal or open a new note on your phone and jot down thoughts on your EI strengths and areas for improvement. Ask yourself:

- When was the last time I effectively managed my emotions during stress?
- How do I react when my son expresses strong emotions?
- Do I actively motivate myself and my son to tackle difficult tasks?
- How often do I truly put myself in my son's shoes?
- Are my social interactions mostly positive, or do they need work?

This self-assessment isn't about judging yourself – it's about setting the stage for personal growth. By understanding your emotional landscape, you're better equipped to guide your son in mapping out his own. Remember, the goal isn't perfection; it's progress. And every step forward is a step toward becoming a better dad and a more emotionally intelligent human being.

One of our favorite family traditions is the "Feelings Jar." A few times a week, we each write down one emotion we felt strongly during the day and why. Then, we share and discuss them over dinner. It's a simple activity, but it opens up so much dialogue and understanding. Plus, it's a fun way to normalize talking about feelings, creating a safe space for everyone to express themselves.

By cultivating emotional intelligence, you're not just raising a son who knows how to handle his feelings; you're shaping a future man equipped to handle life's ups and downs with resilience and empathy. Now, that's a superpower worth developing.

2.2 THE EMPATHY WORKOUT: STRENGTHENING COMPASSION MUSCLES FOR YOU AND YOUR SON

Empathy isn't just about understanding someone else's feelings; it's about stepping into their shoes, even if they're a size too small and covered in mud. As dads, showing empathy in our daily interactions, not only with our kids but everyone around us, sets a powerful example for our sons. Imagine you're at the DMV, and the line is moving slower than a snail on a lazy day or any day for that matter as snails are always slow. We've all been there. Why are those DMV lines so long? Instead of getting visibly frustrated, you choose to be polite and patient, acknowledging the DMV employee's long day. Your son observed this moment, teaching him that kindness and understanding can and should be extended to anyone in any situation.

Empathy-Building Activities

How about some empathy-building activities to bring this concept home? Reading books with diverse characters is a fantastic start. Choose stories that explore a wide range of emotions, cultures, and situations. After each reading session, spend some time discussing the story. Ask questions like, "How do you think the character felt when that happened?" or "What would you do if you were in their place?" This improves his comprehension skills and deepens his ability to empathize with others.

I remember reading "The Giving Tree" with my son. After finishing the book, we talked about the tree's feelings throughout the story. My son said, "I think the tree felt happy giving everything to the boy, but also a little sad when he didn't return for a long time." It was a touching moment that highlighted his growing ability to understand complex emotions. Yes, we talked about the tree's feelings; you read that correctly. Don't be surprised if soon you will be talking about the fish's feelings, the dog's feelings, and the ant's feelings!

Role-Playing Scenarios

Role-playing different scenarios from the books can further solidify this understanding. For instance, if a character is bullied, act out different ways to respond, emphasizing the power of empathy in resolving conflicts. This not only makes the lesson fun but also practical.

Discussing Real-World Issues

Discussing real-world issues also plays a crucial role in developing your son's empathy. Let's say you see a news story about a natural disaster. It's a perfect opportunity to talk about the emotions and struggles of those affected. Encourage him to think about what the children in those situations might feel. Questions like, "What can we do to help?" or "How would you feel if that happened here?" help him connect emotionally with people he has never met, broadening his empathetic reach. This can be extended to discussing family matters or issues at school, always steering the conversation towards understanding different perspectives and nurturing a compassionate outlook. Recently, my son overheard a conversation about a conflict that was occurring on another continent. I could see he was troubled by something, so I asked him if he was okay. He told me about the conversation he had heard and asked, ' 'why are they being mean to other people?' I didn't go into the details, but I explained to him that some leaders are not always in the right and that they sometimes treat people unfairly. Rather than avoid the conversation, I told him it had been weighing on me as well and asked him how he had felt when he heard about the situation. This is a way in which we can be more open and honest as parents, showing our sons that it's ok to talk about difficult issues and that it's not something we need to shy away from.

Providing Feedback and Encouragement

Providing feedback on your son's responses during these discussions is crucial. Suppose he expresses sadness for the victims of a disaster. Acknowledge his feelings with affirmations like, "It's really kind of you to feel for those people," and guide him on channeling those feelings into positive actions, such as writing supportive messages or helping gather supplies for relief efforts. This feedback encourages him to feel empathy and act on it, reinforcing the idea that his emotions can lead to compassionate actions.

Practical Exercises to Teach Empathy:

- **Reading and Discussing Diverse Books:** Choose stories with various emotional and cultural backgrounds.
- **Role-Playing Scenarios:** Act out different responses to situations like bullying or conflict resolution.
- **Discussing Real-World Issues:** Use news stories to explore and empathize with people's struggles.

- **Providing Feedback:** Acknowledge empathetic responses and encourage compassionate actions.

Through these daily practices and discussions, you are not just teaching your son to understand and share the feelings of others; you are helping him to build a worldview that values connection, kindness, and a deep sense of humanity. This skill set will benefit him in his immediate relationships and echo throughout his broader social interactions for years to come.

I've seen this first-hand with my son. One day, after watching a documentary about children in different parts of the world, he asked if we could send some of his toys to kids who didn't have any. We packed up a box together and sent it off, and it was one of those moments where I felt like I was doing something right as a dad. These small, everyday actions build a foundation of empathy and kindness in our children.

2.3 FROM HULK TO HUG: MANAGING KID AND DAD MELTDOWNS

Let's face it, there are days in the dad life when your patience feels like it's been put through a paper shredder. Maybe your little champ has painted the new couch instead of his coloring book, or perhaps the teen drama meter has hit a new high over who-knows-what. It's moments like these that can light the fuse on your temper. But here's the kicker: how you handle these flare-ups can teach your son valuable lessons about managing his own fiery feelings.

Identifying The Button Pushers

First things first, understanding what pushes your buttons or your son's can be a game-changer. It's like piecing together the puzzles and patterns in your own home, working out the 'whys' behind the 'grrs.' This can help you both prepare better for potential blow-ups. For you, it might be the chaos of morning routines that sets you off.

For your son, it could be a last-minute change in plans that throws him off balance. Recognizing these triggers is like mapping out where the landmines are so you can navigate more carefully.

Discuss with your son what makes both of you tick, and talk about the signs which typically indicate that anger or frustration is on the rise. Maybe your clues are clenched fists or a certain tightness in your voice. Your son might get unusually quiet or start tapping his foot rapidly. Spotting these early warnings can help intervene before the emotions boil over. A few weeks ago, I noticed my son was tapping a pen repeatedly on the kitchen surface while I was cooking. He kept doing it repeatedly, until I asked him if he was ok. It turns out he wasn't just apprehensive about my lasagna (It's not that bad!), but that he had had a particularly challenging day at school. Sometimes being receptive to these clues can give our sons the space to express how they are feeling

Healthy Expression Techniques

Now, onto the cool-down strategies. Think of these as your emotional first-aid kit. Deep breathing is a classic that works wonders. It's like hitting the pause button, giving you a moment to step back from the edge. Teach your son to breathe in deeply through his nose, hold it for a second, and then exhale slowly through his mouth. Make it fun by pretending you're both inflating a balloon in your bellies.

Counting to ten is another easy tool that adds a buffer between feeling angry and taking action. It gives your brain a chance to catch up with your emotions. Using words to express feelings is equally powerful. Encourage your son to articulate his frustration with phrases like, "I'm really upset because I can't find my favorite toy," instead of resorting to yelling or lashing out. These techniques aren't just about calming down in the moment; they're about building a toolbox your son can carry into adulthood—equipping him with the skills to handle stress and frustration in a healthy, constructive way.

Practical Cool-Down Techniques:

- **Deep Breathing:** Breathe in through the nose, hold, then exhale slowly through the mouth.
- **Counting to Ten:** Create a buffer between anger and action.
- **Using Words:** Express feelings verbally instead of lashing out.

Problem-Solving Skills

Linking anger to problem-solving can transform a potentially explosive situation into a learning opportunity. It's about shifting the focus from what's wrong to how to fix it. Let's say your son is irate because his video game isn't working. Instead of watching him have a meltdown, guide him through a problem-solving process. Ask questions like, "What do you think is going wrong?" or "What have we tried, and what can we try next?" This approach helps him learn to think critically and creatively about solutions, rather than getting stuck in the frustration loop. It's about teaching him that while it's okay to feel upset, what really matters is how he handles and resolves the situation. This skill is crucial, not just for the broken toys or lost games of childhood but for the complex challenges he'll face as he grows up.

Establishing Rules Around Anger

Finally, setting some ground rules around anger is key. This isn't about denying angry feelings—we all get mad—it's about handling them responsibly. Discuss and set clear guidelines about what's okay and what's not when you're mad. Maybe yelling in the house is off-limits, but punching a pillow or squeezing a stress ball is acceptable. Talk about the importance of respecting each other's physical and emotional space, even when angry. Explain that it's alright to take a timeout—walking away to cool down can be much more productive than hashing it out in the heat of the moment. And, importantly, discuss the consequences of letting anger control our actions. Whether it's hurt feelings, damaged relationships, or things we can't take back, understanding these consequences can motivate both of you to manage anger more constructively.

Rules for Managing Anger:

These rules can be made by writing them down on a sticky note or via your notes app, whatever helps you remember them.

- **No Yelling in the House:** Find alternative ways to express frustration.
- **Respect Physical and Emotional Space:** Give each other room to cool down.
- **Acceptable Outlets:** Use stress balls, punching pillows, or taking a timeout.
- **Discuss Consequences:** Understand the impact of uncontrolled anger.

Real-Life Example

I remember one weekend when the stress levels were high—my son had just spilled juice all over my work papers. Now that I think about it, they were probably some of my rough drafts for this book! Ironic, huh? My first instinct was to yell, but I took a deep breath and counted to ten. Then, I calmly asked him to help me clean up the mess. We turned it into a game of who could wipe up the most juice, and it ended with us laughing instead of crying. It was a powerful reminder that managing anger with calm and patience can turn a potential disaster into a bonding moment.

Navigating anger and frustration successfully is about open communication, mutual support, and a whole lot of patience. It's about showing your son that while anger is a natural emotion, it doesn't have to dictate our actions. By teaching him to recognize triggers, express his feelings healthily, solve problems effectively, and abide by rules relating to anger, you're setting him up not just to manage his emotions but to thrive emotionally, no matter what life throws his way.

2.4 REMOVING THE 'BOYS DON'T CRY' BARRIER: ENCOURAGING EMOTIONAL OPENNESS IN OUR BOYS

Let's face it, the old "boys don't cry" adage is as outdated as polaroid cameras. Today, we're flipping the script, because let's be honest, we want our sons to grow up capable of expressing more than just their favorite color or video game score. We want them to be emotionally articulate, capable of tackling life's ups and downs with a healthy mindset. Breaking down the barriers of traditional male stereotypes about emotional expression is not just good parenting; it's essential for their mental health and the quality of their relationships.

Debunking Emotional Stereotypes

Addressing these stereotypes head-on, we begin by debunking the myth that emotional vulnerability equals weakness. It's quite the contrary. Emotional openness allows for a deeper connection with others and more authentic self-expression. It's like giving your son the tools to build a bridge rather than walls. Think about it—when he's able to express fear, sadness, joy, or anxiety freely, he's better equipped to handle these feelings in a constructive way. This openness not only enhances his mental health but also enriches his relationships, providing a foundation of trust and mutual understanding that can lead to more fulfilling interactions.

Creating a Safe Space for Emotional Expression

Creating a safe, non-judgmental space for these expressions is your next mission. This isn't about creating a physical space, although a comfy, private spot in the house can definitely help. It's more about cultivating an emotional environment where your son knows he can share his feelings without fear of ridicule or dismissal. Regular check-ins can be a great way to foster this environment. Maybe it's over a weekend breakfast or a nightly chat before bed—what's important is that it's consistent and that the focus is on listening rather than solving.

Practical Tips for Fostering Emotional Openness:

- **Regular Check-Ins:** Schedule consistent times for emotional check-ins, such as weekend breakfasts or nightly chats.
- **Ask Open-Ended Questions:** Encourage exploration and expression of emotions with questions like "What made you happy today?" or "Did anything bother you?"
- **Listen, Don't Solve:** Focus on listening and validating feelings, rather than jumping straight to solutions.

Sharing Your Own Emotional Experiences

Sharing your own emotional experiences is equally vital. Let's say you had an unexpected reaction to something minor, like tearing up during a touching commercial or feeling deeply moved by a kind gesture. Share that with your son. Explain what triggered your feelings and how it made you realize the importance of embracing emotions. This doesn't just to normalize having unexpected emotions; it also models healthy ways to handle them. Your openness shows him that it's perfectly normal for anyone, including Dad, to have sensitive moments and to work through them openly. This kind of vulnerability can strengthen your bond and teaches him that emotions are a natural part of life, not something to be feared or suppressed. Remember, kids model what we do, not what we say.

I remember watching a particularly emotional scene from a movie with my son. When I got choked up, instead of hiding it, I turned to him and said, "Wow, that scene really hit me hard. It reminded me of how important family is." We talked about why it made me emotional and shared stories about important moments in our own family. It turned into a meaningful conversation that showed him it's okay to feel and express deep emotions.

Reinforcing Emotional Openness

Finally, reinforcing emotional openness can be as simple as responding positively whenever your son expresses his feelings. This reinforcement can come in many forms—verbal affirmations, a reassuring hug, or even a high five. Let's say he comes to you upset about a falling out with a friend. Listen actively, acknowledge his feelings, and commend him for sharing. You might say, "It sounds like you're really hurt by what happened, and I'm really proud of you for talking about it." These responses validate his feelings and reinforce the trust that sharing emotions is not only accepted but appreciated. This positive reinforcement encourages him to continue communicating openly, building his confidence in expressing his emotions and strengthening his emotional intelligence over time.

Ways to Reinforce Emotional Openness:

- **Verbal Affirmations:** Acknowledge and praise him for sharing his feelings.
- **Physical Comfort:** Offer a hug or a reassuring touch to show support.
- **Positive Feedback:** Commend him for his openness, reinforcing that it's a valued trait.

Through these steps, we're not just teaching our sons to be open about their feelings; we're equipping them with the emotional skills they need to lead healthier, more connected lives. We're showing them that being in touch with their emotions is a strength, not a weakness, and that real bravery comes from facing and sharing what's inside us, not hiding it away.

2.5 Chillax, Dad: The Power of Patience

Patience: it's that magical quality that seems to evaporate just when you need it most, like during a marathon session of "Why?" from your toddler or when your teen is moving at the speed of a slug when you're already late. But here's a little secret—cultivating patience is one of the most powerful tools in your dad arsenal. It's not just about enduring your son's slow pace or repeated questions; it's about embracing these moments as opportunities for growth, connection, and teaching.

Practicing Mindfulness

Let's kick things off with mindfulness—it's like giving your brain a gym workout, only calmer. Mindfulness exercises, such as meditation or mindful walking, can be game-changers for both you and your son. Imagine starting your day with a five-minute meditation together. You both sit, breathe, and simply notice the morning sounds. It's a calming ritual that sets a peaceful tone for the day. It teaches your son to appreciate the moment and gives you both a tool to return to when things get hectic.

Mindful walking is another fantastic way to build patience. Next time you're walking to the park, try focusing on the sensation of walking; the feel of each step, the sounds around you. It's a practice in slowing down and being present—valuable lessons for a world that often seems to be on fast-forward.

Setting Realistic Expectations

Now, about those expectations—we dads are often guilty of setting the bar a bit too high, both for ourselves and our kids. Let's ease up a bit. Understanding and accepting that kids will be kids, and parenting is a messy business, can help reduce frustration and increase your patience. Your toddler isn't going to have perfect manners overnight, and your teen might not keep his room museum-clean. And that's okay. By setting realistic expectations about your son's behavior and development, you're less likely to feel impatient when things don't go as planned. It's about recognizing that progress is better than perfection and that missteps are part of the learning process. Most importantly, remember that no matter how much you love Manchester United, your son may end up supporting Fulham or Arsenal. Now that's something you'll need to prepare for mentally.

The Role of Patience in Teaching

Patience shines brightest in the realm of teaching. Whether it's tying shoelaces or solving math problems, when you teach with patience, you're showing your son that learning is not a race. It's a journey that happens step by step. This approach not only makes the learning experience more enjoyable for your son but also more effective. When he knows that it's okay to make mistakes and take time to understand something, he's more likely to engage fully, and is less likely to give up in frustration. Your patience tells him, "You can do this, I believe in you, take your time to learn it right." This supportive environment fosters confidence and a love for learning that textbooks alone can't teach.

Patience in Daily Interactions

Every day with your son is filled with moments that test your patience. But these moments are also ripe with opportunities to strengthen your bond. For instance, when your son is telling you a story with all the twists, turns, and detours of a labyrinth, resist the urge to hurry him along. Listen, really listen. Your attentiveness shows him that his thoughts and experiences are valuable, which in turn builds his self-esteem and trust in you.

When he's struggling with a task, instead of jumping in to solve it quickly, stand back and offer guidance. Encourage him to try again, demonstrating that you trust his ability to figure it out. This type of patient support not only fosters independence but also deepens the trust between you. He learns that you're his steadfast supporter, not just when things are going smoothly, but especially when they're not.

Practical Tips for Cultivating Patience:

- **Mindful Mornings:** Start the day with a five-minute meditation together.
- **Set Realistic Expectations:** Accept that progress, not perfection, is the goal.
- **Listen Actively:** When your son shares a story, give him your full attention.
- **Encourage Independence:** Guide him through tasks instead of solving them for him.

Incorporating patience into your parenting toolkit isn't just about making life with kids easier on your nerves; it's about building a foundation of trust, respect, and love that will support your father-son relationship through the toddler years, the teens, and beyond. So next time the pace feels too slow or the questions too many, take a deep breath, slow down, and embrace the moment. Your patience is teaching your son more than you know, and the connection you're building is the kind that lasts a lifetime.

Personal Tradition: The Patience Walk

In our family, we have what we call the "Patience Walk." Whenever things get a bit too hectic, or tempers start to flare, we lace up our shoes and head out for a stroll. No destination, no rush—just walking and talking. It's become a cherished tradition that not only cools tempers but also strengthens our bond. This simple practice reminds us to slow down and connect, reinforcing the idea that patience isn't just a virtue; it's a vital part of our relationship.

By embracing these moments of mindfulness and setting realistic expectations, you're not just navigating the challenges of fatherhood with grace; you're modeling behaviors that will help your son grow into a patient, thoughtful, and connected individual.

CHAPTER 3
HEALTHY MASCULINITY AND WHY REAL MEN DO CRY

It's Saturday morning and you're watching a superhero movie with your son. Between the jaw-dropping action scenes, there's a moment where the hero, muscles rippling, saves the day through sheer strength and brute force. Your son turns to you with awe in his eyes, and you can't help but think about the message he's absorbing: that masculinity equals physical power and emotional invulnerability. But here's the twist—real heroism, and real masculinity, are about so much more. It's about empathy, resilience, and the courage to express genuine emotions. This chapter dives into what it means to redefine masculinity for ourselves and our sons, ensuring it's a legacy worth passing down.

3.1 DEFINING HEALTHY MASCULINITY: BEYOND STEREOTYPES

Let's start by smashing some old molds of traditional masculinity—those that tell boys to toughen up and swallow their feelings. These outdated ideals don't just limit our sons; they can actually stifle their emotional and psychological growth. Encouraging a broader, more inclusive understanding of masculinity means acknowledging that true strength lies in vulnerability, in the ability to express and manage emotions healthily, and in nurturing relationships.

Consider public figures like Dwayne "The Rock" Johnson or Chris Hemsworth; both are paragons of physical strength yet openly discuss the importance of mental health, fatherhood, and even their own vulnerabilities. These are the modern heroes we can point to when talking to our sons about masculinity. They show that a man can be both strong and emotionally expressive, can lift weights and also be present at parent-teacher conferences, can save the world on screen and still have time to read bedtime stories.

As fathers, we play a pivotal role in modeling healthy masculinity. It's about showing our sons that caring, empathy, and respect for others and themselves are the hallmarks of true strength. It means having the courage to show love, to speak openly about our struggles, and to seek help when needed. These behaviors teach our sons that being a man is about more than just muscle; it's about character.

Engaging in open discussions about masculinity is crucial. It helps our sons navigate the barrage of mixed messages they receive daily from media, peers, and even other role models who might still adhere to outdated norms. Talk about the pressures they might feel to act a certain way and explore where these pressures come from. Discuss how they can stay true to themselves and develop a sense of identity that respects both their strengths and their vulnerabilities. These conversations can be eye-opening and can strengthen the bond between you as they help your son feel understood and supported in his journey to define his own masculinity.

Interactive Element: Journal Prompt For Movie Lovers

Take a moment to reflect with your son after watching a movie or TV show. Discuss the characters: Who showed strength and how? Was it only physical, or were there instances of emotional strength?

This can be a great way to start a conversation about the different forms of strength and courage.

By expanding the definition of masculinity to include a full range of human emotions and actions, we allow our sons to grow into men who are not only strong but whole. We enable them to build relationships based on mutual respect and understanding, to face challenges with resilience and grace, and to lead lives marked by emotional richness and depth. This new paradigm of masculinity isn't just about changing how we raise our sons; it's about changing the world they will grow up into, one where they can show up as their full, authentic selves without fear or apology.

3.2 STRAIGHT SHOOTERS: RAISING BOYS WHO WALK THE TALK

We all know kids are like sponges, absorbing everything around them. This is especially true when it comes to our behavior. That's why living with integrity and honesty is crucial – it's not just about saying the right words, it's about showing your son what these values look like in action. Because let's face it, the real world can be messy, and sometimes the lines between right and wrong get blurry.

Honesty in Action: Teaching Moments at the Grocery Store

Imagine this: you're at the checkout, groceries bagged, and the cashier accidentally gives you an extra twenty bucks. Sure, that fancy new coffee machine is tempting, but what lesson does your son learn if you pocket the cash? Pointing out the mistake and returning the money is a powerful teaching moment. It shows him that honesty isn't situational; it's a core value, even when it's inconvenient.

Now, think about how you handle mistakes at home or at work. We all mess up—spilled coffee on a new shirt, missed deadlines, you name it. Owning up to these slip-ups in front of your son can be a game-changer. It teaches him that everyone, even Dad, makes mistakes, and that's totally okay. What's important is how we handle them. Apologizing and taking steps to make things right teaches him about accountability and the strength it takes to admit faults. It's about turning "Oops!" moments into "Aha!" moments that build character and resilience.

Discussing the consequences of dishonesty can also be a big eye-opener for kids. Let's use a story to break it down: Imagine two characters, Alex and Chris. Alex cheats during a test and gets a top score, while Chris works hard and scores lower. Initially, Alex is thrilled, but soon realizes he can't keep up in class because he never actually learned the material. Chris, on the other hand, might have scored lower, but his knowledge grows, and he feels proud of his honest effort. Through this story, you can show your son that dishonesty might offer a quick win, but that it will always catch up with you in the long run, while honesty pays off in more fulfilling and lasting ways.

Rewarding honesty is like the cherry on top of the integrity sundae. When you catch your son telling the truth, especially in tough situations, a little recognition can go a long way. Maybe he fessed up to breaking a vase while playing indoors. Instead of focusing solely on the mishap, acknowledge his courage in telling the truth with a hug or a thank you. This positive reinforcement makes honesty more appealing by linking it to positive emotional outcomes, encouraging him to keep being truthful.

By integrating integrity and honesty into your daily lives, and celebrating these values in action, you're doing more than just teaching your son to be truthful. You're helping him develop a moral compass, a sense of inner peace, and the self-respect that comes from living true to his values. And that, dads, is pretty darn important. Now go out there and raise some amazing young men!

3.3 GENTLE GIANTS: BUILDING A LEGACY OF LOVE AND EMPATHY

Let's talk about redefining what it means to be a man. Real strength isn't just about muscles or acting tough. It's also about having the courage to be kind and compassionate – traits often seen as "soft" but that are actually signs of deep emotional strength.

Here's the thing: kindness and compassion are superpowers. They build stronger relationships, make you a better leader, and inspire others. Imagine a leader who crushes goals but also cares deeply about his team. That's the kind of man we want our sons to grow up to be – someone who can lead and achieve, but also empathize and show compassion.

Let's start by framing kindness and compassion as what they truly are—superpowers in their own right. These traits lead to stronger, more effective leadership and more fulfilling relationships. Imagine a leader who not only drives his team towards common goals but also cares deeply about the team members' well-being. This kind of leadership is inspiring and sustainable. It's the kind of example you want to set for your son, showing him that his ability to empathize and show compassion is as important as his ability to lead and achieve.

Cultivating Compassion: Kindness in Action

So how do we raise these compassionate superheroes? Here are a few ideas:

- **Service is the new strength training:** Volunteering at a food bank, cleaning up a park, or simply helping a neighbor are all ways to show that being "manly" involves giving back. These activities teach your son that his actions can make a positive difference, and that true strength is used to uplift others.
- **Bystander Intervention: Standing Up to Bullying**

Bullying is a tough reality. Teaching your son to stand up to it, whether he sees it or experiences it himself, is crucial. Role-play scenarios at home to prepare him. Discuss how to use his words to defend himself or others, and the importance of getting help from trusted adults. This equips him with the courage to intervene and shows him that kindness means standing up for what's right.

Celebrating Kindness: Making Compassion Rewarding

Let your son know his compassionate actions are noticed and valued. Did he share his lunch with a friend? Did he stick up for a classmate? Make a big deal out of it! Create a "kindness chart" where you track these acts. When he reaches a goal, celebrate with a family movie night or a trip to his favorite park. This positive reinforcement encourages him to keep being kind and shows him the importance of his compassionate behavior.

By modeling kindness ourselves and creating opportunities for our sons to practice it, we're raising a new generation of men. Men who are comfortable expressing their emotions, value empathy, and understand that true strength lies in caring for and uplifting others. This isn't just about raising good sons; it's about transforming society into one where kindness is the ultimate superpower. Now go out there and raise some compassionate heroes!

3.4 NEVER SAY QUIT: FUELING YOUR SON'S INNER GRIT

Imagine it's game day, and there you are, cheering from the bleachers. Your son's on the field, and things aren't exactly going his way. Maybe he missed a crucial shot or fumbled a play he's practiced a hundred times. It's not just about the loss on the scoreboard but the look of frustration on his face that tugs at your heartstrings. This, right here, is a prime moment for teaching him about perseverance and grit. It's not just about sports; it's about life. The game is a metaphor, a practice field for real challenges he'll face down the road, be it in academics, personal projects, or any of life's many curveballs.

Building resilience goes way beyond the tired "just try again" speech. It's about helping your son see setbacks as opportunities to grow. A missed goal, a bad grade, a science project gone wrong – each one can be a stepping stone to improvement. The key is to guide him to analyze what went wrong, learn from it, and use that knowledge to do better next time.

Are you struggling with math? Don't let frustration simmer. Grab some snacks, sit down together, and tackle that problem head-on. Break it down into smaller, bite-sized chunks. Show him that sometimes the best solutions come after a few wrong turns. This hands-on approach demonstrates that perseverance isn't just about brute force, it's about trying smarter.

Teaching problem-solving skills is crucial in fostering resilience. Encourage your son to approach problems with a 'detective' mindset. This means observing carefully, asking questions, and experimenting with different solutions. For instance, if he's building a model airplane and the wings keep snapping off, discuss potential reasons and explore various materials or techniques together. This approach shifts his perspective from "I can't do this" to "I haven't figured it out yet." It's a subtle but powerful shift that fuels perseverance by framing challenges as puzzles to be solved, not impassable roadblocks. The other day, my son was trying to untangle some cable leads that had got in a mess in our kitchen, so that he could charge his Nintendo DS, and in the process unplugged my Nespresso coffee machine (the things we do for our loved ones, eh?). He was trying to pull the cables apart vigorously and getting more and more impatient as time passed, huffing and puffing as he went. I asked him if he could think of another method of untangling the cables, rather than pulling them apart from one another as hard as he could. He paused to think, and then started tracing one of the cables back slowly with his finger, so he could see where it came from. Within five minutes, he had untangled the whole mess, and had a wide grin on his face, obviously happy with his success. My gentle prompt in this situation was not to criticize him, but to get him to encourage him to re-think the situation and experiment with different solutions.

The value of hard work often shines brightest through personal stories or historical examples where perseverance turned potential failure into success. Take, for instance, the story of Thomas Edison. Share with your son how Edison faced thousands of unsuccessful attempts before inventing the light bulb. Each failed attempt was a lesson learned, not time wasted. Stories like these highlight that perseverance, coupled with hard work, is often behind many great achievements. They teach that success isn't about never falling but about how many times you're willing to get back up and try again.

One of the toughest parts of parenting? Watching your son struggle and not swooping in to fix everything. It's like teaching him to ride a bike – every instinct screams "hold on!" but real growth happens when he lets go. When he faces a challenge, resist the urge to jump in and be the hero. Instead, offer guidance and tools. Stuck on a decision? Help him create a pros and cons list. Encourage him to think critically about the potential outcomes. This kind of support empowers him, builds his confidence, and strengthens his resilience. It shows him you believe in his ability to tackle challenges, boosting his independence and problem-solving skills.

By integrating these principles into your everyday interactions, you're not just helping your son navigate the hurdles in front of him today; you're equipping him with the tools to face any challenge life throws his way, with grit and a champion's heart. So next time he stumbles, remember, it's not about winning or losing – it's about learning and growing.

3.5 CHORE-N TO BE RESPONSIBLE: ACCOUNTABILITY IN ACTION

When it comes to teaching our kids about responsibility, it often feels like convincing a cat to enjoy a bath – possible, but not always easy. But here's the thing: chores aren't just about keeping the house clean (although a tidy home is nice!). They're about teaching our sons responsibility and pride. Think of chores as training for life's bigger responsibilities. They learn that life isn't all about what you get, it's also about giving back, contributing, and being part of something bigger – a family, a team, a community. Incorporating chores into daily life can start with something as simple as making the bed every morning or helping to clear the table after dinner. These aren't just tasks; they're lessons in discipline and the importance of contributing to the family. The trick is consistency and a clear explanation of why these tasks matter. It's not just about the chore itself, but what it represents—care for personal and shared spaces, and respect for the collective environment. For younger kids, this might mean picking up toys after playtime, while older children can handle more complex tasks like managing their laundry or preparing simple meals. The key is to tailor responsibilities to their age and ability, challenging them enough to keep them engaged without overwhelming them.

Now, let's talk about teaching that actions have consequences, which is where real-life lessons come into play. If your son forgets to feed the family pet, don't rush in to drop the food in the bowl yourself. Instead, use this as a teachable moment about the importance of dependability and the real-world consequences of neglecting responsibilities. It's not about punishment, but about helping him see the impact of his actions (or inactions) on others. This approach helps him understand that his actions extend beyond himself and affect others around him, an invaluable lesson in empathy and social responsibility. One technique I've used to teach my son about contributing to the household, is by asking him to always lay the table on Mondays, Wednesdays, and Fridays. On the other days, I lay the table myself, to demonstrate that we all pitch in. On Monday last week, he forgot to lay the table. Instead of swooping in and laying the table myself, I just left it as it was, and when we sat down for dinner, none of us had knives and forks. My son quickly realized that he had forgotten to lay the table, and rushed to the cutlery drawer so that he could prepare the table. In this situation, it would have been less effective if I had lay the table myself. Leaving it as it was reinforced to my son the importance of his contribution to our household.

We don't bribe our kids to do chores, but we do celebrate their efforts and successes. This could be a simple "thank you" or a hug, showing appreciation for their commitment. For ongoing chores, consider a reward system that culminates in something fun, like a family outing or a small prize. For instance, if your son consistently takes out the recycling without being reminded, maybe a trip to his favorite ice cream shop is in order. Positive reinforcement makes responsibility rewarding and something to strive for.

By integrating chores and accountability into daily life, we're not just teaching our sons to do laundry or clear the table. We're preparing them for life. They learn that being part of a family means contributing, that their actions have consequences, and that responsibility is rewarding. These are lessons that will serve them well as they grow into men who can take care of themselves and contribute positively to the world around them. So next time you hand out chores, remember, you're not just cleaning the house, you're building a responsible young man.

3.6 RITE ON TIME: CELEBRATING MILESTONES WITH STYLE

Remember those milestones – the first wobbly steps, the nervous first day of school, the triumphant graduation march? They fly by in a blur, but each one is a glittering marker on your son's journey to manhood. These milestones aren't just about getting older; they're about the emotional and mental leaps he makes as he moves from one stage to the next. Celebrating them isn't just about parties (although who doesn't love a good bash?); it's about acknowledging his journey, reinforcing his growth, and setting the stage for the next adventure.

Think about the first day of school. It's a monumental step for any kid (and let's be honest, for us parents too). This isn't just about learning ABCs and 123s; it's a major emotional adjustment. Your little guy is stepping into a new world, independently managing relationships and responsibilities outside the cozy cocoon of home. Recognizing and celebrating this milestone helps him understand its importance and reassures him that he's got this—and that you're cheering him on all the way. It's about boosting his confidence so that he strides into that classroom with his head held high.

Creating meaningful rites of passage can enhance the impact of these milestones. These rituals, steeped in personal or cultural significance, can vary widely, but they all serve to highlight a transition and cement a memory. For instance, a 'bicycle ceremony' the day a training wheel comes off could involve a special ride through a favorite park followed by handing down the family 'Cyclist's Handbook' (a simple homemade guide filled with biking tips and trails). These ceremonies don't have to be grand, but they should resonate with personal meaning and celebrate the skills and maturity gained.

Involving family and community in these celebrations can turn personal achievements into cherished communal joys. When your son hits a milestone, like scoring his first goal in soccer or acing his first big test, involve loved ones in the celebration. Maybe it's a family dinner where everyone shares stories of their own first successes, or a community soccer game where he's the guest of honor. This inclusion strengthens his sense of belonging and support, showing him that his achievements are a big deal not just to him, but to his whole 'team.'

Looking back at past milestones is just as important as celebrating new ones. It's like reaching the top of a mountain and looking back to see how far you've climbed. Pull out photos, certificates, or other keepsakes and talk about the challenges he faced and how he grew from them. Then, set your sights on the next peak – maybe a tougher subject in school or a new sports goal. This reflection boosts his pride in his accomplishments and fuels his ambition for the future.

These celebrations are more than just happy memories. They're building blocks that reinforce his growth, bolster his confidence, and prepare him for the road ahead. They remind him that every challenge he overcomes isn't just about getting older, it's about personal development. As you guide him through these celebrations, you're crafting a legacy of achievement and resilience that will equip him for whatever life throws his way.

Dads, remember, these milestones are more than calendar entries or party excuses. They're moments that shape your son into the man he'll become. They strengthen your bond, celebrate his achievements, and prepare him for a bright future. Let's carry these lessons into everyday interactions, recognizing every small success and celebrating every big moment. Onwards to the next chapter, where we'll explore even more ways to raise these incredible young men!

CHAPTER 4
PRACTICAL PARENTING STRATEGIES

Let's face it, navigating the maze of fatherhood isn't always about those big, hallmark moments that you see in movies. Often, it's about the day-to-day rhythms, the routines that you establish that help shape your son's world, providing him with a sense of security and stability. It's about laying down a beat that he can groove to, even when you're not around. This chapter is going to dive into the groove of creating consistent routines, why they're crucial for your little guy's development, and how you can master the art of routine-making like a pro.

4.1 CONSISTENT ROUTINES FOR SECURITY AND STABILITY

Establishing Daily Routines

Think of daily routines as the drumbeat to your son's day-to-day symphony. It's what keeps the music flowing smoothly rather than turning into a cacophony of missed cues and clashing chords. Establishing and maintaining these routines—from regular meal times to a set bedtime—helps your son know what to expect each day and provides a comforting predictability amid the chaos of growing up.

Starting with the morning routine, consider how a consistent wake-up time followed by a structured series of events (like brushing teeth, having breakfast, and packing the school bag) can set a positive tone for the day. It's like setting the first domino in a chain; get it right, and the rest follows more smoothly. And it's not just about getting to school on time; it's about teaching him the importance of punctuality and preparedness.

Real-Life Story: Morning Mayhem to Morning Mastery

Before we got our morning routine sorted, it was like a scene from a disaster movie. My son would be running around looking for his homework, my wife and I would be playing detective to find missing shoes, and breakfast would be an afterthought. Then we implemented a simple checklist: wake up, brush teeth, eat breakfast, pack bag. It transformed our mornings from chaos to calm. Well, mostly calm. There's still the occasional shoe hunt.

Meal times are more than just about feeding the body; they're about nourishing the soul. Having regular meal times is a chance to connect, to talk about the day, and to reinforce the value of family. Then there's the bedtime routine—arguably one of the most critical routines. A consistent bedtime routine (which could include a bath, storytime, and a few minutes of bedside chat) not only helps him wind down from the day but also sets the stage for a good night's sleep, which is crucial for his growth and development.

Analogy: The Bedtime Routine Orchestra

Think of the bedtime routine as conducting an orchestra. Each step —bath, pajamas, storytime—is like a different section of the orchestra playing its part. When done right, it creates a symphony that leads to peaceful sleep. Miss a step, and it's like forgetting to cue the violins—chaos ensues.

Benefits of Structured Environments

The benefits of such structured environments are backed by heaps of psychological research. Routines are shown to imbue children's lives with a sense of security and stability. They help reduce anxiety because the predictability of routines provides a safety net, highlighting the knowns amidst the unknowns of daily life. Moreover, routines foster an environment where positive behaviors can thrive. For instance, a study from the American Academy of Pediatrics suggests that children in households with regular routines have better emotional health and exhibit fewer behavioral problems. It's about giving your son the structure he needs to navigate his world confidently.

Research Insight: Routine Magic

A study from the American Academy of Pediatrics found that children in households with regular routines have better emotional health and exhibit fewer behavioral problems. It's like giving your son a map in a world of chaos—he knows where he's going and feels safer getting there.

Adapting Routines as Children Grow

Of course, as your son grows, his needs will change, and so should your routines. The bedtime story that worked like a charm at age five might not hold the same allure at ten. This is where you, as a dad, need to be flexible and adaptive. For example, as your son moves into school age, his homework and social activities might require tweaks to the existing routine. Maybe it's adjusting bedtimes or finding new ways to spend quality time together in the evenings. The key is to evolve these routines without losing the underlying consistency that holds them together.

Personal Tradition: The Evolving Bedtime Routine

When my son turned ten, bedtime stories gave way to "Dad and Son Debates." We'd pick a topic—Marvel vs. DC, pizza toppings, best video game—and go at it. It kept the connection strong and made bedtime something to look forward to.

Involving Sons in Routine Planning

And here's a pro tip: get your son involved in the planning and adjustment of these routines. This not only makes the routines more likely to stick but also teaches him valuable lessons about responsibility and time management. Sit down with him and discuss what parts of the current routine are working and what might need changing. Maybe he wants more time for after-school activities, or perhaps he's finding it hard to wake up in the morning. Use this input to adjust routines accordingly. It's a collaborative approach that respects his growing autonomy and makes him feel valued, boosting his willingness to stick to these routines.

Interactive Tip: The Routine Planning Meeting

Every few months, we have a "Family Routine Meeting." We sit down with some snacks, review what's working, and discuss what needs changing. It's a democratic process where my son gets a say, and it's amazing how much more invested he is in the routine when he's helped create it.

By embedding consistent routines in your son's life, you're not just keeping the ship steady; you're also teaching him how to steer it himself. You're showing him the value of structure, the importance of adaptability, and the strength of collaboration. And the best part? You're doing it together, beat by beat, building a rhythm that will guide him toward becoming not just a well-rounded individual but a master of his own symphony.

4.2 EFFECTIVE DISCIPLINE TECHNIQUES: GUIDANCE OVER PUNISHMENT

When it comes to discipline, think of it less like laying down the law and more like coaching a mini-human on the more nuanced points of life. It's about guidance and growth, not just correction. One of the most effective ways to approach this is through positive discipline techniques that focus on teaching and guiding rather than punishing. Imagine you're not just trying to stop bad behavior, but you're aiming to foster good behavior. This isn't about being a buddy; it's about being the wise guide who uses tools like logical consequences and positive reinforcement to help shape a young mind and heart.

Real-Life Scenario: The Wall Art Incident

Consider the scenario where your son has just drawn a masterpiece... on your living room wall. Traditional punishment might dictate a time-out or revoking some privileges. But positive discipline takes a different tack. First, acknowledge his creative effort—yes, even if it's on your lovely white wall that's just had a fresh coat of paint. Then, guide him to understand why walls aren't canvases and involve him in the cleanup process. Discuss what appropriate outlets for his creativity could look like, such as large sheets of paper taped to the walls or a designated art space. Here, the logical consequence—cleaning up the wall—naturally follows from the misbehavior, teaching him that actions have consequences, while also respecting his creative impulse. This method not only addresses the behavior but also redirects it in a positive way.

Communicating Expectations Clearly

Now, none of this works without crystal-clear communication. It's crucial that your son knows what's expected of him. Without clear rules, every day is a guessing game, and that's a game no one wins. Let's say bedtime needs to be at 8 PM. If that's communicated clearly and consistently, your son knows what's expected and can begin to incorporate that into his internal schedule. Clarity reduces confusion and, by extension, reduces the opportunities for misbehavior. It's about setting the stage for success from the get-go, rather than just dealing with problems as they arise.

Role of Empathy in Discipline

Incorporating empathy into discipline might sound like a soft approach, but it's actually about making discipline more effective. When your son understands that you recognize and care about his feelings, even when he's in trouble, he's more likely to listen and take the lessons to heart. Let's revisit the wall-drawing scenario. If you approach it with empathy, acknowledging his desire to express himself artistically, he feels understood. Then, when you guide him toward appropriate ways to channel this expression, he's more receptive. He understands that you aren't just laying down rules because you can, but because you care about him and the home you share. This kind of empathetic engagement helps him understand the reasons behind rules, which can make all the difference in how he views discipline.

Personal Tradition: Empathy in Action

When my son gets upset because he has to stop playing video games, my wife and I have a tradition. We sit down with him and explain why it's important to balance fun and responsibilities. We share stories from our own childhoods, making him see that we understand his frustration. It turns what could become a battle into a bonding moment instead.

Consistency in Enforcing Rules

Finally, let's talk about consistency because it's the glue that holds all your discipline strategies together. If one day you enforce a rule and the next day you let it slide, what you're teaching isn't discipline, it's confusion. Consistency means that the rules are the same day after day, situation after situation. It provides a reliable framework within which your son can operate. It builds trust, too. He knows that you mean what you say and that you'll follow through, whether it's a promise of a trip to the park or a consequence for scribbling on walls. Consistency in discipline helps your son understand the world as a stable, predictable place, which is incredibly comforting and necessary for his development.

Summary

Navigating the path of discipline with your son is all about balance, understanding, and a whole lot of consistency. By focusing on teaching rather than punishing, clarifying expectations, empathizing with his feelings, and applying rules consistently, you're not just managing behavior—you're raising a responsible, thoughtful individual who knows his actions have meaningful consequences. This approach doesn't just solve problems in the now; it builds the foundation for a lifetime of good decision-making and self-discipline.

4.3 SCHOOL OF HARD KNOCK: FROM HOMEWORK HEADACHES TO BULLY BATTLES

Ah, school days! Remember when your biggest worry was whether you'd nailed that spelling test or if you'd be picked last for dodgeball? Well, now as a dad, you're on the other side of the equation, helping your son navigate his way through homework, teachers, and yes, even the modern-day dodgeball equivalent—social dynamics. Let's kick things off with the homework hustle because, let's face it, getting your son to sit down and focus after a long day can sometimes feel like negotiating peace talks. And while there's the temptation to resign yourself and let him play video games all evening so you can sneak off for a couple of cheeky beers and watch the soccer, we know this isn't what's best for his well being in the long run.

Supporting Homework Habits

Creating a conducive environment for homework is all about crafting a space where concentration comes naturally. Think about setting up a dedicated 'homework zone' in your home. This doesn't mean you need a lavish study; a quiet corner of the dining room or his bedroom can do the trick. Make sure it's well-lit, supplies are at hand, and distractions are at a minimum. Yes, this means the TV and gadgets are off, unless they're needed for research (and by research, I mean researching biology and math techniques, not the most recent viral trend on TikTok).

Personal Story: The Homework Nook

When my son started getting regular homework, we created a homework nook together. It wasn't anything fancy—just a small desk, a comfortable chair, and a good lamp. We let him pick out a few decorations, making it his own special space. The first few weeks were rough, but soon it became a routine. Now, he heads to his nook right after school like it's second nature.

Tips for Supporting Homework Habits:

- **Create a Dedicated Space:** A consistent spot for homework helps establish routine.
- **Keep Supplies Handy:** Ensure all necessary tools—pencils, paper, calculator—are within reach.
- **Minimize Distractions:** Keep the area free from noise and screen distractions.
- **Be Available:** Offer help without taking over, encouraging independence and confidence.

Addressing School Bullying

Switching gears to a tougher topic—bullying. It's something we all hope our kids will never face, but the reality is, it happens. The key here is open communication—making sure your son knows he can talk to you about anything. If he does come to you about being bullied, take a deep breath and listen. Keep calm and thank him for being brave enough to tell you. Validate his feelings and reassure him that it's not his fault.

Personal Story: Standing Up Together

My wife and I once had to deal with a bullying incident. Our son came home quiet and withdrawn, not his usual chatty self. After some gentle probing, he shared what had been happening. We sat down as a family, listened to him, and made a plan together. We contacted his teacher and the school counselor. It was a tough process, but he knew he wasn't alone, and that made all the difference.

Steps to Address Bullying:

- **Listen Actively:** Give him your full attention and show empathy.
- **Reassure:** Let him know he's not alone and it's not his fault.
- **Take Action:** Work with teachers and school staff to address the issue.
- **Follow Up:** Keep the lines of communication open and monitor the situation.

Enhancing School Communication

While we're on the topic of school, staying in regular communication with teachers and school staff can make a world of difference. Attend those parent-teacher meetings, not just as a formality, but to genuinely understand your son's school environment and progress. Ask specific questions, not just about his grades, but about his participation in class, his social interactions, and any areas he might be struggling with.

Personal Tradition: Parent-Teacher Coffee Chats

My wife and I started a tradition where, after every parent-teacher conference, we'd take our son out for a treat. We'd discuss what the teacher said and ask for his thoughts. It became a fun way to stay engaged with his school life and showed him we were interested in his day-to-day experiences.

Tips for Enhancing School Communication:

- **Attend Meetings:** Be proactive in attending school events and parent-teacher conferences.
- **Ask Specific Questions:** Go beyond grades to understand your son's overall school experience.
- **Discuss Insights:** Share what you learn with your son and encourage his input.
- **Stay Informed:** Regularly check in with teachers via email or scheduled meetings.

Encouraging Academic Motivation

And speaking of motivation, fostering a love for learning is about praising the effort, not just the outcome. Celebrate the hard work he puts into a project or the extra reading he does, not just the A on the paper. This kind of encouragement helps him value persistence and hard work, qualities that are crucial not just in school but in life.

Personal Story: The Science Fair Triumph

One year, my son decided to enter the school science fair. We spent weeks on his project, from brainstorming ideas to the final presentation. The night before, he was a bundle of nerves. We talked about how proud we were of the effort he'd put in, regardless of the outcome. When he won third place, it was the icing on the cake, but the real victory was seeing his confidence grow through the process.

Ways to Encourage Academic Motivation:

- **Praise Effort:** Focus on the hard work, not just the results.
- **Set Goals:** Help him set and achieve realistic academic goals.

- **Celebrate Milestones:** Acknowledge his progress and accomplishments, big or small.
- **Encourage Curiosity:** Foster a love of learning by exploring new topics together.

Navigating school challenges is a significant part of parenting during the school years. It's about more than just making sure homework gets done or stepping in when there's a problem. It's about actively participating in your son's educational journey, helping him navigate the highs and lows with a supportive, guiding hand. Whether it's creating the right environment for study, tackling bullying head-on, communicating with his teachers, or encouraging his love of learning, your involvement is key to his success. And through it all, you're not just helping him get through school; you're teaching him valuable life skills that will prepare him for whatever challenges come his way.

4.4 WINGMAN DAD: HELPING YOUR KID SOAR WITH CONFIDENCE

Imagine this: your young lad is growing up, and he's starting to show flashes of independence. Maybe he's tying his shoes without help, choosing his own outfits, or even making his own peanut butter sandwiches (smooth, not crunchy, of course). It's bittersweet, right? You're proud to see him becoming his own person, but part of you might also want to keep him safely under your wing. That's where the art of fostering independence with supportive oversight comes into play. It's about giving him the room to grow and make decisions, but still being there to guide, support, and jump in when absolutely necessary.

Gradual Release of Responsibility

Let's talk about the gradual release of responsibility. It's like teaching your son to ride a bike. Initially, you're holding onto the back of the seat, running alongside him. Gradually, you start letting go, but you're still jogging beside him, ready to catch him if he wobbles. Eventually, you're just watching from the sidewalk, cheering him on as he pedals away. Apply this analogy to daily tasks and larger decisions. Start with small responsibilities, like picking out clothes for school or organizing his backpack. As he shows he can handle these, increase the complexity of the tasks. Let him plan how he spends his allowance or manage his homework schedule. Each step builds his confidence and shows him that you trust his judgment, which is crucial for his development into a self-reliant individual.

Personal Story: The Allowance Experiment

When my son was about eight, my wife and I decided it was time for him to learn about money management. We started giving him a small allowance each week. The first few weeks, he blew it all on candy and cheap toys, but we resisted the urge to step in and manage his spending. Instead, we sat down and talked about saving for bigger items he wanted. It took some time, but eventually, he got the hang of it. Now, he's pretty savvy with his money, and that early lesson in financial independence has paid off.

Tips for the Gradual Release of Responsibility:

- **Start Small:** Begin with manageable tasks to build confidence.
- **Increase Complexity:** Gradually introduce more complex responsibilities as he shows readiness.
- **Provide Guidance:** Be available for support but encourage independent problem-solving.
- **Celebrate Milestones:** Acknowledge and celebrate his achievements to boost confidence.

Teaching Decision-Making Skills

Teaching decision-making skills is another crucial aspect of fostering independence. Start with scenarios that require him to make choices and discuss the potential outcomes. For example, if he's torn between going to a friend's birthday party or a family outing, weigh the pros and cons together. Discuss factors like commitment, relationships, and personal enjoyment. Encourage him to think about how his decision affects not just him but others involved. This process not only sharpens his decision-making skills but also teaches him to consider the broader implications of his actions, a vital skill in all aspects of life.

Personal Story: The Birthday Dilemma

I remember a weekend when my son had to choose between attending his best friend's birthday party or going on a family trip to the zoo. We sat down and listed the pros and cons of each choice. He learned to weigh his options and consider his commitments. In the end, he chose the family trip but made sure to call his friend and explain. It was a great lesson in decision-making and consideration for others.

Tips for Teaching Decision-Making:

- **Discuss Scenarios:** Talk through various choices and their potential outcomes.
- **Weigh Pros and Cons:** Help him list the advantages and disadvantages of each option.
- **Consider Others:** Teach him to think about how his decisions impact those around him.
- **Encourage Reflection:** After making a decision, discuss what he learned from the experience.

Encouraging Problem-Solving Independence

Nurturing problem-solving independence involves stepping back and allowing your son to handle challenges on his own. This might be one of the harder aspects of parenting—watching your child struggle without immediately rushing in to help. But there's immense value in this struggle. When he comes to you with a problem, like a disagreement with a friend or a difficult homework question, resist the urge to provide a solution. Instead, guide him with questions that encourage him to think independently. Ask, "What do you think is a fair solution?" or "How could you approach this problem differently?" This not only develops his problem-solving skills but also reinforces his confidence in his ability to handle challenges. It's also important to be patient with your son always, not just in words but in your actions. Remind yourself that though the challenges he faces may seem simple when compared to your own, such as meeting tight deadlines at work, or fixing your old Ford that's on its last legs, his problems are real and tangible to him, as he approaches them for the first time.

Personal Story: The Puzzle Challenge

One rainy afternoon, my son decided to tackle a 500-piece puzzle. After an hour of frustration, he came to me for help. Instead of jumping in, I asked him what strategies he had tried and what parts he found hardest. We talked through different approaches, and he went back to work with renewed determination. When he finally finished the puzzle, the pride on his face was priceless. It was a reminder that sometimes the best help is simply guiding them to find their own solutions.

Tips for Encouraging Problem-Solving:

- **Ask Guiding Questions:** Encourage him to think through solutions rather than providing answers.
- **Support Efforts:** Show appreciation for his attempts and persistence.
- **Discuss Strategies:** Talk about different approaches to solving problems.
- **Reflect on Outcomes:** After resolving an issue, discuss what worked and what didn't, in order to build on his experiences.

Balancing Oversight with Autonomy

Balancing oversight with autonomy is a delicate dance. You want to monitor his activities enough to ensure he's safe and on track, but not so much that he feels smothered. It's about knowing when to step back and let him try, even if it means making mistakes. Say he's working on a school project. Instead of taking over and doing it for him, be available for guidance. Ask probing questions that encourage him to think critically and solve problems on his own. This balance helps him learn from his experiences and understand that while you're always there as a safety net, you trust him to take the lead.

Personal Story: The Science Fair Project

When my son had his first science fair project, my wife and I were tempted to take charge to ensure it was perfect. Instead, we decided to let him lead. We asked questions to guide his thinking, like, "What materials do you need?" and "How will you present your findings?" He took ownership of the project, and although it wasn't flawless, the pride he felt from doing it himself was invaluable.

Tips for Balancing Oversight with Autonomy:

- **Provide Supportive Oversight:** Be present and available without taking over.
- **Encourage Independent Thinking:** Ask questions that guide his critical thinking.
- **Allow for Mistakes:** Let him learn from his errors and offer support in finding solutions.
- **Celebrate Independence:** Acknowledge and praise his efforts and successes, big or small.

Navigating the path of fostering independence with supportive oversight is about trusting the process. It's about believing in the foundations you've laid through your parenting and trusting your son to build upon them. It's not about cutting the cords all at once but gradually untangling them, allowing your son to freely navigate his own path with the assurance that you're always there, ready to support when needed. As you watch him make decisions, solve problems, and take on responsibilities, you'll find that your role as a parent isn't diminishing—it's evolving, celebrating each step he takes towards becoming a capable, independent young man.

4.5 TECH AND THE TEEN: FINDING THE BALANCE IN SCREEN TIME

Ah, technology. It's the double-edged sword of modern parenting. On one hand, it's a magical portal to knowledge and creativity, and on the other, it's a vortex that can suck in even the most studious and outdoorsy kid into a never-ending loop of swipe and scroll. As dads, it's our job to manage this delicate balance, ensuring our sons reap the benefits of the digital age without falling into its pitfalls. So, let's talk about setting realistic and enforceable limits on screen time, using parental controls wisely, encouraging activities that break the screen cycle, and, most importantly, modeling the digital behavior we want to see in our kids.

Setting Reasonable Limits

Setting limits on screen time isn't about being the tech police; rather, it's about guiding your son to use technology as a tool, not a crutch. The key here is to set boundaries that make sense for your son's age and developmental needs. For young kids, this might mean 30 minutes of tablet time after homework and chores are done. For older kids, the rules might evolve into a more flexible arrangement, like screen time limits on school nights versus weekends. But here's the clincher—whatever rules you set, they need to be clear, consistent, and jointly discussed. Bring your son into the conversation. Discuss why these limits are necessary, focusing on the benefits of diversified activities and the importance of face-to-face interactions.

It's about making him see these limits not as punishments but as steps towards a balanced life. When my son was eight, we sat down together and set up a screen time schedule. We talked about why it's important to spend time outdoors and how too much screen time can affect sleep. By involving him in the process, he felt a sense of ownership over the rules, making it easier for him to stick to them.

The Role of Parental Controls

In an era where a kid can stumble from a video about science experiments into the deep end of YouTube, parental controls are your best friend. But here's the trick—they should be used to protect, not to pry. Tools like content filters, time limits, and activity monitors can help you keep your son's online experiences positive and safe, without feeling like you're constantly looking over his shoulder. Explain to your son why these controls are in place; it's about safety, just like wearing a helmet while biking. It's not about distrust; it's about ensuring the digital playground is as safe as the physical one. And as he grows older, you can adjust these controls, gradually giving him more freedom as he shows responsibility. Think of it like teaching him to ride a bike—starting with training wheels and slowly letting go as he gains confidence.

Encouraging Alternative Activities

Now, for the fun part—getting your son off the screen without a battle. The goal is to make the offline world as engaging as the online one. It's not just about telling him to go outside and play; it's about making the great outdoors appealing to him. Plan family hikes, bike rides, or even a simple game of catch. Be involved. Your participation not only makes these activities more fun but also shows that they're important. For quieter times, encourage hobbies that don't involve screens. Maybe it's building model airplanes, starting a rock collection, or drawing. When my son was younger, we started a Saturday morning tradition called "Craft and Create." We'd pick a project—anything from building a birdhouse to painting canvases. It became something we both looked forward to, and it was a great way to limit screen time without it feeling like a punishment.

Role Modeling Digital Behavior

Finally, and perhaps most importantly, let's talk about walking the walk. Our kids are always watching and learning from us—even when we wish they weren't (like that one time you accidentally hammered your thumb and let out a word that was definitely not "ouch"). If we're glued to our phones during family dinners or constantly checking emails during their soccer games, what message are we sending (in real life, not on our phones)? Set tech-free times or zones in the house where everyone, parents included, puts away their devices. Show your son that there's a time to connect digitally and a time to disconnect. By modeling the balance between digital and real-life interactions, you're teaching him habits that will help him navigate the digital world as he grows. My wife and I have a rule—no phones at the dinner table. It's our time to connect with each other and with our kids, and it sets a clear example of prioritizing family time over screen time.

By setting boundaries, using tools wisely, promoting engaging alternatives, and leading by example, you're not just managing his screen time; you're helping him build a healthy relationship with technology—a skill that will serve him well into adulthood.

4.6 BRAINSTORM BROS: TACKLING PROBLEMS TOGETHER

Hey there, super dad! Ready to turn your little guy into a problem-solving whiz? This isn't just about fixing stuff around the house (though that's a bonus); it's about nurturing a mindset that sees challenges as opportunities and puzzles waiting to be solved. Teaching your son critical thinking and problem-solving skills equips him not just for school or hobbies, but for life.

Teaching Critical Thinking

So, how do you start? Well, it's about encouraging your son to think outside the toy box. When a problem pops up, resist the urge to jump in with a solution. Instead, turn it into a brainstorming session. Say his favorite action figure's arm snaps off. Instead of super gluing it back immediately, ask him, "What do you think we can do to fix this?" or "Can you think of any other ways we might repair this without glue?" This kind of questioning encourages him to think critically and creatively about possible solutions, evaluating their effectiveness before trying them out.

It's also about teaching him to think ahead and consider consequences. For example, if he's about to build a tower out of blocks, discuss what could happen if he builds it too high without a stable base. Ask questions like, "What do you think will happen if we add another block here?" This doesn't just apply to physical activities (or Jenga); use similar questions when he's facing decisions about friendships or school projects. It's all about making him pause and consider the 'if I do this, then that might happen' scenarios, which is a cornerstone of critical thinking.

Shared Problem-Solving Activities

Now, let's put these skills into action with some fun, hands-on activities that you can both tackle together. Building projects are fantastic for this. Whether it's a Meccano creation, a LEGO set, or a birdhouse, these projects require you to follow instructions, figure out where each piece fits, and solve problems when pieces don't fit as expected. Puzzles are another great tool. They're not just for rainy days; they're excellent for teaching patience and the process of elimination, piece by piece.

How about some strategic games? Games like chess or even some video games that require planning and strategy can be incredibly beneficial. They teach forward thinking, strategy, and the anticipation of consequences. Plus, they're a great way for you to bond and have fun while fostering a love for thinking and problem-solving. Remember, the goal here isn't just to win the game but to engage with the process and each other.

Encouraging Questions and Curiosity

Curiosity didn't just kill the cat; it made the scientist. Encouraging your son to ask questions about how things work instills a deep-seated love for learning and discovery. Start with everyday things. How does the TV remote work? Why does the moon change shape (and is it really made of cheese)? Encourage him to come up with hypotheses, and then explore answers together. Maybe it's looking up information in books or online, or conducting little experiments at home.

Remember, there's no such thing as a silly question—every query is a stepping stone to knowledge. By valuing his curiosity, you're telling him that his thoughts and questions are important. This not only builds his confidence but also deepens his engagement with the world around him.

Learning from Mistakes

Lastly, let's talk about the goldmine that comes from making mistakes. Yes, mistakes—the things most of us dread. In the world of problem-solving, mistakes are not just inevitable; they are invaluable. Teach your son that each mistake is a lesson in disguise. Instead of getting frustrated when something goes wrong, encourage him to analyze what happened. What went wrong, and why? How can it be done differently next time? This approach takes the sting out of mistakes and turns them into learning opportunities.

For instance, if a science project doesn't go as planned, instead of focusing on the failure, focus on the why. Maybe the hypothesis was off, or perhaps the materials were not used correctly. Discuss what he learned from the experience and how it can be applied in the future. This kind of reflective thinking enhances his ability to tackle problems and reduces fear of failure, fostering a mindset of being open to taking risks and trying new things.

The Joy of Collaborative Problem-Solving

When my son and I faced the daunting task of building his first model rocket, it was a mixture of excitement and trepidation. We laid out all the parts, carefully read the instructions, and then the unexpected happened—the launch pad didn't fit together as smoothly as the diagram promised. Instead of taking over, I turned to him and said, "Okay, buddy, what do you think we should try next?" We experimented with different configurations, discussed why some didn't work, and finally found a solution together. Not only did we successfully build that rocket, but we also celebrated our teamwork and problem-solving triumph with a launch in the backyard. Moments like these aren't just about the task at hand; they're about building a foundation of trust and collaboration.

By the end of this chapter, you've not only given your son tools to solve problems, but also the mindset to approach life as an exciting puzzle. These skills—critical thinking, problem-solving, curiosity, and learning from mistakes—are his toolkit for not just tackling academic challenges or building cool stuff, but for navigating the complexities of life. This isn't just about making him smarter; it's about making him wiser. And as we wrap up this chapter, remember, every problem faced, every question asked, and every mistake made is a step towards becoming a more thoughtful, resilient, and capable person. Now, let's carry these lessons forward, as we continue to explore more ways to empower and guide our sons through the adventure of growing up.

CHAPTER 5
NAVIGATING THE DIGITAL AGE

Welcome to the jungle, dads! No, not the wild outdoors, though sometimes the digital landscape feels just as untamed and unpredictable. It's a place where pixels meet parenting, where screen time battles are as real as they get, and where navigating the World Wide Web feels more complex than a treasure hunt. But fear not! This chapter is your trusty map, crafted to guide you through the maze of gadgets, games, and gigabytes, helping you to set healthy digital boundaries without becoming the family tech tyrant.

5.1 WI-FI WHISPERER: KEEPING SCREEN TIME IN CHECK

Assessing Screen Time

So, let's talk screen time. It's like Halloween candy: a little can be a treat, but too much can lead to a pretty nasty stomachache—or in the case of screens, a headache, quite literally. But how do you decide what's just right? It starts with a clear-eyed assessment of how much digital sugar your son is consuming. Consider his age, his needs, and how screens fit into the broader nutritional chart of his daily activities. For little ones, the American Academy of Pediatrics suggests sticking to one hour a day for those under age six. Older kids can handle more, but it's crucial to balance screen time with other activities that feed their brains, bodies, and souls.

Replacing Doom-scrolling with Micro-learning

Think about what your son is viewing. Is it passive scrolling, or is it interactive and educational? There's a world of difference between zoning out in front of endless YouTube videos and, say, participating in an online science tutorial. Discuss with your partner and maybe even involve your son in the conversation. What does he think about his screen time? Are there better ways in which he could be spending his screen time? You might be surprised by his insights. This isn't just about laying down rules; it's about helping him understand his own digital habits, which is a crucial step toward self-regulation.

Creating a Family Media Plan

Alright, it's strategy time! Creating a family media plan isn't just practical; it's empowering. It's about setting up a framework that everyone in the house understands and agrees on. Here's how you can start: Gather the crew for a family meeting and lay out the goals. Maybe it's ensuring screen time doesn't interfere with sleep, homework, or family meals (unless it's the Super Bowl of course). Then, draft up a plan that includes screen time limits, acceptable content, and perhaps most importantly, tech-free zones and times. Maybe the dinner table becomes a phone-free zone, or perhaps after 8 PM, screens go off to help everyone wind down before bed.

Get everyone to pitch in. When kids have a say in the rules, they're more likely to follow them. Plus, this plan isn't just for the kids; it's for the whole family. That means your work emails can wait during family game night, too. Post the plan somewhere visible—a reminder that everyone's on the same digital page. It's about creating a family culture where technology is managed collectively and consciously, making sure it enhances rather than dictates your family life.

Enforcing Boundaries Consistently

Consistency is key—yeah, you've heard it before, but with screen rules, it's golden. Once you've set your boundaries, stick to them like super glue. Consistency means your son knows what to expect, and when kids know the boundaries, they're less likely to push them. But, let's be real, enforcement isn't about being the bad guy; it's about being the guide. When rules are broken, and they will be, handle it with a mix of firmness and understanding. Reiterate why the boundaries exist and the benefits of sticking to them, like better sleep or more time for hobbies.

And what about when you meet resistance? Because let's face it, you will. Stay calm, dad. Reflect back what your son is feeling. Maybe he's upset because he can't finish his game, or his favorite episode of a TV show Acknowledge his frustration but reiterate the importance of balance and sticking to the plan. Sometimes, a little empathy can defuse a standoff and turn it into a teaching moment.

Evaluating Media Content

Not all screen time is created equal. As the dad, think of yourself as the curator of a high-quality digital diet. Just as you wouldn't let your son eat junk food for every meal, you don't want his brain dining on junk content. Be proactive. Know what games, apps, and programs your son is into. Watch an episode with him, play the game, or explore the app together. Discuss the content. Ask questions like, "What do you enjoy about this show?" or "What skills are you learning from this game?" This doesn't just help you assess the value of the content; it also shows your son that you're interested in his world.

Look for content that is age-appropriate and aligns with your family values. Does it encourage creativity, problem-solving, or learning? Or is it passive, violent, or filled with ads? Make this evaluation a regular part of your digital routine, and don't be afraid to pull the plug if something doesn't measure up. Remember, you're the dad, and part of your job is to help your son navigate to the good stuff—a task that's a lot easier when you're exploring the digital world together, setting boundaries that protect, guide, and sometimes, liberate both of you from the digital jungle.

5.2 ONLINE SAFETY: PROTECTING YOUR SON FROM DIGITAL THREATS

Navigating the internet can sometimes feel like steering a ship through murky waters, especially when you've got your young one on board. The digital realm is vast and filled with wonders, but let's face it, there are also pirates lurking in the form of cyberbullies, inappropriate content, and online predators. As dads, our role isn't just to set sail but to ensure that our kids can navigate these waters safely, understanding the risks and knowing how to handle problematic situations if they arise.

Understanding Online Risks

First things first, let's chat about the kind of choppy waters your son might encounter online. Cyberbullying is a biggie—it's not just about the schoolyard anymore; it can follow him home on his phone or computer. Then there's the exposure to inappropriate content—stuff that he might stumble upon even during innocent searches. And let's not forget about online predators, who often disguise themselves as friendly faces. It's crucial to educate yourself about these risks, not to scare the living daylights out of yourself, but to be prepared and vigilant. Knowledge is power, right? Understanding these risks is the first step in teaching your son how to handle them.

Implementing Safety Measures

Now, onto the action plan. Setting up parental controls isn't about spying; it's about safeguarding. Most devices and platforms offer these controls, and they can be real lifesavers. You can filter out inappropriate content, set time limits, and monitor activity without being overly intrusive. Think of it as putting bumpers up when you go bowling—it's not cheating; it's making sure your kid doesn't end up in the gutter! Set up these controls together with your son. This can be a great way to discuss why they're necessary, and it shows him that you trust him enough to involve him in the process.

I remember when my son first got his tablet. We sat down together and set up the parental controls. It turned into a mini tech lesson where I explained why certain restrictions were in place. We joked about how it was like setting up a virtual fort, keeping out the "bad guys" while letting him have fun inside safely.

Teaching Internet Safety Skills

While parental controls are great, they're not foolproof. That's why teaching your son how to navigate the internet safely is key. You can think of this in the same way as teaching yourself to fix things around the house. While you can hire a plumber or an electrician to fix your toilet or oven, developing your own DIY skills means that you can always troubleshoot problems yourself, allowing you to become self-reliant. Start with the basics: recognizing unsafe websites and understanding why sharing personal information online is a no-go. Make it relatable. Show him how just as he wouldn't give out his house keys to a stranger, he shouldn't share personal info online. You can even make a game out of spotting suspicious links or ads to turn these lessons into interactive learning sessions.

Here are some basic rules to cover:

- **Personal Information:** Never share personal details like home address, phone number, or school name.
- **Password Protection:** Use strong passwords and never share them, even with friends.
- **Safe Browsing:** Stick to websites you know are safe and report anything suspicious.

- **Social Media Smarts:** Be cautious about who you friend or follow and what you post.

Open Communication about Online Activities

Last but definitely not least, keep the lines of communication as open as the ocean. Regular chats about what your son is doing online can do wonders. It's not about interrogation; it's about interest. Show curiosity about the games he plays, the friends he chats with, and what he loves about the internet. This keeps you connected to his digital world and makes it easier for him to come to you if something troubling pops up. And if he does come to you with a problem, handle it with calm and care, not panic or punishment. This reassures him that he's done the right thing by telling you, strengthening his trust and encouraging him to always keep you in the loop.

I remember when my son encountered his first online scam email. He came to me worried, and instead of freaking out, we sat down and dissected it together, identifying the red flags and discussing what to do in the future. It turned into a teachable moment and reassured him that he could always come to me with his online concerns.

Navigating the wide expanse of the digital sea doesn't have to be a daunting voyage. With a good map (knowledge), reliable tools (safety measures), great skills (internet safety education), and an excellent communication crew (open dialogue), you can ensure that your son not only enjoys his digital explorations but also stays safe from the storms out there. Now, let's keep sailing forward, as there's much more to explore in guiding our sons through the digital age.

5.3 VIDEO GAMES AND VIRTUAL PLAY: PROS AND CONS

Alright, let's level up and talk about something that's probably as much a part of your household as that mystery box of mismatched socks: video games. Now, before you roll your eyes, thinking about the countless hours your son might be spending with a controller in hand, let's pause and reload. Video games aren't just digital candy. Managed wisely, they can be a part of a balanced 'play diet' that includes plenty of real-world adventures and learning experiences. So, how do we strike that balance and ensure that video game time doesn't turn into a free-for-all? It's all about setting some ground rules that adapt to your family's rhythm and your son's needs.

Balancing Video Game Time

Balancing video game time starts with understanding that not all screen time is created equal. Like the difference between snacking on chips and chowing down on carrots, the quality of screen time matters. Consider what games your son is playing—are they mindless button mashers, or do they challenge him with puzzles and strategy? The next step is setting limits that fit with your son's daily routine. Does he need to unwind after school? Sure, a half-hour quest can be just the ticket. But make sure it's framed by clear boundaries, like homework and chores first, gaming later. And remember, the aim here isn't to vilify gaming but to integrate it healthily into his life. Discuss these plans with him; make him part of the conversation so he understands that it's not about taking away fun, but about adding to his overall well-being.

Tips for Balancing Screen Time:

- **Set clear rules**: Define when and how long your son can play.
- **Use a timer**: Helps in maintaining the agreed-upon limits.
- **Create a schedule**: Include other activities like outdoor play, reading, and family time.
- **Be flexible**: Adjust rules based on special circumstances like holidays or exceptional behavior.

Benefits of Video Games

Now, onto the perks of picking up that game controller. Video games are like the broccoli of the digital world—often misunderstood, surprisingly nutritious. They can sharpen problem-solving skills, especially games that involve puzzles or strategic planning. Think of games like 'The Legend of Zelda' or 'Minecraft,' where players explore, experiment, and learn through trial and error. These games encourage critical thinking and creativity, offering real cognitive workouts. There's also the teamwork angle. Many games require players to cooperate to achieve common goals, promoting skills like communication and cooperation. Plus, in a world that's increasingly tech-driven, fluency in technology is a significant advantage. Gaming can improve hand-eye coordination, tech literacy, and even multitasking skills.

Key Benefits:

- **Problem-solving skills**: Games that require strategy and puzzles.
- **Teamwork**: Multiplayer games that foster communication and cooperation.
- **Tech literacy**: Familiarity with digital interfaces and problem-solving.
- **Creativity**: Games that allow building and exploration encourage creative thinking.

The Pitfalls of Gaming

However, it's not all power-ups and victory dances. The dark side of gaming—addiction, isolation, and exposure to inappropriate content—needs to be managed. Video game addiction is real and can lead to issues like poor academic performance, social withdrawal, and even health problems like obesity or repetitive strain injuries. Keep an eye on how much time your son spends gaming and watch for signs that it's becoming more than just a hobby.

Encourage diverse interests, ensuring that gaming is part of a wider array of activities. Social isolation can also creep in if gaming replaces face-to-face interactions. Encourage your son to maintain a healthy social life outside of the virtual world, perhaps by blending interests—joining a gaming club at school where he can interact with peers in person, not just online.

In my household, we've developed a system called Game and Grift. For every different sport or activity my son tries out with me, I let him pick a new game to play, and I help him put towards the cost. We try to pick a game that is similar to the activity we've enjoyed. We recently tried skateboarding together, which was followed by him trying out Skate 3 on his Xbox. In this way, he feels encouraged to try out real sports and activities, as well as games with different content and learning opportunities, ensuring he consumes a well-balanced digital diet as well as a varied lifestyle.

Pitfalls to Watch For:

- **Addiction**: Excessive gaming leading to neglect of other activities.
- **Isolation**: Preferring virtual interactions over real-life socializing.
- **Inappropriate content**: Exposure to violent or age-inappropriate material.
- **Health issues**: Poor posture, repetitive strain injuries, and lack of physical activity.

Co-Playing as a Strategy

Co-playing can be your secret weapon in the parenting arsenal. Jumping into the game with your son does more than give you street cred—it lets you directly experience the gaming environment. You can monitor the content, understand the appeal, and even discuss aspects of the game like strategy and storytelling. This shared activity can strengthen your relationship, giving you insight into his world and opening up new avenues for conversation and connection. It shows him that you're inquisitive about his interests and that you're willing to meet him on his turf, even if that turf is a digital battlefield or a fantasy kingdom.

Benefits of Co-Playing:

- **Monitoring content**: Ensuring games are appropriate.
- **Understanding**: Gaining insight into your son's interests.
- **Bonding**: Strengthening your relationship through shared activities.
- **Guidance**: Teaching strategies and discussing game elements.

Navigating the realm of video games as a parent can feel like stepping into a new version of 'Jumanji'—slightly overwhelming, unpredictably exciting. But with a strategy in place—a balance of oversight, engagement, and healthy limits—you can help your son reap the benefits of his gaming experiences without falling prey to the pitfalls. It's about guiding him to be not just a gamer but a discerning digital citizen who can navigate both the virtual and real world with confidence and skill.

5.4 SNAP, TWEET, REPEAT: GUIDING YOUR SON THROUGH THE SOCIAL MEDIA JUNGLE

Navigating the ever-expanding universe of social media with your son can feel a bit like trying to tame a wild beast. It's huge, it's lively, and it can be dangerous if not handled with care. But here's the deal: just like any tool, when used wisely, social media has the power to enrich lives, broaden horizons, and connect us in ways like never before. So, how do you guide your son through this digital social landscape without stifling his explorations or leaving him to wander alone? Let's dive into some strategies that can help you both make the most of this digital age.

Age-Appropriate Social Media Use

First up, figuring out the right time for your son to start using social media is crucial. This isn't just about age; it's about maturity. Each platform has its own age requirements, typically starting at 13 due to the Children's Online Privacy Protection Act (COPPA), which helps protect the privacy of younger kids online. However, just because your son hits that magic number doesn't necessarily mean he's ready to handle everything that social media throws at him. Consider his ability to navigate interpersonal relationships, his sense of responsibility, and how well he understands the concept of digital footprints. It's about ensuring he can handle the good, the bad, and the ugly of social media with a level head.

Start with a conversation about what social media is and why it's appealing. Discuss the platforms his friends use and what interests him about social media. This can be a great way to gauge his readiness. If you decide he's ready, begin with platforms that offer robust parental controls or family accounts, so you can guide him through the initial stages of his digital journey. Gradually introduce him to more platforms as he shows he can handle them responsibly, always keeping the lines of discussion open about his experiences and the things he encounters online.

Building a Positive Digital Footprint

The concept of a digital footprint can be pretty abstract, especially for a young mind. Explain it like this: everything he posts, likes, or comments on leaves a trace, kind of like digital footprints in the sand. Only, unlike footprints on the beach that wash away, these can stick around forever. Help him understand that his online actions are like public, permanent records. Encourage him to ask himself, "Would I be okay with grandma seeing this?" before he posts anything. It's about teaching him to create a digital persona that reflects his best self.

One effective way to convey this is through examples. Show him news stories about how social media behavior impacted individuals' lives, both positively and negatively. You can also have him create a "positive posting plan" where he thinks of things he enjoys or is good at, like a sport, a hobby, or a school subject, and explores how he can share that online in a positive, constructive way. This not only builds his digital footprint but also enhances his self-esteem and his sense of responsibility towards his online presence.

Navigating Social Dynamics Online

Social media isn't just about posting; it's a complex web of social interactions. From the pressure of likes and follows to the dynamics of online friendships, it can be a lot for a kid to handle. Start by explaining that online interactions can be very different from real-life conversations. Things can be misinterpreted without the context of tone of voice or facial expressions. Teach him to be thoughtful and kind in his comments and posts, reminding him that behind every profile is a real person who has feelings just like he does.

Discuss the concept of peer pressure in the context of social media. Just because everyone is sharing something doesn't mean he has to. Help him develop the confidence to make choices that align with his values, not just go along with the crowd. Role-playing can be a useful tool here. Create scenarios where he might feel pressured to act against his better judgment and walk through how he can handle them. This not only prepares him for potential challenges but also reinforces his decision-making skills.

Me and my son recently discussed a trend that was occurring across social media through the Covid pandemic, where children and teenagers were deliberately licking handrails on public transport, as an act of rebellion, and ultimately to show off. They were recording this and posting it on social media. I asked my son what he thought about the trend, and we discussed the danger of the transmission of germs, and the fact that these children were ultimately putting other more vulnerable people at risk. On reflection, my son told me he thought it was silly and that he wouldn't do it himself. Giving him the space to allow him to think critically about this trend enhanced his own ability to reason and make good decisions for himself.

Role Modeling Responsible Use

As with so many aspects of parenting, kids learn a lot by watching us. If you're constantly checking your phone at dinner or posting everything you do online, your son will notice and likely mimic your behavior. Make a conscious effort to model responsible social media use. Share stories about how you use social media at work or in your hobbies in positive ways. Let him see you putting your phone away during family times and being responsible with your own use of social media.

I'd encourage setting up "social media-free zones" in your home and times when the whole family unplugs. Maybe it's during meals or an hour before bedtime. Use these times to connect offline, showing that while social media is a part of life, it doesn't run your lives. By setting this example, you're not just telling your son how to use social media responsibly; you're showing him.

Navigating social media with your son doesn't have to be a daunting task. With open communication, clear guidelines, and responsible modeling, you can help him use social media in a way that enhances his life and doesn't overrun it. It's about mentoring him to navigate not just the fun and connectivity but also the challenges and responsibilities of his online world effectively.

5.5 TECH-ING CARE OF BUSINESS: THE BEST APPS FOR DIGITAL DADS

Hey, let's face it, navigating fatherhood in today's technological world can sometimes feel like trying to solve a Rubik's cube blindfolded. But guess what? There's an app for that! Well, maybe not for the Rubik's cube thing, but definitely for making the dad gig a bit smoother. From educational tools that turn boring old homework into an adventure, to apps that keep your family organized better than a seasoned drill sergeant, technology is here to serve up some serious parenting hacks. So, let's dive into some of the best apps and tools that can help you level up your parenting game. Ready to tech-care of business?

Leveraging Educational Apps

First off, let's talk educational apps. These aren't just digital pacifiers; they're your secret weapon for turning idle screen time into brain-boosting adventures. Take language learning apps, for example. Apps like Duolingo or Babbel can introduce your son to new languages through fun, interactive lessons that feel more like games than education. It's about making learning engaging and accessible, and hey, you might even pick up a bit of Spanish or French along the way!

Then there are problem-solving games. Apps like Lightbot offer puzzles that teach basic coding skills through fun, challenging games that require logical thinking and strategy. It's like sneaking veggies into a smoothie—so much learning is happening and they don't even know it! Integrating these tools into your son's daily routine can boost his academic skills while also satisfying his digital appetite. It's about smart screen time, where every tap and swipe is an opportunity to learn something new.

Me and my son are currently having a Duolingo competition to see who can learn the most Spanish in six months. It's a great way to bond while also learning a useful skill.

The Art of Boundaries And Child Surveillance

Now, onto the somewhat tricky topic of parental monitoring tools. Navigating this can feel like walking a tightrope between being protective and respecting your son's privacy. Tools like Qustodio or Net Nanny can help you keep an eye on what your son is up to online without feeling like you're spying on him. You can set filters, monitor usage, and even block harmful content, all while keeping the lines of communication about online safety wide open.

The trick here is balance. Discuss the use of these tools with your son. Explain that they're not about distrust but about ensuring he has a safe online experience. Use these tools judiciously, always being upfront about what you're monitoring and why. We don't want them to feel like we just planted spyware on them. But rather it's about building trust, not breaking it, and helping your son learn to navigate the internet responsibly.

Organizational Tools for Family Management

Keeping a family organized can sometimes feel like herding cats, but thanks to technology, there are tools to help keep the chaos at bay. Apps like Cozi or TimeTree can be lifesavers for managing family schedules. From soccer practices to doctor appointments to family movie nights, everything can be conveniently synced in one place. These apps allow every family member to add events, set reminders, and even share shopping lists. It's like having a personal assistant in your pocket, one that doesn't complain about working overtime!

Using these tools can help teach your son about time management and organization. He can see firsthand how planning and coordination lead to a smoother-running family life. Plus, it's a great way for him to start taking responsibility for his own appointments and activities. Encourage him to add his own events and set his reminders. It's a good small step towards independence, with the safety net of family oversight. If you can't tell already, I'm all about encouraging baby steps when it comes to learning any skills. This helps avoid overwhelm.

Health and Wellness Apps

Last but certainly not least, let's talk health and wellness apps. In a world where screens often contribute to sedentary lifestyles, apps like MyFitnessPal or Nike Training Club can motivate both you and your son to stay active. These apps offer everything from workout routines that you can do together, to tracking and planning healthy meals. It's about making health and fitness accessible and engaging. Though there will be evenings when your son wants chicken nuggets and you wouldn't mind a greasy takeout yourself, these apps can offer inspiration for healthier alternatives such as cooking a 'fakeaway' at home with quality ingredients. Following my son's football practice a few weeks ago, we were both starving, but we abstained from visiting our local fast food joint and instead cooked up a delicious carbonara that we found a recipe for on MyFitnessPal.

Mental well-being is just as important as your physical health, and apps like Headspace provide guided meditations that can help both you and your son learn to relax and manage stress. Incorporating these apps into your daily routines can not only improve your physical and mental health but also set an example for your son of the importance of taking care of both body and mind.

Tips on Using Apps and Technology Effectively

- **Organizational tools**: Ensuring a schedule which is healthy and well planned.
- **Health and wellness**: Boost physical and mental wellbeing with health-focused apps.
- **Parental monitoring Tools**: Monitor digital consumption to ensure safe usage.
- **Educational apps**: Enhance learning with engaging educational apps.

Personal Story: Tech Traditions

In our house, tech traditions have become a fun part of our family routine. Usually around the holidays or during family gatherings Every Sunday, we have what we call the "App Swap." My wife and I, along with our son and our daughter, share new fun apps that we've discovered during the last few months. It's our little way of staying connected and tech-savvy together. Sometimes we find a great new game; other times, it's a productivity app or a new way to learn. It's a simple tradition, but it keeps us engaged and opens up new conversations about technology and how we use it.

Conclusion

Incorporating these tech tools into your parenting arsenal can make you feel like you've got a superpower, turning potential parenting pitfalls into opportunities for growth, learning, and connection. Whether it's through learning apps that make education interactive and fun, monitoring tools that keep your son safe online, organizational apps that keep your family on track, or health and wellness apps that promote a healthy lifestyle, technology is there to help you be the best dad you can be. So go ahead, embrace the digital age, and watch as both you and your son learn, grow, and thrive together in this connected world.

5.6 USING TECHNOLOGY TO BOND: SHARED DIGITAL ACTIVITIES

Hey there, tech-savvy dads! Let's face it, technology isn't just about navigating the digital dangers or managing screen time—it's also an incredible tool for bonding with your son. Think of it as your digital Swiss Army knife, handy for more than just cutting down screen time squabbles. From interactive learning escapades to crafting digital stories together, technology can turn an ordinary afternoon into an adventure, strengthening your bond while you both have a blast. So, let's plug in and power up some truly engaging activities that are perfect for father-son time.

Interactive Learning Activities

Imagine transforming your tablet or computer into a dynamic classroom where the lessons are so engaging, your son doesn't even realize he's learning. Interactive websites and apps can turn subjects like science and math into hands-on experiments and puzzles that you both can solve together. For instance, dive into websites like National Geographic Kids or the NASA Kids' Club where you can explore everything from the depths of the ocean to the far reaches of space. Engage in science experiments that you can conduct with common household items, courtesy of sites like Science Bob. You can watch volcanic eruptions unfold on your kitchen table or create a tornado in a bottle.

Coding doesn't have to be a solitary activity either. Platforms like Scratch or Tynker offer coding games designed for kids and parents to learn the basics of programming through interactive storytelling or game creation. These platforms allow you to work together to solve puzzles and build simple programs, turning screen time into a creative and educational experience. It's not just about coding; it's about thinking logically, solving problems, and expressing yourselves digitally.

Digital Storytelling

Now, let's switch gears to storytelling. Digital storytelling tools like Storybird or My Storybook give you and your son the canvas to create your own stories. Whether it's a wild adventure with pirates and aliens or a personal story about a day at the park, crafting a narrative together can be a powerful way to connect. These tools often offer a mix of writing, art, and technology, allowing you to add illustrations, animations, and even music to your stories. It's a fantastic way to foster creativity, improve writing skills, and have a lot of fun in the process. Plus, you get to know more about what sparks your son's imagination and share a bit of your own.

Virtual Travel and Exploration

Last but not least, who says you need to leave the house to explore the world? Virtual tours can take you and your son to museums, historical sites, and even other planets. Platforms like Google Arts & Culture offer virtual tours of museums like The British Museum in

London or the Van Gogh Museum in Amsterdam. You can explore ancient ruins with virtual reality apps or take a virtual walk on Mars with the help of NASA's VR tours. It's a great way to explore new cultures and histories, sparking discussions about the world and its diverse heritage. Plus, it's a fantastic way to plan future travels; maybe one day soon you'll visit these places in person!

Using technology to bond with your son offers both fun and educational opportunities. It turns the digital world into a playground of learning and creativity, where each click represents an opportunity to learn and grow together. Whether you're solving science puzzles, crafting epic stories, practicing internet safety, or traveling the globe virtually, these activities can enhance your relationship, making every moment spent together not just fun, but meaningful. Now, let's gear up for the next chapter where we'll explore more ways to strengthen family bonds, creating memories that last a lifetime.

CHAPTER 6
MAXIMIZING HEALTH AND WELLNESS FOR DADS AND SONS

6.1 LEADING BY EXAMPLE: FITNESS AND NUTRITION

Picture this: it's a sunny Saturday morning and you're in the park, chasing your son up the hill—both of you laughing breathlessly, your legs feeling like they're made of both springs and lead. Later, you're in the kitchen together, tossing a salad, and he's wrinkling his nose at the sight of spinach but is curious enough to give it a taste because, well, you're eating it too. This isn't just about fun and food—it's your masterclass in fatherhood where you're teaching by doing, showing your son the ropes of living a healthy, active life.

Modeling Healthy Behaviors

As dads, we're the first heroes our sons ever know, and with great power comes great responsibility—especially when it comes to setting a lifestyle example. Kids are like sponges; they absorb everything they see us doing, for better or for worse. If they see us sprawled on the couch for hours with a bag of chips within arm's reach, that's a snapshot of normal life for them. On the flip side, if they see us lacing up our sneakers for a run, or chomping on an apple instead of a candy bar, those images stick too.

It's all about making sure the behaviors they're copying are the ones we're proud to pass on. Think about what habits you want your son to inherit. Is it the dedication to keep fit? The willpower to choose a well-balanced meal? Or maybe the enthusiasm for trying out a new sport? Whatever it is, let him see you doing it, and not just as a one-off but as a regular part of your routine. Remember, actions speak louder than words, and when it comes to teaching our kids about health and fitness, this couldn't be truer. So set a positive example, and when you do decide to grab a scrumptious Five Guys on your way home from work, scoff it down before your son sees you!

Joint Fitness Activities

Now, transforming these observations into joint activities is where the real magic happens. It's one thing for your son to see you in action, and another for him to join in. This isn't just about getting fit together; it's about building memories, strengthening your bond, and setting up a foundation for lifelong health.

So, what can you do together? If you're into running, consider mini-races in the park. If you're a gym enthusiast, some facilities offer family-friendly sessions where kids can learn age-appropriate exercises. Even home workout videos can be a fun way to get moving together—just clear some space in the living room, roll out a couple of mats, and press play. For something less structured, how about a bike ride around the neighborhood? Or perhaps a hike on a nearby trail? These activities not only boost physical health but also give you both a chance to disconnect from screens and connect with nature—and each other.

Nutritional Guidance

When it comes to food, being a role model gets a bit trickier—especially if your culinary skills are limited to microwaving leftovers. But fear not, you don't have to be a gourmet chef to teach your son about good nutrition. It starts with the basics: incorporating fruits and veggies into meals, choosing whole grains, and swapping out soda for water or milk.

Involve your son in meal planning and preparation. Even young children can help with washing veggies or setting the table. As he grows, he can take on more complex tasks like mixing ingredients or even cooking simple dishes. Use this time to talk about why you choose certain foods over others and what benefits they bring to the body. This hands-on approach not only teaches him about nutrition but also equips him with cooking skills that'll serve him well beyond childhood.

Remember that even making small healthy choices adds up over time. It is about consistency, not perfection. If your son wants the occasional chocolate bar, and you are impartial to a large pizza with stuffed crust once a month, that's fine, as long as it's in moderation. Teaching your son about realistic and balanced choices will ensure that he takes these healthy habits with him into the rest of his life.

Setting Fitness Goals

Setting fitness goals together can be a great way to stay motivated and track progress. It's like a buddy system, but better because it's with your son. Start with setting simple, achievable goals. Maybe it's a daily 15-minute walk after dinner, or doing 30 sit-ups each morning. Track these activities on a calendar somewhere that your son can see, and mark off what's been accomplished—it's incredibly satisfying for kids (and let's be honest, for us too) to see this progress visually.

Celebrate when you reach these goals. Did you both stick to your walk schedule for the whole month? Reward yourselves with something special, like a trip to the ice cream shop or a new soccer ball. These celebrations reinforce the idea that fitness isn't just good for you; it can be fun, too. They also teach goal-setting—a valuable skill in all areas of life, from academics to personal growth.

In this way, you're not just improving your health; you're enhancing your relationship. You're building a foundation of healthy habits for your son, showing him that fitness and nutrition aren't chores, but parts of a fulfilling lifestyle. And through every jog, every bike ride, and every healthy meal, you're showing him that the best way to take care of himself is by enjoying the journey—side by side with you, his dad, his first and forever hero.

Tips to Promote Health and Wellness

- **Modeling healthy behaviors:** Living a healthy lifestyle yourself, leading by example.
- **Joint fitness activities:** Combining your workouts, sharing in the experience.
- **Nutritional guidance**: Ensuring a healthy diet which promotes wellbeing.
- **Setting fitness goals**: Striving to improve, having fun while staying healthy.

6.2 MENTAL HEALTH MATTERS: RECOGNIZING SIGNS IN YOUR SON

Let's talk about something that often hangs out in the quieter corners of parenting discussions—mental health. As dads, we're usually on the front lines when it comes to teaching bike riding or how to throw a perfect spiral, but we're also crucial players in recognizing and supporting our sons' mental well-being. Understanding the signs of mental health issues like anxiety and depression in our kids is as crucial as knowing how to put on a Band-Aid. It's about being vigilant, empathetic, and proactive because early recognition can make a world of difference.

Awareness of Mental Health

First off, knowing what to look out for can help you catch potential issues before they grow. Signs that might raise a flag include changes in mood that are more intense and persistent than typical moodiness associated with growing up. If your usually chatty son becomes withdrawn, or if his energetic spirit dims without explanation, these could be cues worth paying attention to. Other signs might include changes in eating and sleeping habits, expressions of hopelessness, or a drop in performance at school. It's about tuning into those subtle changes in his usual pattern that might indicate something is up.

But this isn't about becoming a helicopter parent, hovering over every frown. It's about being present, engaging in real conversations, and creating a space where feelings can be discussed openly. Ask about what's going on in his life, not just academically but socially and emotionally as well. Sometimes, just knowing someone is there to listen without judgment can open up a dialogue about what's troubling him.

Just recently, my son was being particularly quiet on an otherwise sunny and cheery Saturday. I was leaving him to his devices and respecting his space, but his behavior persisted. I decided to ask him if he was ok, and told him I was here for him if he needed me. He ended up sharing with me that he had had a rubbish week at school and that a boy had said something nasty to him in class. Picking up on his social cues in this situation gave rise to a really helpful and important conversation where he could share his struggles with me, and I could make sure he was heard and understood.

Creating a Supportive Environment

Creating an environment where your son feels safe to express his feelings and admit when he's not okay is vital. This starts with how you handle emotions yourself. Showing that it's okay to talk about feelings, and that you're not immune to life's ups and downs, sets a powerful example. Use everyday situations to model positive emotional responses and resilience. If you had a tough day at work, share that with him—not in a way that burdens him with your stresses, but in a way that shows him that everyone has challenging days and that it's okay to talk about them.

Encourage activities at home that foster communication. Family dinners can be a great time to check in with everyone's mental state. Make it a routine where each family member shares one good thing about their day and one thing that might have been challenging. This not only promotes gratitude but also normalizes discussing struggles and seeking support.

Professional Help and Resources

Knowing when to seek help from professionals is another key aspect of supporting your son's mental health. If you notice persistent sadness, a significant drop in school performance, or disinterest in activities he once loved, it might be time to consult a professional. Start with your family doctor who can recommend a child psychologist or psychiatrist if necessary.

Organizations like the National Alliance on Mental Illness (NAMI) offer great tools and information for understanding various mental health conditions. Websites like Psychology Today can help you find local therapists and counselors. Also, apps like Headspace offer guided meditations that can help manage anxiety and stress, making them great tools for both prevention and management of mental health issues.

Preventative Mental Health Practices

Lastly, integrating preventative practices into your daily life can help maintain and support mental well-being. Establishing a routine provides a sense of security and predictability, which can be comforting in a world that often feels chaotic. Ensure that he has a supportive social environment by encouraging friendships and social activities that boost his mood and self-esteem.

Teach coping skills that can help him manage stress. Simple techniques like deep breathing, mindfulness, or even physical activities like yoga can be effective ways to manage stress. Encourage him to keep a journal where he can express his thoughts and feelings, which can be a powerful tool for mental health.

By tackling mental health head-on, maintaining open lines of communication, and modeling healthy emotional behaviors, you're setting your son up not just to succeed, but to thrive. Remember, taking care of his mental health is just as important as any other aspect of his upbringing. It's about equipping him with the tools to not only cope with life's challenges but to emerge stronger, more resilient, and more connected to those around him.

6.3 UNWIND & REWIND: STRESS RELIEF FOR DADS AND LADS

Hey there, super dads! When was the last time you felt like your day needed a few more hours, or your to-do list looked more like a novel? Stress—it's like that one guest at your BBQ who just won't leave, right? And guess what, our kids, they feel it too. From school pressures to that relentless stream of social media, our sons are navigating a world that's buzzing non-stop. But here's the kicker: just as we can share laughs and games, we can also share ways to tackle stress together. Let's roll up our sleeves and turn stress management into another bonding experience that's both rewarding and fun.

Identifying Sources of Stress

First off, let's play detective and identify what's really grinding our gears. It's like when you're trying to find the remote—sometimes the search reveals a lot more than what you were looking for. Sit down with your son and have a chat about what aspects of his day trigger stress. Is it homework? A certain class or maybe social situations at school? For you, maybe it's juggling work deadlines or managing household chores. Write these down. Seeing them on paper can sometimes make them feel less daunting and more like a puzzle you both can solve. Plus, it's a great way to show your son that everyone deals with stress, and it's perfectly okay to talk about it.

Discuss how these stressors make you both feel. Is there a stomach knot before a math test or a sense of dread on Sunday nights? Recognizing these physical cues is about tuning into your body's way of saying, "Hey, something's up," and using that awareness to manage stress before it manages you.

Relaxation Practices

Next up, let's talk chilling out—dad and lad style! Ever tried deep breathing exercises? They're like hitting a reset button for your body and mind. And the beauty is, you can do them anywhere. Whether it's during a quiet moment after dinner or in the car before school drop-off, take a few minutes to breathe deeply together. Count to four as you inhale, hold for four, and then exhale for four. It's a simple trick, but you'd be amazed at how it can melt away tension.

Yoga and meditation are other fantastic tools. No need to be a yoga guru here; just start with some basic poses or even a guided meditation app. Make it fun by setting a challenge—who can hold a tree pose longer, or who can stay quite the longest during meditation? These activities aren't just great for stress relief; they enhance focus and bring a sense of calm that can help both of you handle whatever the day throws your way. You'll quickly realize that you don't need to be the Dalai Lama for these exercises to have a huge impact on your day-to-day stress levels.

Time Management Skills

Now, let's tackle the beast that is time management. It's like figuring out a strategy in a video game. You've got to plan your moves, manage your resources, and sometimes, beat the clock. Start by setting priorities. Help your son understand what needs his attention first and what can wait. Maybe homework and chores come before video games and TV time. And dads, this applies to you too—

modeling good time management is key. Show him how you prioritize your day, maybe by making lists or setting reminders on your phone.

Avoid over-scheduling. It's tempting to pack the day with back-to-back activities, but where's the fun in that? Ensure there's downtime for both of you. It's like leaving space between the chapters of a book—it gives you a moment to breathe and get ready for what's next.

A few weeks ago, I had a really busy week ahead of me. I remember looking at my schedule on Monday morning and seeing that I had one gap left in my Friday evening. I had a friend ask me if I wanted to play some five-a-side football that evening, and though I could have fit it in, I didn't want to cram my week too much, so I declined the invite. When Friday rolled around, I ended up watching a great movie with my son and enjoying some popcorn together. This was an important reminder to me that sometimes you need to leave a breathing room in your schedule, so you can enjoy chill time with your family.

Fun and Unwinding

Finally, let's not forget the fun factor! Stress reduction doesn't have to be all serious. It's also about laughing and letting loose. Plan activities that you both enjoy and that give you a break from the daily grind. Maybe it's a weekend bike ride, watching a movie together, or just tossing a baseball in the yard. These moments of fun play a massive role in unwinding and reconnecting.

Consider creating a "chill zone" in your home—a spot where you both can relax, free from the buzz of everyday tasks. Fill it with comfy cushions, maybe some good books, or even some art supplies. This can be your go-to spot when you sense the stress levels rising.

By integrating these stress reduction techniques into your daily routine, you're not just helping dodge the stress bullets—you're building a toolbox of strategies that your son can carry into adulthood. And the best part? You're doing it together, strengthening that father-son bond, one shared deep breath, one laughter-filled afternoon at a time. So here's to less stress and more high fives, knowing that you're tackling one of modern life's biggest challenges side by side

Techniques to Reduce Stress

- **Identifying stress:** Being aware of stresses, so they can be managed effectively.
- **Relaxation practices:** Promoting relaxation through regular practices like breathing.
- **Time management skills:** Managing time effectively to avoid stressful situations.
- **Fun and unwinding:** Having fun and relaxing, preventing stress from building up.

6.4 THE GREAT OUTDOORS: ENCOURAGING PHYSICAL PLAY

Remember those days when the phrase "Go play outside!" was all the permission you needed to embark on an epic adventure, whether it was building forts, exploring streams, or just lying on the grass watching clouds sail by? It's time to pass that torch of outdoor exploration to your son, injecting a healthy dose of nature into his life which, let's be honest, often revolves a bit too much around pixels and less around pinecones. The great outdoors isn't just a playground; it's a vast, open-ended classroom where lessons in physics, biology, and personal growth happen in the most natural way possible.

Just the other day, my son had gone hiking with friends in the forest. He had noticed a pine cone fall to the floor, seemingly unprovoked. Later on, he asked me what had happened to cause the pine cone to fall, and we ended up having an educational conversation about gravity and the laws of physics. This is an example of how the natural world can inspire learning.

Benefits of Outdoor Activities

Spending time outdoors isn't just fun—it's foundational. The physical benefits are the most obvious, with activities like climbing trees and playing tag burning energy and building muscles in a way no gym class can. But the perks extend far beyond the physical. Nature enhances mental and emotional well-being, reducing stress and boosting mood dramatically. It's like Mother Nature's own brand of mood medicine, available and free for all. On top of that, being outdoors sparks creativity. Ever watched a kid turn a stick into a sword, a laser gun, or a magic wand? That's creativity on the fly, fueled by simple, unstructured play in the great wide open.

Moreover, outdoor play strengthens your son's connection to the environment, fostering an appreciation for the beauty and complexity of the natural world. This connection can cultivate a sense of responsibility for taking care of the environment as he grows. Each hike through the woods, each day spent at the beach, builds a bond with nature that can last a lifetime, encouraging him to become not just a steward of the earth but also an advocate for its preservation.

Ideas for Outdoor Adventures

So, what exactly can you do to get this all-natural party started? Well, the possibilities are as vast as the great outdoors itself. For starters, think about what's accessible to you. If you're near mountains, plan a family hike. If the sea is closer, a beach day can be just as adventurous. Don't forget about your local parks—they're often packed with potential for fun and exploration.

Seasons can dictate your activities, but they don't have to limit them. Summer is great for swimming and kayaking, while winter snows set the stage for sledding or building snowmen (or snow forts for the more competitively inclined). Spring and fall are perfect for biking or kite flying when the weather is mild and the scenery is spectacular. And if you're feeling adventurous, why not try camping? It's an all-in-one package of outdoor skills, from setting up a tent to cooking over a fire. Plus, it's a fantastic way to bond, sharing stories under the stars, far from the glow of screens and the buzz of everyday life. Don't forget your marshmallows for toasting!

Safety in Outdoor Settings

Now, as much as we're boosting the benefits of the outdoors, let's not sidestep safety. It's all fun and games until someone ends up with a sprained ankle—or worse. Always check the weather before you head out, dressing appropriately and planning activities that suit the conditions. Make sure both you and your son understand the basics of outdoor safety. This includes everything from wearing helmets while biking to knowing what to do if you encounter wildlife.

Bring along a basic first aid kit for those inevitable scrapes and scratches. Teach your son how to use each item safely. It's not just about patching up wounds; it's about empowering him with knowledge and the confidence to handle unexpected situations.

On a camping trip with my son a couple of years back, we were lucky enough to encounter a wild boar with its young. Thankfully, I had educated myself on how to behave when coming across a boar, and so I instructed my son to keep a good distance and not get between the boar and their young. Though this was a harmless encounter, being educated on the right way to deal with this situation ensured that we remained safe and out of harm's way, highlighting the importance of being prepared.

Respecting Nature

Finally, instilling a respect for nature goes hand-in-hand with enjoying it. Practice the 'leave no trace' principle on all your outdoor adventures. Show your son how to enjoy the outdoors without leaving a mark, like taking all your trash home and avoiding picking plants or disturbing wildlife. Discuss why these practices matter. It's about more than keeping places nice for other people; it's about preserving them for other creatures and for future generations.

Incorporating these elements into your outdoor adventures not only maximizes the fun and the benefits but also sets a foundation for responsible, respectful interaction with the natural world. It's about teaching your son that the great outdoors is a gift we all need to share, one that requires our care and respect. So, grab your gear, prep your knowledge, and step outside—the world is waiting, and it's time to play.

6.5 SNORE WARS: THE EPIC QUEST FOR THE ULTIMATE SLEEP ROUTINE

Ah, sleep—the magical realm where our bodies and minds go to recharge, grow, and sort through the day's adventures. As dads, we often focus on the hustle of daytime activities, but let's not forget the silent powerhouse of health and well-being: a good night's sleep. Establishing and maintaining healthy sleep routines for both ourselves and our sons is like ensuring our cars have enough quality fuel for the long haul—it's essential for our performance, mood, and overall health.

Establishing Healthy Sleep Habits

Creating a sleep-friendly routine isn't just about telling your son bedtime is at 8 PM; it's about creating a rhythm that winds down the day with calm and consistency. Start with a bedtime routine that might include quieter activities as the evening progresses, like reading a book together or discussing the day's highs and lows. This gradual wind-down helps signal to his body and brain that it's time to slow down, making the transition to sleep smoother and more natural.

It's also about consistency—going to bed and waking up at the same time every day, yes, even on weekends, can significantly improve the quality of sleep. This regularity helps set your son's internal clock, making it easier for him to fall asleep and wake up naturally. And hey, while you're at it, model this behavior yourself. Let him see that dad also prioritizes good sleep, not just by enforcing rules but by practicing them, even if that means cutting a Breaking Bad rewatch short. It's a team effort, after all.

Personal Tradition Example: In our house, we have a little bedtime routine that's become a beloved tradition. My son and I do a "wind-down hour" where we read a chapter of his favorite book and then talk about our favorite parts of the day. It's a perfect way to signal the end of the day and prepare for sleep.

Dealing with Sleep Challenges

Now, onto tackling those pesky sleep challenges like nightmares or insomnia, which can turn nighttimes into a less-than-dreamy scenario. For nightmares, it's about reassurance first—letting your son know it's okay and that everyone gets them once in a while. A little comfort goes a long way. Keep a 'monster spray' (just a spray bottle of water) handy to ward off bad dreams, or invent a bedtime ritual that includes checking under the bed or in the closet to ensure a monster-free zone.

For insomnia, which can be trickier, start by looking at daytime activities. Too much screen time, especially before bed, can make it hard for him to wind down. Encourage activities that expend energy —like playing outside. If the insomnia persists, consider a consultation with a pediatrician to explore further solutions. Sometimes, just tweaking the daily routine or the bedroom environment can make a world of difference.

The Role of Technology

Speaking of screen time, let's dive into how tech affects sleep. Screens emit blue light, which can mess with the body's ability to prepare for sleep because it mimics daylight. This can delay sleep onset and disrupt sleep quality. So, set a tech curfew—an hour before bed where screens go off, and quieter activities take over. Maybe replace game time with storytime or drawing. This not only helps his brain gear down for sleep but also gives you both a perfect time to connect offline.

Story: One of our best decisions was establishing a "tech-free hour" before bed. My wife suggested it, and now it's a staple in our routine. We put away all screens and focus on calming activities, and it's made a noticeable difference in how quickly our son falls asleep.

Creating a Restful Environment

Lastly, creating a sleep-conducive environment can play a huge role in how well both you and your son sleep. This means looking at factors like lighting, noise, and temperature in his bedroom. A cool, dark, and quiet room is ideal for sleeping. Consider blackout curtains if street lights peek through his window or a white noise machine if there's noise from the street or the house. And make sure his mattress and pillows are comfortable—it's hard to sleep well if he's tossing and turning all night.

Investing in good sleep is like investing in a high-yield bond—it pays off in numerous, sometimes surprising, ways. From better mood and behavior to improved attention and learning, the benefits of quality sleep go far beyond just not feeling sleepy. It's laying a foundation for good health, not just for now but for life. So here's to good nights and bright, energetic mornings—may they be as regular as clockwork in your household, setting the stage for days filled with energy and nights filled with dreams.

Tips to Improve Sleep Quality

- **Establishing healthy habits:** Maintaining a regular sleep schedule and bedtime routine.
- **Dealing with challenges:** Soothing any concerns around sleeping.

- **Limiting technology:** Reducing screen time to promote a natural wind down.
- **Creating a restful environment:** Ensuring a calming and relaxing bedroom.

6.6 HANDLING HEALTH CHALLENGES: FROM MINOR ILLNESSES TO MAJOR CONCERNS

Navigating the choppy waters of health issues, whether they're the sniffles or something more persistent, is part and parcel of the dad gig. It's about being ready with both the band-aids and the big-hearted hugs. But beyond kissing boo-boos to make them better, there's a real knack to handling health challenges effectively. It starts with a solid understanding of first aid and knowing when to switch gears from home care to professional help.

First Aid and Basic Care

Let's start with the basics. First aid—it's like the dad's emergency toolkit. Knowing how to clean a cut, bandage a bruise, or manage a fever can make all the difference. These aren't just handy skills; they're your first line of defense in keeping minor issues from turning into major problems. Make sure you have a well-stocked first aid kit at home and in the car. Include the essentials: bandages, antiseptic wipes, gauze, and over-the-counter medications for pain and fever. But it's not enough to just have the tools; you need to know how to use them. Consider taking a basic first aid course if you haven't already. Many local community centers or hospitals offer them, and they can equip you with the confidence to handle common injuries and ailments. I found the information from one of these courses really useful when my son came over dizzy one day when he was four. It was brought on by a temporary low blood sugar, and I knew to put him in the right position lying down so he wouldn't fall over if he fainted. We never know when this sort of information might come in useful, so it's better to be safe than sorry. Teach your son the basics too. Depending on his age, he can learn to clean a scratch or put on a bandage. It's about making him an active participant in his health care, not just a bystander. This not only educates him but also helps reduce any anxiety associated with injuries. Make it a regular father-son learning session, and who knows? You might just spark an interest in medicine or healthcare!

When to Seek Medical Attention

While a stocked first aid kit and a cool head can handle many a scrape and cough, knowing when to seek professional medical attention is crucial. Not every health issue can or should be tackled at home. If your son has persistent symptoms that don't improve with home treatments, or if he experiences more severe symptoms like difficulty breathing, severe allergic reactions, or intense pain, it's time to call the doctor.

But it's not just about responding to symptoms. Regular check-ups are vital. They keep you informed about your son's health and provide a baseline for what's normal for him, which can be invaluable in spotting potential issues early. Encourage openness during these visits. Make sure your son feels comfortable discussing anything that's on his mind, no matter how small it might seem. This open dialogue can often uncover health issues that might have been missed otherwise.

Managing Chronic Conditions

Dealing with chronic conditions such as asthma, diabetes, or allergies requires a tailored approach. It's about more than just managing symptoms; it involves creating a lifestyle that accommodates and mitigates the impact of the condition. Work closely with healthcare providers to understand your son's needs and the best ways to support him. This might mean dietary adjustments, activity modifications, or regular medication.

Educate yourself about his condition. The more you know, the better equipped you'll be to help him manage it. And involve him in the management plan as much as possible. Whether it's teaching him to recognize the early signs of an asthma attack or understanding how food affects his diabetes, empowering him with knowledge gives him a sense of control over his condition.

Emotional Support During Illness

Lastly, never underestimate the power of emotional support. Being sick, especially with a chronic condition, can be frustrating and scary for a child. Your role as a comforter is just as important as your role as caregiver. Keep the atmosphere positive and uplifting. Focus on what he can do rather than what he can't. Celebrate small victories, like a good day at school or the successful management of a flare up..

Create a support system not just within the family but with friends and caregivers who understand his condition and can provide encouragement and understanding. Knowing he's not facing this alone can make a significant difference in how he copes with and manages his health challenges.

Navigating health challenges with your son requires a mix of practical knowledge, proactive management, and, most importantly, a whole lot of heart. It's about more than just treating symptoms; it's about nurturing a spirit of resilience, educating for independence, and ensuring emotional well-being through every sniffle and sneeze. As you equip yourself and your son with the knowledge and skills to manage health challenges effectively, you reinforce the foundation of trust and care that defines your relationship, ensuring that no matter what health issues come your way, you'll face them together, stronger and more connected.

As we wrap up this exploration of health and wellness, remember that these lessons in taking care of physical and mental health are invaluable, not just for now, but for a lifetime. What we instill in our sons today—resilience, awareness, and proactive care—prepares them not just to cope with life's challenges but to thrive through them. As we turn the page to our next chapter, let's carry forward this spirit of proactive care and deep connection, ensuring that our journey as fathers is as healthy and fulfilling as it can be, for both us and our sons.

Tips on Handling Health Challenges

- **First aid and basic care:** Ensuring timely first aid in the first instance of illness.
- **Seeking medical attention:** Knowing when it is appropriate to seek medical help.
- **Managing chronic conditions:** Promoting health and resilience over time.
- **Providing emotional support:** Showing emotional support always, through all trials.

CHAPTER 7
FOSTERING LIFELONG LEARNING AND GROWTH

7.1 SMARTY PANTS DANCE: CELEBRATING THE JOY OF LEARNING

Remember the thrill of your first bike ride without training wheels? That "aha!" moment wasn't just about the bike; it was about discovery and learning. Now, as a dad, you're in the co-pilot seat, helping your son navigate the exhilarating path of learning and curiosity. But how do you transform the sometimes mundane task of learning into an adventure that rivals his favorite video game? It's all about fostering curiosity, learning through play, incentivizing learning correctly, and exploring diverse environments. Let's dive into these concepts, ensuring your son's educational journey is as thrilling as his first solo bike ride.

Cultivating Curiosity

Curiosity is the engine of intellectual achievement—it's the spark that ignites the passion for exploration and learning. But it's important to realize that curiosity doesn't always maintain itself; it needs to be nurtured. One of the simplest yet most profound ways to do this is by encouraging questions. Yes, even those "Why is the sky blue?" inquiries during a long car ride. Every question your son asks is an opportunity to explore answers together. This doesn't mean you need to have all the answers. In fact, admitting that you don't know something and proposing, "Let's find out together," can be incredibly empowering. It shows him that learning is a lifelong process, even for dads. After all, there's no shame in admitting that you don't know why ostriches can't fly, or what a female camel is called. Use resources like educational websites, library books, or even documentaries to explore these questions. This approach not only answers his immediate queries but also teaches him how to find information and satisfy his curiosity independently. I recently found myself researching hamburgers when my son asked me where they were invented. Who would have thought they actually originated from Hamburg, a city in Germany. You learn something new every day, eh?

Learning through Play

For younger children, play is the language of learning. It's through play that children understand the world around them. Integrating learning into play is like hiding cauliflower in mac and cheese - nutritious but delightful.. Consider educational toys like building blocks (Lego, for example), which can be used to teach basic engineering concepts, or puzzle games that enhance spatial reasoning. Interactive science kits that allow children to conduct safe experiments can turn your kitchen into a laboratory, making science exciting and accessible. These playful learning experiences are crucial—they engage your son's natural curiosity and joy in a way that more formal education sometimes struggles to capture.

Incentivizing Learning

While gold stars and a chart can be effective, true motivation often comes from within. Intrinsic motivation—learning because it's enjoyable or satisfying, not just because it leads to a reward—is key to fostering a lifelong love of education. To cultivate this, praise the effort rather than just the outcome. Comments like, "I'm so proud of how hard you worked on this project," emphasize the process of learning, which is filled with challenges and improvements. This approach helps build resilience and a growth mindset, key ingredients for academic and personal success. Moreover, involve your son in setting his own learning goals. Whether it's reading a certain number of books a month or mastering a new math skill, having a say in his goals makes achieving them that much more satisfying. My wife and I once set a family reading challenge where we all chose a book to read within a month. The reward wasn't a prize but a special family outing to our favorite ice cream parlor. The journey, the discussions about the books, and the shared goal made the experience enriching (well, and the mint choc chip double cone).

Diverse Learning Environments

Why limit learning to the four walls of a classroom when the whole world can be your son's educational oyster? Diverse learning environments, from museums to nature parks, provide unique opportunities for experiential learning. A trip to the museum isn't just about observing; it's about engaging with history, science, and culture in a tangible way. Nature walks can turn into lessons on biology and environmental science. Even a day out in the city can be educational if you discuss the architecture, history, or the functioning of public transport. These experiences make learning dynamic and deeply ingrained, showing your son that education isn't just about textbooks—it's about the immersive and interactive world around him. My wife often joins us on these explorations, turning them into family adventures that bring learning to life.

In essence, the joy of learning is about sparking that innate curiosity, integrating play into education, motivating wisely, and stepping out into the world as your classroom. By adopting these approaches, you're not just teaching your son about the world; you're showing him how to learn from it passionately and persistently. As you both embark on this educational adventure, remember, every day holds the possibility of a lesson, every curiosity a chance to grow, and every moment spent together is a step towards a future where he embraces learning not just as a task, but as a thrilling part of life.

7.2 BOOKS AND BEYOND: BUILDING A HOME LIBRARY TOGETHER

Ah, books—the timeless portals to other worlds and minds. But here's the twist: building a home library with your son isn't just about stacking shelves with dusty tomes; it's about laying the foundation for a lifelong journey into the realms of imagination, knowledge, and beyond. Think of it as crafting a treasure chest where each book is a gem, sparkling with potential and adventures. Let's embark on this literary expedition, curating a collection that not only entertains but enlightens, creating routines that turn the page on how you both view reading.

Selecting Diverse Materials

When it comes to building your library, variety isn't just the spice of life; it's the main ingredient. Diverse materials mean books that span genres, cultures, and subjects, painting a broad picture of the world. Start with genres—mix it up with mysteries, science fiction, fantasy, biography, and non-fiction. Each genre offers different benefits: mysteries hone problem-solving skills, science fiction sparks imagination, biographies teach history and resilience, and non-fiction expands general knowledge.

Cultural diversity in books is crucial. Include stories that reflect different cultures and voices. This not only broadens your son's worldview but fosters empathy and understanding. Look for books that celebrate stories from around the globe, offering windows into lives both similar to and different from his own. And don't shy away from subjects that challenge—books that tackle historical events or social issues can provoke important thoughts and conversations about the world.

My son recently read a book about cultures from around the world, and it inspired all sorts of questions that he had about different faiths, customs, and traditions that other countries have developed. I could see the curiosity in his eyes as he asked me these questions. This one book had the power to spark his curiosity so much that he now wants to see other parts of the world (he'll have to get saving because we all know how expensive flights are these days...).

Creating a Reading Routine

Establishing a reading routine is like setting the stage for a daily mini-adventure. Make it a special time of the day, free from the distractions of chores, screens, and outside noise. Maybe right before bedtime or on a lazy Sunday afternoon. This isn't just about reading; it's about bonding. As you both curl up with a book, you're signaling that this is important, enjoyable, and a priority.

Make this routine anticipated. Perhaps, every time you finish a book, you and your son can pick the next one out together, make some hot cocoa, and make a big deal of starting a new journey. This ritual not only makes reading together something to look forward to but also solidifies it as a cherished part of your family culture.

Interactive Reading Sessions

Turn reading into an interactive dialogue, not a monologue. As you read, pause to discuss the story. Ask questions like, "What do you think he'll do next?" or "How would you feel if that happened to you?" This transforms reading from a passive to an active experience, enhancing comprehension and critical thinking. Predicting plot developments keeps your son engaged, turning the pages not just to follow along, but to see if his guesses were right.

Relate the stories to his experiences. If a character is dealing with a bully or a big move, draw parallels to similar situations he might have faced. This not only deepens understanding of the text but helps him apply literary lessons to real-life scenarios. It shows that books aren't just stories; they're life lessons in disguise.

Library and Bookstore Visits

Regular visits to libraries and bookstores can turn the task of building a library into an adventure. Libraries are treasure troves of free resources, and most librarians are more than happy to recommend books suitable for your son's age and interests. Make these trips regular events. Many libraries also host story hours or book clubs that can further enrich his experience.

In bookstores, allow him to wander, explore, and pick out books that catch his eye. This autonomy makes him feel invested in what he reads and teaches him how to make choices. It's like giving him a map and letting him discover his own path, which can be incredibly empowering.

Building a home library is more than just an educational task; it's a way to travel the world from your living room, explore conflicts and resolutions, and understand diverse perspectives, all while bonding over shared stories and adventures. Each book you read together lays down another brick in the foundation of his lifelong relationship with learning, turning each story into a stepping stone on the path to understanding the complex, beautiful world around him.

How to Build a Home Library and Promote a Love of Reading

- **Creating a reading routine:** Promote regular reading sessions.
- **Selecting diverse books:** Learn about a wide range of subjects and stories.
- **Reading interactively:** Read together to share the experience.
- **Visit libraries:** Visit local libraries and bookstores to find exciting new books.

7.3 BRUSH STROKES AND BELLY LAUGHS: MAKING ART A FAMILY AFFAIR

Imagine transforming your living room into a vibrant studio where colors splash and music flows, where dance moves shake up the daily routine, and where craft projects turn ordinary afternoons into exhibitions of imagination. Yes, we're talking about diving into the world of artistic expression with your son, transforming your home into a space where creativity knows no bounds. It's about giving him the tools to paint, draw, dance, and play his way through the vast landscapes of his imagination. Let's explore how different forms of art can not only entertain and engage your son but also enrich his emotional and cognitive development, making every dab of paint, every note of music, and every dance step a building block for his growth.

Exploring Different Mediums

First up, let's set the stage for creativity by introducing a variety of artistic mediums. Start with the classics like drawing and painting. Grab those crayons, markers, and paints, and join your son in creating everything from family portraits to alien landscapes. Don't worry about messes or masterpieces; it's all about the process, about putting thoughts and visions onto paper. Then, there's music. Whether it's banging on a bongo drum, strumming a guitar, or exploring sounds on a keyboard, music offers a profound way to connect emotionally and intellectually. If your son is shy about performing, consider starting with music appreciation. Play different genres at home, from classical symphonies to rock anthems, and discuss what you both like about different songs.

Dance might seem a bit daunting if you consider yourself more of a 'sit and watch' kind of guy, but it's incredibly liberating. Turn up the tunes after dinner and have a dance-off. Or if you prefer something more structured, enroll in a father-son dance class. It's a great way to get active and have a laugh together. Lastly, don't overlook crafts.

Building models, assembling puzzles, or even simple woodworking projects can enhance fine motor skills and teach patience and precision. Plus, these activities provide tangible results that your son can be proud of, which can be a huge boost to his confidence. And who knows, you might find a hidden dancer within you. I recently found myself attempting the worm in my kitchen. Suffice it to say, I'm going to stick to the day job for the moment, but you might have more luck!

Benefits of Artistic Expression

Now, let's paint a broader picture of why these activities matter. Engaging in the arts is like a workout for the brain. It enhances problem-solving abilities and cognitive flexibility—think about deciphering the steps of a new dance or figuring out which colors to mix to get just the right shade of green. These activities also provide a unique way to handle emotions. Creating art can be incredibly therapeutic; it offers a safe outlet for expressing feelings that might be hard to put into words, thus supporting emotional regulation.

Moreover, the arts can improve academic performance. Yes, you heard that right. The skills learned through artistic expression—like focus, perseverance, and attention to detail—translate into better performance in school. And let's not forget the joy and satisfaction that comes from creating something on your own. This joy fosters a positive attitude towards learning and exploration, which can influence all areas of life.

Showcasing Artistic Work

Every artist deserves an audience, and every piece of art deserves a spotlight. Organizing a home art exhibition can be a fantastic way to showcase your son's artwork. Dedicate a wall or a shelf for his creations, and have regular "gallery openings" where family members can view and discuss the art. You could even invite friends and extended family to these events, either virtually or in person. This not only celebrates his efforts but also encourages him to keep creating. For a digital twist, create an online gallery. This can be a fun project where you both learn a bit about digital photography and web design as you upload his artwork and share it with loved and admired ones.

Art in Education

Finally, let's bridge the gap between art and formal education. Art is not just an extracurricular activity; it's a vital part of learning that complements traditional academic subjects. For instance, drawing maps or scenes from history can deepen his understanding of social studies, while building models can enhance his grasp of scientific concepts. Advocate for arts education, emphasizing how it cultivates not just a well-rounded education but a well-rounded individual.

By integrating arts into your home and your son's education, you're doing so much more than just filling time with activities. You're opening a door to self-expression, emotional growth, and cognitive development. You're giving him the tools to not just navigate but to color his world in vibrant, dynamic ways. So, grab those paintbrushes, tune those instruments, and let the dance of creativity begin, transforming every note, every stroke, and every step into a celebration of learning and growth. I got immersed in the artistic spirit myself recently, when me and my son attempted to make some papier-mache dinosaurs. I can honestly say his tyrannosaurus rex was much more realistic than mine... but sometimes part of being a great dad is just humbling yourself and getting stuck in.

7.4 SCIENCE AND DISCOVERY: EXPLORING THE WORLD TOGETHER

Ah, the thrill of discovery! There's something about the sparkle in your son's eyes when he learns something new about the world around him that just can't be beaten. Whether it's understanding why the sky is blue or how bridges stand up, these moments are pure gold. Let's channel that natural curiosity and enthusiasm into fun, educational activities that turn everyday moments into science lessons and lay the groundwork for a lifelong love of learning. From bubbling volcano experiments in your kitchen to exploring the great outdoors, science is about to become one of the coolest adventures you and your son embark on together. Below are some of my personal favorite activity hacks.

Conducting Home Experiments

Every dad's home can be a mini laboratory, a place where vinegar and baking soda aren't just for cooking but are the key ingredients for an erupting volcano. Imagine the fun of watching your son's face light up as you create a tornado in a jar or a balloon rocket that zooms across the living room. These aren't just entertaining tricks; they're gateways to understanding scientific principles like chemical reactions, physics, and more. For instance, that vinegar and baking soda volcano? It's a perfect way to discuss the concept of reactions and the properties of acids and bases. Each experiment not only feeds his curiosity but also strengthens his analytical thinking and problem-solving skills. Plus, using everyday materials makes these lessons accessible and shows him that science is everywhere, not just in textbooks or laboratories.

Nature Walks and Observations

Now, take your scientific adventures outside with regular nature walks. Whether it's a stroll through your neighborhood, a day trip to a nearby nature reserve, or just exploring your backyard, the natural world is a fantastic classroom. Equip yourselves with a magnifying glass and maybe a notebook for your son to jot down or sketch what he sees. Discuss the types of trees, the insects bustling about, and why certain plants grow in some areas but not in others. These walks are great for teaching him about ecosystems, biodiversity, and the importance of environmental conservation. They also offer a fantastic way to bond, sharing discoveries and fostering a deep appreciation for the natural world. Plus, they're a healthy dose of exercise!

Science and Technology

In today's tech-driven world, a basic understanding of technology and engineering is invaluable, and guess what? You can start teaching these concepts early on. Use simple examples like explaining how a remote control sends signals to the TV or how bridges are designed to hold up weight. Toys like building blocks or engineering kits for kids can turn these lessons into hands-on projects, making complex ideas more tangible and a lot more fun. Apps that teach basic coding or games that involve problem-solving can also be great tools, introducing him to the digital side of technology in an engaging and educational way.

Visiting Science Centers and Museums

For a deeper dive into the world of science, plan visits to science centers and museums. These places are designed to spark curiosity and inspire awe, making them perfect for inquisitive young minds. Interactive exhibits allow him to get hands-on experience with concepts you've talked about at home, from gravity to electricity. Many museums also offer workshops and educational programs tailored to children, making learning both fun and engaging. These trips can make the abstract concepts in science books come alive, showing your son the real-world applications of what he's learning. Plus, they're a great excuse for a family day out, full of learning and bonding opportunities.

Through these activities, science becomes more than just a subject in school—it becomes a shared adventure, a series of discoveries that you and your son make together. Whether it's mixing ingredients at home to see them react, exploring the great outdoors, tinkering with technology, or marveling at the wonders in a museum, each experience is a building block in his understanding of the world and a memory that you both will cherish. And though these experiences may not be as predictable as playing video games or watching college football on a Saturday night, you can be sure that over time, they will enrich your lives in a powerful way. So, grab your experiment kits and your walking boots, and get ready to explore the fascinating world of science together.

Tips to Build Science Into Your Lives

- **Conduct home experiments:** Turn your home into a mini-laboratory by conducting simple experiments. This hands-on approach makes science tangible and fun.
- **Walk in nature:** Promote a sense of curiosity in your lives through observing nature.
- **Visit museums:** Spend time in science museums, natural history museums, or planetariums. These places often have interactive exhibits that make learning about science engaging and memorable. Many museums also offer educational programs and workshops.
- **Talk about scientific ideas:** Engage in discussions about scientific concepts and fun scientific discoveries.

7.5 FINANCIAL LITERACY: TEACHING MONEY MANAGEMENT EARLY

Ah, money—it makes the world go 'round, right? But somehow, even though it's crucial in virtually every aspect of life, it's often one of the last things we think about teaching our kids. Now, I'm not saying your five-year-old needs to balance your checkbook, but introducing basic concepts of money management early on can set him up for a lifetime of financial literacy. Let's break open the piggy bank and explore how to give your son a head start on becoming a mini money maestro.

Starting with Basics

Kick things off with the basics: earning, saving, and spending. It sounds simple, but these are foundational concepts that even adults struggle with (I can admit this is something I am continuing to improve at daily!). Start by explaining money as a tool—we work to earn it, we save it for bigger goals, and we spend it on our needs and wants. A great way to introduce this is through an allowance. Whether he earns it through chores or is given a weekly stipend, an allowance can be a powerful tool for teaching financial responsibility.

Discuss what it means to earn money. Even simple tasks like feeding the pet or tidying up can be linked to earning a small amount. This not only teaches him the value of work but also begins to instill a strong work ethic. Then comes saving. Get a clear jar for his savings to make it visual and exciting. Every time he adds money, he'll see his savings grow. Set a goal together, maybe a new toy or a book he's been eyeing, and calculate how saving his allowance can help him reach that goal. This tangible representation of saving teaches patience and planning.

When I started giving my son a small amount of pocket money per week, he initially felt tempted to buy candy, like many of his friends were doing. He managed to resist, decisively saved up for a new game for his Xbox. To me, the game he bought was insignificant. What was more important was the experience this gave him, of having control over his money, and the power to save up for something through discipline and making good financial choices.

Using Financial Games

Now, let's make learning about money fun—yes, it's possible! Board games like Monopoly or The Game of Life are fantastic for introducing concepts of money management, investment, and budgeting in a playful environment. These games simulate real-life financial decisions, like buying property or managing unexpected expenses, which can spark great conversations about financial strategies and consequences.

Online games and apps designed to teach financial concepts can also be engaging tools. Look for apps that simulate stock market investments or allow him to manage a virtual business. These platforms offer safe environments where he can make financial decisions and see the outcomes without real-world risks. Plus, they're a fun way for you both to learn together. Engage with him as he plays, discuss decisions and strategies, and reinforce the learning process by making it a shared activity.

Setting Financial Goals

Teaching your son to set and achieve financial goals is like giving him a roadmap to success. Start with short-term goals, which are more tangible for younger children. Maybe he wants a new skateboard or a video game; discuss how saving a portion of his allowance can help him get there. As he matures, introduce longer-term goals. This could be saving for a special class trip or even starting a college fund.

Involve him in family financial planning sessions to make it more practical. Show him how household budgets are set and how you save for family goals, like vacations or a new car. This transparency not only educates him on managing money but also helps him understand the financial dynamics of his own home, making the concept of money management more relevant and real.

Real-Life Financial Learning

Finally, let's put all this knowledge into practice. Involve your son in real-life financial activities. Take him grocery shopping and show him how to comparison shop, explaining why you choose one product over another based on price and value. Discuss the household bills; explain what utilities are and why conserving resources like water or electricity saves money.

Plan a family outing and let him help budget for it. Give him a set amount and guide him through allocating money for different expenses like tickets, food, and souvenirs. These practical experiences are invaluable. They not only reinforce the concepts he's learned but also give him a sense of involvement and achievement in real-world financial planning.

Incorporating financial literacy into your parenting toolkit might seem daunting at first, but it's as crucial as teaching him to ride a bike or tie his shoes. By starting early, keeping it fun, setting clear goals, and involving him in real-life financial decisions, you're not just teaching him how to handle money—you're setting him up for a future where financial worries are reduced, and financial opportunities are vast. So, let's raise the next generation of savvy savers and smart spenders. After all, a little financial wisdom goes a long way, and who knows? Maybe he'll be the one managing your retirement fund someday!

7.6 CULTURAL AWARENESS AND SOCIAL SENSITIVITY: RAISING A GLOBAL CITIZEN

Hey there, Super Dad! Ready to take your fatherhood skills global? In today's beautifully tangled world of cultures, nurturing a global citizen in your son is more crucial than ever. It's not just about teaching him to appreciate sushi or enjoy Bollywood movies; it's about cultivating a deep-rooted respect and understanding of diverse cultures and viewpoints. This isn't just about making him a well-rounded individual—it's about preparing him to thrive in a connected world where empathy and understanding cross all borders.

Introducing Global Cultures

So, how do you introduce the wide world to your living room? Start with the universal language of humanity: food. Cooking together can be a fantastic way to explore global cultures. Whip up a Mexican taco night, an Italian pizza evening, or a Japanese sushi party. As you mix spices and roll dough, chat about the origins of these dishes and the people who created them. It's a delicious way to make learning about different cultures both engaging and literally digestible. And while we can all agree that Domino's pizza always hits the spot after a busy week at work, who knows, you may find a new dish which you prefer and can even cook from scratch.But don't stop at food. Dive into the arts—music, dance, and movies from around the world can all be eye-opening experiences. Have a movie night featuring films from different countries, and discuss the themes and how they might differ from your local cinema. Play music from other parts of the world during your home activities; let the rhythms of African drums or the melodies of a Chinese guzheng fill your home. Each note and scene offers a chance to discuss and appreciate the creativity and expression of different cultures.

Discussing Social Issues

Now, on to the tougher stuff. Discussing global and social issues might seem daunting, but it's essential for raising a socially sensitive son. Whether it's poverty, inequality, or climate change, these conversations can help your son understand the complex world around him and his role in it. Approach these talks with honesty and empathy, and use age-appropriate language. For instance, if you're discussing homelessness, you can talk about the importance of empathy and how different societies handle social welfare.

Encourage questions and offer simple, clear explanations. If he's curious about why certain countries face famine, discuss geography, climate, and even politics in simple terms. These discussions can teach him critical thinking and, importantly, empathy. They can also inspire him to think about how he might make a difference, even in small ways, like donating part of his allowance to a charity.

Participating in Cultural Events

One of the best ways to learn is by doing, right? Dive into the cultural tapestry of your community by participating in cultural festivals and events. Whether it's a Chinese New Year parade, a Diwali festival, or a Native American pow-wow, these events offer immersive experiences that are as educational as they are exhilarating. Encourage your son to ask questions, interact with participants, and learn about the significance of the festivities.

These outings can be fun adventures, but they also serve as live-action lessons in diversity and inclusion. They show your son that despite our many differences, we all celebrate, we all have traditions, and we all value community. These experiences can foster a sense of global community and show him that his own cultural background is just one thread in the vibrant tapestry of humanity.

Language Learning

Lastly, let's talk tongues. Learning a second language is about more than just expanding vocabulary; it's about opening doors to other cultures. Language is a key that unlocks the subtleties of a culture in ways that are profound and personal. Encourage your son to learn a new language, whether it's through classes, apps, or by practicing with friends who are native speakers.

Discuss the benefits with him—not just the practical advantages of being bilingual but the deeper understanding and connections it fosters with people from different backgrounds. Make it fun and relevant. If he's learning Spanish, maybe plan a family trip to Spain or a Spanish-speaking country. If he's into anime, explore Japanese. This not only enhances his communication skills but deeply enriches his cultural appreciation.

In raising a global citizen, you're doing so much more than teaching tolerance; you're celebrating diversity, encouraging empathy, and opening your son's eyes to the vast world beyond his doorstep. It's about preparing him not just to live in the world but to appreciate its myriad peoples and to contribute positively to the global community. So, here's to world cultures, broader horizons, and the joy of discovery—may your journey together be as rich and varied as the world itself.

As we close this chapter on fostering lifelong learning and growth, remember, every topic explored— from science and creativity to financial literacy and cultural awareness—is a step toward nurturing a well-rounded, informed, and compassionate individual. These aren't just lessons; they're investments in your son's future, equipping him with the knowledge, skills, and sensitivity he needs to navigate and contribute to the world effectively. As we turn the page, let's continue this incredible adventure of fatherhood, filled with learning, laughter, and lots of love.

CHAPTER 8
PLANNING FATHER-SON ESCAPADES

8.1 ADVENTURE TOGETHER: PLANNING TRIPS AND OUTINGS

Imagine this: it's a Saturday morning, and instead of your typical pancake breakfast, you and your son are plotting a course on a map, your fingers tracing the routes to your next great adventure. Maybe it's the mountains calling your name or the whispers of the sea beckoning you to explore its depths. Wherever the compass points, the thrill isn't just in the destination but in the journey you're about to undertake together.

Selecting Destinations Together

Involving your son in the planning process isn't just about teaching him the logistics of travel; it's about giving him a voice in the adventures you undertake. This inclusion boosts his confidence and shows him that his opinions and ideas matter. Start by laying out some options that are feasible and intriguing. Whether it's a hiking trip to a national park or a cultural dive into the nearest city's museums, discuss what each destination has to offer and what he might enjoy most. You could turn this into a fun evening activity, with brochures spread out on the living room floor and a globe or map to pinpoint locations, turning the planning itself into an adventure.

Learning Through Travel

Travel is one of the richest forms of education, offering lessons that the four walls of a classroom could never contain. It's about history, geography, biology, and so much more, all rolled into the real-world experience. When you visit historical sites, talk about the stories behind them, perhaps dressing up the tales in the dramatic flair that kids so love. At nature reserves, discuss the wildlife and ecosystems. What role does each animal play in its environment? Why is it important to protect places like this? Museums offer hands-on experience with science and history, and many have interactive sections designed especially for kids. Before each visit, you might read up on a few key exhibits or events tied to the location to make the trip more meaningful and engaging.

Packing and Preparation

Preparing for a trip can teach a multitude of skills, from the basics of packing to the responsibilities of travel. Have your son participate in packing his own luggage. You can create a checklist together, which not only ensures that he has everything he needs but also teaches him how to organize and prioritize. Discuss each item's importance and use, turning a simple task into a learning opportunity. Moreover, talk about travel safety—why it's important to stay close in crowded places, what to do if he gets lost, and how to identify safe sources of help. These discussions are crucial, not just for the trip, but as life skills that instill safety awareness.

Capturing Memories

In today's digital age, photos are snapped in seconds, but there's something uniquely special about keeping a travel journal. Encourage your son to document your travels with both photos and words. This could be as simple as a notebook where he can paste tickets, postcards, and write down what he enjoyed most about each day. Not only does this reinforce his literacy skills, but it also encourages him to reflect on his experiences, capturing details that a photograph might miss. For a fun twist, you could both have cameras (or use phones, if appropriate) and compare shots at the end of the day, discussing what you chose to capture and why. This not only preserves memories but also enhances his observational skills.

Traveling together is more than just taking a break from the usual routine; it's a series of moments woven into the ongoing journey of your relationship. Each trip, each experience is a thread in the fabric of your bond, colored with the hues of sunsets watched together, the textures of roads traveled, and the echoes of laughter shared. These are the journeys that define us, that strengthen our connections and remind us that no matter where we roam, the best part of every adventure is who we share it with.

Tips to Plan and Enjoy Adventures Together

- **Select destinations together:** Enjoy a shared and collaborative traveling experience.
- **Learn through travel:** Discuss thoughts and ideas about the places you visit.
- **Pack and prepare:** Pack and prepare effectively, learning vital planning skills.
- **Capture memories:** Take photos and keep a scrapbook of your adventures.

8.2 SPORTS AND TEAMWORK: LEARNING TO WIN AND LOSE TOGETHER

Think back to your childhood—chances are some of your brightest memories involve tossing a ball around or racing down the street with friends. Sports have this magical way of teaching life's big lessons, like teamwork, resilience, and the sweet taste of victory (and yes, the occasional sour bite of defeat). Now, as a dad, you've got front-row seats (and a starring role) in guiding your son through these experiences. Whether he's the next soccer prodigy or he just likes to shoot hoops in the driveway, sports can be a fantastic way to bond, learn, and grow together.

Choosing Sports Activities

When it's time to pick a sport, think of it less like drafting for the big leagues and more like choosing the right superhero suit—it has to fit just right. Start by exploring a variety of sports with your son. This could be anything from traditional team sports like soccer and baseball to individual activities like swimming or martial arts. The key is to gauge his interest and enthusiasm. Does he light up when he kicks a soccer ball, or does he seem more engaged when focusing on his own in a swim lane?

This exploration phase is crucial because it helps him discover not just what he's good at but what he truly enjoys. Remember, the goal here isn't to train an Olympian (unless that's where his talents and interests take him), but to cultivate a love for physical activity and the valuable life lessons that come with it. Plus, participating in both team and individual sports can offer the best of both worlds. Team sports teach cooperation, communication, and working towards a common goal, while individual sports can foster self-reliance, personal goal setting, and self-discipline.

I tried to give my son the chance to try lots of different sports as he grew up, and in a strange turn of events, he ended up enjoying curling, which is a very niche sport played by very few people, and even less commonly enjoyed by young boys. However, it didn't matter what sport he picked up; it was the process that he went through to learn new skills, and the experience of working within a team, that held the valuable lessons.

Teaching Teamwork and Fair Play

Now, let's talk about teamwork. It's like being part of a band—each member may play a different instrument, but it takes everyone working together to create a harmonious sound. In sports, this means passing the ball, cheering on teammates, and learning that sometimes, you assist, and other times, you score. Playing sports with your son, whether you're tossing a football in the yard or joining a community soccer team, gives you a golden opportunity to model these behaviors.

Discuss the importance of fair play. It's about respecting teammates, opponents, and referees, even when decisions don't go your way. These moments on the field are more than just game play; they're the building blocks for integrity and respect—qualities that extend far beyond sports. Use examples of sportsmanship from professional athletes as teachable moments: the basketball player who helps an opponent up after a fall, or the soccer player who admits to a foul even when the referee doesn't catch it.

Handling Winning and Losing

Handling wins and losses can be tricky, but think of it as a critical part of your son's emotional education. Celebrate victories with enthusiasm, but keep the focus on effort and improvement rather than just the scoreboard. "I saw how hard you worked to improve your passing this season," can be more impactful than, "Great job on winning!"

But what about when the game doesn't go as hoped? Losses are inevitable, but they're not just obstacles; they're opportunities— opportunities to teach resilience and grace. Encourage him to congratulate the winners and to think about what can be learned from the loss. Maybe it's a skill that needs refining, or perhaps it's recognizing how far the team has come even if the score sheet doesn't show it. This balanced approach helps him appreciate the effort over the outcome, a lesson that's valuable both on and off the field.

Active Participation

Lastly, your involvement is crucial. It shows him that you value his interests and his growth. This doesn't mean you need to coach every team (though if you do, hats off to you!), but be present. Attend his games, practice with him in the backyard, offer to help with team activities. Your presence matters—it shows him that you're his biggest fan, and it provides ongoing opportunities to reinforce lessons about teamwork, perseverance, and sportsmanship.

Whether it's through celebrating a well-earned win, learning from a tough loss, or just enjoying the game together, sports offer a dynamic setting for father-son bonding. These experiences aren't just about building athletic skills; they're about nurturing character, crafting memories, and enjoying the ride, bumps and all. So lace up those sneakers, warm up those cheers, and get ready for a fantastic, fulfilling adventure in sports and teamwork with your son. You can be sure it will be even more enjoyable than watching the cricket during the holidays.

8.3 DIY PROJECTS: BUILDING AND FIXING AS A TEAM

Imagine a Saturday where the usual cartoon marathons turn into a hands-on DIY adventure with your son, as you transform a pile of wood into a birdhouse, or maybe even a small fort. Not only does this create a physical token of your time together, but it also cements valuable life lessons and skills. But before you start dreaming of hammering nails and painting walls, let's nail down how to pick the right projects and turn this into a safe, fun, and educational experience.

Project Selection: Picking the Perfect Project: Size Matters!

The key to a successful father-son project is choosing something age-appropriate. Think about your project as though it were a video game for your son – he needs the right level of challenge to stay engaged and avoid frustration. Here's a quick cheat sheet:

- **Little Dudes (Ages 5-8):** Start simple! Birdhouse kits, mini planters, or even decorating pre-cut wooden toys are all winners. These projects focus on basic skills like using glue or hammering a few nails – perfect for little hands and short attention spans.
- **Big Dudes (Ages 9 and Up):** Ready to level up? Think building a bookshelf, a shelf for his trophies, or maybe even a shoebox city! The key here is to get your son involved in the selection process. Talk to him about what interests him and browse plans online or in DIY books together. This is a fantastic opportunity to teach him about planning and seeing a project through from start to finish.

Learning by Doing: Building Skills, Not Just Stuff

Once you've chosen your project, it's time to roll up your sleeves and get to work! But remember, it's not just about the finished product – it's about teaching valuable skills along the way. Here's where Dad wisdom comes in:

- **Mastering the Basics:** Think measuring, following a plan, cutting wood – these are all essential skills that translate into everything from cooking to car repair. Turn each step into a mini-lesson. Explain why measuring twice is crucial (avoid wonky birdhouses!), and demonstrate proper technique before letting him take over. Patience is key here, Dad – it might take a few tries to get it right, and that's okay.

The most important part here is to involve your son in the selection process. Discuss what you both want to build and what each project requires. This can be a great opportunity to gauge what he's excited about and to teach him how to plan a project from start to finish. You can look up plans together online or in DIY books, which often include a detailed list of materials and tools, along with step-by-step instructions. This research phase can be as educational as the building itself, introducing concepts like preparation, foresight, and the satisfaction of seeing a project come to life from just a blueprint.

Learning Practical Skills

Once you've figured out what you're going to try and build,, it's time to jump right in—but keep the focus on teaching practical skills along the way. Skills like measuring accurately, following a design plan, cutting wood, or even basic electrical work if you're fixing an old lamp, are incredibly valuable. Each step of the project offers a chance to explain why these skills matter. For example, measuring accurately is crucial not just for the project at hand, but it's a skill that translates into everything from sewing to engineering.

Walk through each step together, demonstrating techniques first and then letting him try. For instance, show him how to measure twice before cutting, explain why this is important, and then watch as he does it. This hands-on learning is vital, and it's okay if it takes a few tries to get it right. The goal isn't perfection on the first go but building competence and confidence through practice.

Safety First

Before the hammering commences, address the elephant in the room: safety.. Every great builder knows safety is priority number one. Here's how to keep your project zone hazard-free:

- **Safety Gear Showdown:** Goggles, gloves, ear protection – make sure your son is suited up for the job.

- **Tool Talk:** Walk him through the safe use of each tool, and never let him use something he's not comfortable with. Complexity can wait – it's better to introduce new tools gradually as his skills develop.
- **Tidy Up Time:** A clean workspace equals a safe workspace. Keep your project area organized and free of tripping hazards like loose nails or stray tools. This is also an important lesson in responsibility and preparedness.

Pride in Accomplishment

Finally, as your project nears completion, emphasize the value of effort and teamwork. Celebrate the work you've done together, regardless of how the final product turns out. Maybe the paint job isn't perfect, or the corners aren't exactly square—what matters is the process and the learning that happened along the way.

Take a moment to reflect on what you both learned. What would you do differently next time? What skills has he mastered? This reflection is crucial as it turns every project, successful or not, into a stepping stone for improvement. And when you do nail it, make sure to celebrate that success. Hang the birdhouse in a prominent place or use the bookshelf in his room to remind him daily of what you accomplished together, reinforcing the pride in creation and the bonds built not just in wood and nails, but in patience, effort, and shared experiences.

One of the most memorable experiences I have shared with my son was crafting a bow and arrow from wood and flint. This wasn't the first project we undertook, we started with much simpler tasks like making a wooden spoon. The bow took us several weeks to make but the time spent and lessons learned together were priceless, and I know we will both always cherish that memory. The bow is hung in our hallway, so if you're a home invader, think again!

Tips to undertake DIY Projects

- **Learn by doing:** Learn new skills by trying new things.
- **Select a project:** Pick a project which resonates with you.
- **Safety first:** Make sure you take the necessary precautions before creating.
- **Take pride:** Take pride in the learning process, not just the end result.

8.4 VOLUNTEERING: THE VALUE OF GIVING BACK TOGETHER

Remember that warm, fuzzy feeling you get after helping someone? Imagine sharing that feeling with your son – now that's a Saturday well spent! Volunteering isn't just about giving back; it's a golden opportunity to bond with your little dude, teach valuable lessons, and open his eyes to the world around him.

Finding the right volunteer gig can turn a simple weekend chore into a life lesson that sticks with him way longer than any textbook learning. Here's how to make it a win-win for both of you.

Finding the Perfect Fit: Volunteering for Tiny Dudes and Big Dudes

The key is to pick something that excites your son and is age-appropriate. Make sure it's the right combination of challenging but enjoyable. This will keep him engaged. Here's a quick guide:

- **Little Dudes (Ages 5-8):** Start simple! Packing care packages at a homeless shelter or decorating cards for senior citizens are fantastic options. These activities are easy for young hands and short attention spans, and they allow them to make a tangible difference.
- **Big Dudes (Ages 9 and Up):** Ready to level up? Consider tutoring younger kids, participating in a community clean-

up, or helping out at an animal shelter. Older children can handle more complex tasks and interact directly with those they're helping. The key here is to find something that challenges them but doesn't overwhelm them.

Bonus Tip: Share Your Passions! Does your family love animals? Look into volunteering at a local rescue. Are you passionate about the environment? Beach clean-up days might be your perfect fit. Sharing the causes you care about can be incredibly inspiring for your son.

Lessons in Emphasis and Compassion

Volunteering is a powerful way to teach empathy and compassion. There's something about stepping into someone else's shoes, even for a moment, that can shift a young person's perspective dramatically. Discuss with your son how the people you are helping might feel and what their lives might be like. For example, if you're volunteering at a food bank, talk about what it might be like to worry about where your next meal is coming from. Encourage him to imagine a day in the life of someone facing challenges different from his own. You could ask him to reflect on the things he is grateful for such as being able to play Fortnite, ride his bike, or play in the garden at home. Then ask him to imagine how life would be without these things. The aim isn't to make him feel gloomy, but to encourage him to reflect on how life might be for less fortunate people.

These conversations can deepen his understanding of the world and spark a genuine desire to help others. It's also a chance to discuss the importance of action—how each small effort contributes to a larger good. This can be incredibly empowering for a young person, knowing that their actions, no matter how small, can make a difference.

Building Social Awareness

Volunteering also helps build social awareness and a sense of responsibility towards others. It opens up a broader view of society and the myriad ways people live and struggle within it. For your son, seeing these realities firsthand can be much more impactful than reading about them or watching them on TV. It teaches him about diversity and the complexities of social issues in a very hands-on way.

Use these experiences as a springboard for discussions about social issues and what it means to be a responsible citizen. Talk about the role of various community services and non-profits, and how these organizations work to improve lives. Discuss how he might be able to contribute now and in the future. Perhaps he's inspired to start a fundraiser or organize a community project. Encouraging him to think about solutions to social issues can foster a strong sense of agency and responsibility.

Reflecting on Experiences

After each volunteering experience, take some time to reflect on what you both learned and felt during the activity. Ask him what he enjoyed the most and what was challenging. Discuss the impact of your efforts and what you both might do differently next time. These reflections not only enhance the learning experience but also help cement the memories you've made together.

Consider keeping a journal or a scrapbook of your volunteering adventures. This can be a great way to preserve memories and track the different activities you've engaged in over time. Looking back on this can be incredibly rewarding, and it can serve as a reminder of the journey you've both taken towards becoming more compassionate and socially aware citizens.

Volunteering together provides a unique blend of personal bonding, educational experience, and the joy of helping others. It's about more than just giving back; it's about growing together, learning about real-world issues, and understanding the power of compassion and empathy. Through each activity, you're not just shaping a more informed and caring individual; you're enhancing the bond between you, built on shared experiences of meaningful impact. My son recently started volunteering as a 'big buddy' at his school, where he mentors younger pupils and helps them find their way around and settle into their surroundings. He has found this incredibly rewarding and I have watched him grow so much through the process. It's important to remember that you don't need to do something drastic when it comes to volunteering, you can do something simple and straightforward. It's the taking part that counts.

8.5 DAILY RITUALS TO CHERISH: FROM MORNING ROUTINES TO BEDTIME STORIES

Imagine the scene: the sun peeks just over the horizon, a fresh new day tiptoes quietly into your home, and there you are, the captain of this ship, steering the morning towards a treasure trove of small but golden moments with your son. It starts with a morning routine that's less about the hustle and more about the harmony. How about flipping pancakes together while dancing to some classic rock? Or maybe planning the day over a bowl of cereal, discussing who can make the most epic sandwich for lunch? These moments, simple yet profound, set the tone for the day, infusing it with positivity and a sense of shared purpose.

Morning Routines: Launching Pads for Connection

Starting your day with shared activities isn't just about ticking chores off the list; it's about building a foundation of connection and teamwork. Whether it's picking out outfits with a mini fashion show or deciding on breakfast together, each activity strengthens your bond. This shared start teaches cooperation, responsibility, and decision-making skills, all while making him feel like he has a say in the day's flow.

Consider making this routine a mix of fun and function. While part of the morning might be dedicated to necessary tasks like packing school bags or sorting laundry, ensure there's a slice reserved for something enjoyable. Perhaps it's a quick game of tic-tac-toe or a short story read together. This balance keeps the morning from feeling like a checklist of chores and more like a series of moments to cherish.

Importance of Daily Conversations

As the day unfolds, the magic doesn't have to fade. Instituting a habit of daily check-ins can act like the glue that holds the day's experiences together. It's about touching base, heart to heart, without distractions. Maybe it's a chat over an after-school snack where you share the highs and lows of the day or a discussion during a drive to soccer practice. These conversations are invaluable. They offer a window into each other's worlds, providing insights into feelings, thoughts, and experiences.

This daily dialogue ensures that no concern is too small to be shared and no achievement goes unnoticed. It's also a perfect time to gently guide your son through any difficulties he's facing, whether it's trouble with homework or a disagreement with a friend. By making these conversations a regular part of your day, you send a clear message: I'm here, I'm listening, and I care. Plus, it's a great way to teach your son about empathy and understanding, showing him how to listen actively and respond thoughtfully.

Bedtime Routines

As night falls and the world quiets, a bedtime routine can be the gentle close to the day's chapter. This is more than just brushing teeth and getting into pajamas. It's a sacred time for you and your son to wind down, reconnect, and prepare for a restful night. Reading bedtime stories, for instance, is a classic activity that does wonders not just for his literacy skills but also for his ability to dream and imagine. As you turn the pages, let the stories whisk you both away to lands filled with dragons, heroes, or mysteries.

Alternatively, discussing the day's highlights can be a soothing end to the evening. Reflect on what went well, what was learned, and what could be improved. This not only helps your son develop a habit of reflection but also ends his day on a note of positivity and growth. Make sure this time is free of screens and distractions. This is your moment together, a bubble in time where the world's hustle is muted, and the focus is solely on the bond you share.

Customizing Rituals

While these rituals provide a framework, the real beauty lies in tailoring them to fit your and your son's unique rhythm and needs. Maybe your son thrives on long conversations, or perhaps he prefers quiet activities that require less verbal interaction. Observing and adapting these rituals to suit his temperament and interests shows that you value his comfort and preferences.

Customizing these rituals might mean tweaking the timing, the activities, or even the frequency. What matters is that these rituals feel right for both of you, nurturing a connection that's based on mutual respect and love. So, whether it's through shared pancakes or whispered stories, remember, it's these daily rituals that weave the strong, vibrant threads of your relationship, making every day a tapestry of shared moments and memories.

Tips to Cherish Daily Rituals

- **Develop morning routines:** Create a solid morning routine that you can enjoy.
- **Have conversations:** Have daily conversations to check in with each other.
- **Create a bedtime routine:** Develop a cozy bedtime routine.

- **Customize rituals:** Customize your daily rituals to suit your preferences.

8.6 CELEBRATING EACH OTHER: APPRECIATING MUTUAL GROWTH AND ACHIEVEMENTS

When you pause and reflect on the journey you're on with your son, it's not just about marking milestones—it's about celebrating the steps you've taken together, both big and small. Think of it as a high-five for the soul, a way to acknowledge and appreciate the growth you've both achieved through shared experiences and challenges. It's not just about giving a pat on the back for acing a math test or scoring a goal; it's about recognizing the effort, the persistence, and the love that's woven into these achievements.

Recognizing Achievements

Start by making it a habit to celebrate achievements regularly. Whether it's a successful bike ride without training wheels or a well-handled disagreement with a friend, each accomplishment offers a chance to boost your son's self-esteem and reinforce your role as his cheerleader. But here's a twist—celebration doesn't always mean throwing a party. Sometimes, it's a quiet acknowledgment, a special note in his lunchbox, or a story shared at dinner about how proud you are. These moments of recognition teach him to value his own efforts and to see growth in his abilities, character, and understanding of the world.

Make these recognitions specific. Instead of a generic "good job," point out what exactly he did well. Did he show great teamwork during a soccer game? Did he handle a tough homework problem with impressive persistence? Highlighting these specifics not only makes your praise more meaningful but helps him understand and internalize what behaviors and efforts are truly commendable.

Father's Achievements

Now, let's flip the script. Just as you celebrate his achievements, let him celebrate yours. Whether it's a promotion at work, a successful DIY home project, or even your efforts to manage stress better, sharing your achievements with your son can strengthen your bond. It shows him that growth and learning are lifelong processes. When he sees you striving to improve and succeed, he learns the value of setting and pursuing goals, regardless of age.

Involve him in your celebrations in simple ways. Perhaps you can have a small family celebration when you achieve a personal goal, or you can share a special activity together like a movie night or a day out. These moments of sharing joy can foster mutual respect and admiration, showing him that achievement is not just about personal success but about sharing that success with those who support and cheer for you.

Annual Reflections

Consider establishing an annual tradition where you both sit down at the end of the year to reflect on your achievements and challenges. It could be on New Year's Eve, a birthday, or any significant date that holds meaning for you both. Discuss what goals were met, what challenges were faced, and what lessons were learned. This isn't just about recapping events; it's about understanding the journey you've shared, appreciating the growth, and setting sights on new horizons.

During these reflections, set goals for the coming year together. What does he hope to achieve? What do you aspire to do, both personally and as a father? Setting these goals together not only motivates you both but also strengthens your partnership, showing him that you're in this together, supporting each other every step of the way.

Me and my son have created an annual reflection day which we refer to as 'thought Thursday.' We have this on the first Thursday of

July to represent the mid-way point through the year. We talk about how we feel the year is going, what we have achieved already, and what we would like to achieve in the second half of the year. Though it might seem small, this tradition is something special that we both cherish, enhancing our bond and partnership.

Creating a Culture of Appreciation

Finally, cultivate a household culture where appreciation is a regular part of your daily lives. Make it a routine to express gratitude for each other's efforts, whether it's thanking him for doing his chores without being asked or him appreciating the extra effort you put into making his favorite dinner. These small expressions of gratitude can significantly reinforce the bonds of love and respect, creating a family atmosphere where everyone feels valued and appreciated.

Incorporate simple practices like a gratitude jar, where each family member can drop notes of appreciation for others to read at the end of the week, or a gratitude board displayed prominently in your home. These visual reminders of appreciation can be incredibly uplifting and serve as constant reminders of the love and respect that flow within your family.

Celebrating each other's growth and achievements is about more than just acknowledging success—it's about reinforcing the journey you're on together, fostering an environment of mutual support, and teaching the values of perseverance, gratitude, and respect. It's these values, celebrated and shared, that strengthen your bond and prepare both of you for the challenges and triumphs that lie ahead.

As we wrap up this chapter on celebrating each other, remember that every high-five, every congratulatory hug, and every word of encouragement builds a foundation of confidence, love, and mutual respect that will support both of you throughout your lives. It's not just about celebrating achievements; it's about celebrating each other, every day. Now, let's turn the page and continue our journey into the next chapter, where we explore new adventures and lessons in fatherhood, armed with the strength of our shared successes and the joy of our mutual growth.

CONCLUSION

Well, fellas, we've been through quite the journey together in these pages, haven't we? From those first moments of "What have I gotten myself into?" to feeling like a seasoned pro who can handle bedtime tantrums and heart-to-heart talks with equal finesse. We've navigated the changing tides of fatherhood, transforming apprehension into confidence, and I hope you're starting to feel that deep, unshakeable bond with your son that only strengthens with each passing day.

Let's not forget the powerhouse duo of emotional intelligence and effective communication. These aren't just buzzwords; they're the scaffolding for building secure, resilient young men who aren't afraid to express a full range of emotions. By fostering open dialogue and showing a willingness to understand and share feelings, you're setting the stage for your son to thrive in a world that often sends mixed messages about what it means to be "manly."

And speaking of manliness, we've taken some old stereotypes about masculinity and turned them on their heads, haven't we? Showing that vulnerability, practicing empathy, and offering compassion are now part of your dad toolkit. These qualities lead to richer, more authentic relationships—not just with your son but with everyone in your life. It's about being real, being you, and showing up fully, even when it's tough.

Of course, bonding isn't just about the deep stuff. It's also about those shared adventures and everyday moments that fill your days with joy and laughter. Whether you're exploring the great outdoors, building a fort in the living room, or simply sharing a home cooked meal, these experiences are the glue that binds your relationship and creates memories that both of you will cherish for a lifetime.

As we've seen, the path of fatherhood is also a path of continuous learning and growth. It's a journey that doesn't end when your son grows up but evolves as you both do. Keep feeding that curiosity, keep learning, and keep supporting each other. Every day brings a new opportunity to grow together.

Health and wellness have been a recurring theme, and with good reason. Staying active, eating right, and keeping those stress levels in check are as crucial for you as they are for your mini-me. Role modeling a healthy lifestyle sets your son up for success from the get-go. Plus, staying fit means you can keep up with him, whether he's sprinting around the soccer field or challenging you to a game of chess.

We've covered a ton of practical parenting strategies throughout this book, designed to give you the confidence to handle whatever fatherhood throws your way. From discipline to play, education to emotional well-being, you now have the tools you need to navigate the complexities and joys of raising a boy in today's fast-paced world.

Now, if you take anything away from our time together, let it be this: Dive into fatherhood with all your heart. Be present, be engaged, and cherish every moment. The bond you build with your son now lays the groundwork for the man he will become.

Reflecting on my own journey, I've had my fair share of ups and downs, missteps and victories. But each moment has been a lesson, each challenge a chance to learn and grow. And I wouldn't trade it for the world.

So here's to you, dads—new and seasoned alike. Embrace the chaos, embrace the quiet moments, and most of all, embrace your child. The road ahead is as rewarding as it is challenging, and believe me, it's worth every step.

Keep up that "rockin' dad energy"

Your friend,

~ Alex

EXCLUSIVE BONUS (FOR THE ELITE DAD READERS ONLY!)

You thought I was done? No way! First off, congrats on finishing my book. You've come further than most.

As a thank you for joining this journey of "fatherhood" with me, I have a special gift for you.

Community is very important to me. So, I'm actively building a team of legendary dads (or soon-to-be dads) to join this elite opportunity.

Here's why this Exclusive Dad Reader Team is a must-join:

- **Early Access to My Unreleased Books:**

Be the first on your block (or at the pediatrician's office) to brag about the amazing books you're reading.

- **Pay It Forward:**

Help me make my books even better for other new dads by sharing your honest (and hopefully dad-joke-filled) opinions.

- **The Dad Zone:**

Connect with other committed boy dads in our exclusive Facebook group where you can share tricks, tips, and some extra punny dad jokes.

So are you ready to take your rockin' dad game to the next level?

Just scan the QR code below and apply for our Exclusive Dad Reader Team.

P.S. I promise not to cry if you tell me the dialogue is cheesier than movie theater popcorn.

Join me and let's build up the boy dad community together.

For access to all of my free resources, go to thealexgrace.com for more details.

I'm done now! Be well and hopefully I see you on the team.

~ Alex

REFERENCES

- *Emotional Intelligence Creates Loving and Supportive Parenting* https://www.gottman.com/blog/emotional-intelligence-creates-loving-supportive-parenting/
- *Decoding the father-son relationship* https://www.manifest.me/insights/decoding-the-father-son-relationship/
- *Teaching Kids to Be Smart About Social Media (for Parents)* https://kidshealth.org/en/parents/social-media-smarts.html
- *How to Make Discipline a Positive Experience* https://fathers.com/blog/topics/discipline/how-to-make-discipline-a-positive-experience/
- *Emotional Intelligence Creates Loving and Supportive Parenting* https://www.gottman.com/blog/emotional-intelligence-creates-loving-supportive-parenting/
- *Key Strategies to Teach Children Empathy (Sorted by Age)* https://biglifejournal.com/blogs/blog/key-strategies-teach-children-empathy
- *Helping your child with anger issues - NHS* https://www.nhs.uk/mental-health/children-and-young-adults/advice-for-parents/help-your-child-with-anger-issues/
- *How to Raise Boys Who Are in Touch With Their Feelings* https://greatergood.berkeley.edu/article/item/how_to_raise_boys_who_are_in_touch_with_their_feelings
- *How Pedro Pascal Became a Symbol of Modern Masculinity* https://www.menshealth.com/entertainment/a43315760/pedro-pascal-modern-masculinity/
- *Resilience guide for parents and teachers* https://www.apa.org/topics/resilience/guide-parents-teachers
- *Part I Benefits of Chores* https://centerforparentingeducation.org/library-of-articles/responsibility-and-chores/part-i-benefits-of-chores/
- *How to Create Your Own Rites of Passage* https://www.artofmanliness.com/character/advice/how-to-create-your-own-rites-of-passage/
- *The Importance of Schedules and Routines | ECLKC - HHS.gov* https://eclkc.ohs.acf.hhs.gov/quienes-somos/articulo/importance-schedules-routines
- *Examples of Positive Discipline Techniques* https://www.verywellfamily.com/examples-of-positive-discipline-1095049
- *How to foster independence in children* https://www.health.harvard.edu/blog/how-to-foster-independence-in-children-2019110518223
- *Media and Young Minds | Pediatrics | American Academy ...* https://publications.aap.org/pediatrics/article/138/5/e20162591/60503/Media-and-Young-Minds
- *5 ways slimming screen time is good - Mayo Clinic Health ...* https://www.mayoclinichealthsystem.org/hometown-health/featured-topic/5-ways-slimming-screen-time-is-good-for-your-health
- *Parental controls & privacy settings guides* https://www.internetmatters.org/parental-controls/

REFERENCES

- *Best Video Games for Bonding With Your Child* https://www2.grm.net/2023/05/11/best-video-games-for-bonding-with-your-child/
- *Teaching Kids to Be Smart About Social Media (for Parents)* https://kidshealth.org/en/parents/social-media-smarts.html
- *Benefits of Physical Activity - CDC* https://www.cdc.gov/physical-activity-basics/benefits/index.html
- *How Parents Can Support a Child's Mental Health* https://discoverymood.com/blog/10-ways-to-support-your-childs-mental-health/
- *Managing stress for a healthy family* https://www.apa.org/topics/stress/managing-healthy-family
- *A Child's Need for Sleep | Harvard Medicine Magazine* https://magazine.hms.harvard.edu/articles/childs-need-sleep
- *Learning Through Play: Benefits, Ideas, And Tips For ...* https://www.beginlearning.com/parent-resources/learning-through-play/
- *8 tips to develop children's curiosity - Mayo Clinic Health System* https://www.mayoclinichealthsystem.org/hometown-health/speaking-of-health/8-tips-to-develop-childrens-curiosity
- *How Racially Diverse Schools and Classrooms Can Benefit All Students* https://tcf.org/content/report/how-racially-diverse-schools-and-classrooms-can-benefit-all-students/
- *9 Tips for Teaching Kids About Money* https://www.schwab.com/learn/story/9-tips-teaching-kids-about-money
- *How Traveling With Kids Can Help Them Later in Life* https://www.travelandleisure.com/trip-ideas/family-vacations/why-travel-is-important-for-kids
- *The Importance of Developing Good Sportsmanship in Youth ...* https://redlineathletics.com/athletic-development/good-sportsmanship/
- *Father Son Projects to Build* https://teachingwoodwork.com/projects/father-son-projects-to-build/
- *The Benefits of Teen Volunteerism: Transforming Lives and ...* https://www.nvfs.org/benefits-of-teen-volunteerism/

Printed in Great Britain
by Amazon

BRITISH GEOLOGICAL SURVEY

A walkers' guide to the geology and landscape of western Mendip

Andy Farrant

with contributions from
Elaine Burt, Sharon Pilkington, Ian Thomas and Mark Woods

Bibliographical reference

Farrant, A R. 2008. A walkers' guide to the geology and landscape of western Mendip. Book and map at 1:25 000 scale. (Keyworth, Nottingham: British Geological Survey.)
ISBN 978 085272576 4

© NERC 2008 All rights reserved

Keyworth, Nottingham: British Geological Survey

Contents

Introduction	3
Rocks of Mendip	4
The Ice Age	10
Geology and man	12
Cheddar Gorge	14
The Charterhouse area	20
Blackdown	26
Burrington Combe	30
Shipham and Rowberrow	36
South flank: Crook Peak and Axbridge	40
North flank: Banwell to Churchill	44
The Priddy area	48
South flank: Draycott and Westbury	52
Wookey Hole and Ebbor Gorge	58
Wells	62
North flank: Harptree and Smitham Hill	66
Geological glossary	68
Useful information	70
Further reading	72
Acknowledgements	75

Introduction

Welcome to western Mendip

The Mendip Hills are a special landscape where a wide variety of rock types and wildlife habitats occur within a relatively small area. Such diversity makes it one of the best areas in the country to appreciate the relationships between geology, landscape and natural history.

The region has a fascinating geological history that stretches back many millions of years, through frozen tundra, arid deserts and tropical lagoons. Rocky outcrops, coupled with the legacy of mining and quarrying, provide opportunities for you to see the geology and landscape at first hand.

This book and accompanying map will introduce you to the rocks and landscape of western Mendip, and through a series of described localities, will help you explore the area. The guide is divided into a number of areas, which can be explored separately or combined into a tour that can be made on foot or by car. For those interested in finding out more about the geology and natural history of the region, more information and links can be found on the accompanying website **www.mendiphills.com** and in the companion guidebook and map for eastern Mendip.

Exploring the geology and landscape of the Mendips

Please remember that much of this ground is an Area of Outstanding Natural Beauty (AONB) and many of the sites described in the text are either protected nature reserves or Sites of Special Scientific Interest (SSSIs).

Many of sites described here can be seen from roads and public footpaths or are on open-access land. The exceptions are the large working quarries. Access to some of the localities is via footpaths across farmland, so please respect the interests of the landowner and if you have a dog, keep it under control. Visits to any localities on private land need permission from the owner, and in this guide the mention of a footpath does not imply a right of way.

Always remember that the cliffs, quarries and caves that so often provide the best exposures for study are also inherently dangerous places. Never enter a working quarry without obtaining permission and first visiting the quarry office. Caves should not be entered except in the company of an experienced caver. Many caves and old quarries are on private land. The use of a geological hammer is not necessary at any of the localities, and hammers should not be used at SSSIs. If a hammer is used, please do so sparingly and with appropriate safety equipment.

Contact the Mendip Hills AONB Service (01761 462338) www.mendiphills.org.uk for more information on access to the countryside and details of caving and climbing clubs.

Numbered locations [1] are shown on the accompanying map and where possible in the illustrations. National Grid References are given in the form [489 123], and all lie within Grid Zone ST.

Finally, always remember:

'leave only footprints; take only photographs'

Rocks of Mendip

Sedimentary rocks

The western Mendips are made up of sedimentary rocks ranging in age from Devonian to Jurassic. Sedimentary rocks are formed by the accumulation of debris, such as sand and mud or the remains of organisms such as shells, in a range of different environments. Over time sediments are buried and harden into rock, thus forming sandstone, mudstone or limestone, depending on the original sediment; this process is known as diagenesis.

Sediments are usually deposited in layers or beds, which may vary in thickness and character and contain features, such as ripple marks, that are diagnostic of certain environments. A sequence of beds that forms a mappable unit of rock is known as a 'formation' and is given a name, for example the Charmouth Mudstone Formation. Several formations that show broadly similar characteristics are known collectively as a 'group' or 'subgroup', and also given a name, for example the Avon Group.

The Mendips are characterised by a wide variety of sedimentary rock types formed in a range of different settings from tropical seas to coal swamps and arid deserts. This section describes the major rock units that can be seen as you explore the area.

The story of the Mendips

The story of the Mendip Hills begins some 416 to 359 million years ago during the Devonian Period. At this time, the Mendip region was part of a landmass lying south of the Equator. Rivers draining mountains to the north deposited a thick sequence of sediments across the area; part of this is preserved as the Portishead Formation.

Tropical seas, corals and limestone

A change in the environment occurred at the beginning of the Carboniferous Period about 359 million years ago when the sea flooded, or transgressed, across the area. Britain lay close to the Equator. Conditions would have been warm with most of the region covered by shallow sea or lagoons. As the sea rose, the muddy limestone and mudstone of the Avon Group (also known as the Lower Limestone Shale) was deposited, but as the sea-water cleared of sediment the Carboniferous Limestone accumulated. Many fossils are found in the limestone, including corals, bivalves, crinoids (sea lilies), brachiopods and trilobites.

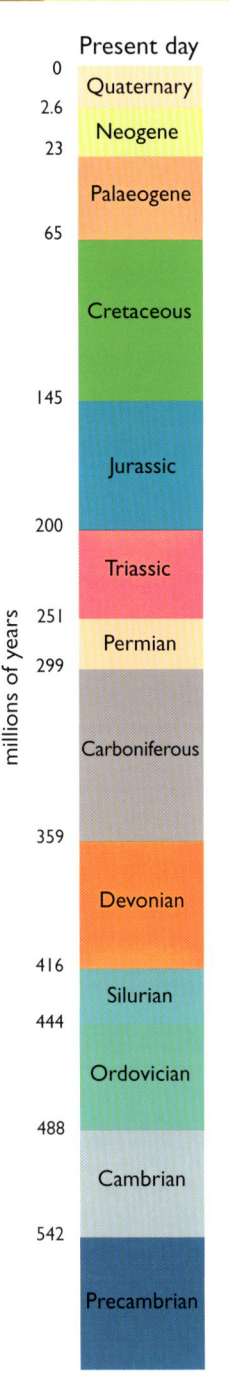

Geological timescale.

River deltas, muddy swamps and fossil forests

During the late Carboniferous (327–299 million years ago) huge rivers washed sand and mud into the region. The water flowed across wide river deltas allowing the sediments to settle out as thick layers of sand and mud — now the Quartzitic Sandstone and the Coal Measures. Large areas of swampy tropical forest developed on the deltas. The remains of the forests are preserved as thin coal seams, which contain exquisitely preserved fossil plants and insects. Some of these coal seams were worked in the Somerset Coalfield.

Mountains, rocky ravines and arid deserts

Following the Carboniferous, a major period of uplift and mountain building occurred. The

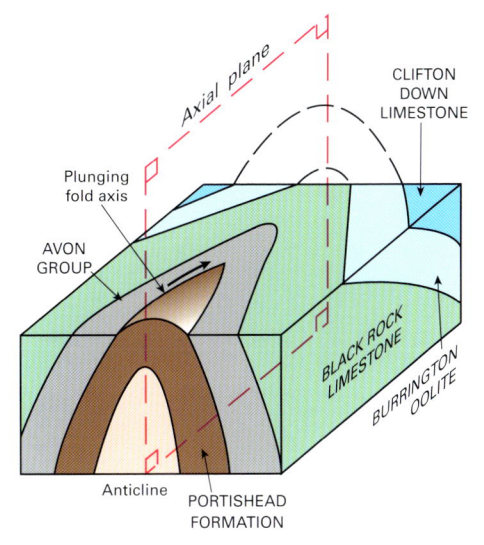

Block diagram of a pericline.

Devonian and Carboniferous rocks were folded into a series of four asymmetric folds known as periclines (a pericline is a type of anticline which plunges at each end, resembling an upturned boat). These four periclines are centered on Blackdown, North Hill, Pen Hill and Beacon Hill. The rocks were also faulted, with thick slices of rock thrust up over younger strata, creating a series of thrust faults (see map-face section through Priddy and Ebbor).

This folding and faulting created a range of steep rugged mountains. During the Triassic (251–200 million years ago) the climate was hot and dry. Occasional storms incised many deep steep-sided ravines or wadis into the flanks of the mountains. The mountain flanks and valleys were buried by material eroded from the mountains which was subsequently cemented by calcite to form the Dolomitic Conglomerate. These slope deposits thin rapidly away from the Mendips, grading into red mudstone — the Mercia Mudstone Group, which was deposited in the surrounding lowlands. At the end of the Triassic, the sea began to encroach into the area once again, and the youngest Triassic beds are coastal and shallow marine in origin.

Rising seas and the Mendip archipelago

At the start of the Jurassic (200–145 million years ago), the marine transgression continued, at times submerging almost the entire area and leaving only a few areas of land to create the 'Mendip archipelago'. Limestone accumulated in a series of shallow lagoons, together with beach (littoral) deposits of the Lower Jurassic Lias Group. Much thicker sequences of Jurassic sediments accumulated in the deeper water that lay to the south. Eventually sea level rose to submerge the entire area, depositing hundreds of metres of Middle and Upper Jurassic and then the Cretaceous strata that are seen to the east of Frome. Only in the last few million years, during the Quaternary, following uplift and extensive erosion, have the Mendip Hills re-emerged from their deep burial to give the present 'exhumed' topography we see today.

Rocks of Mendip

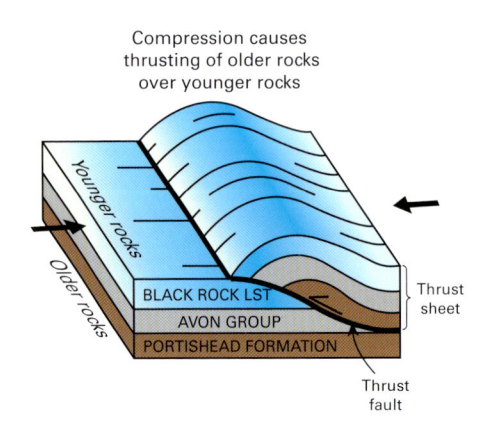

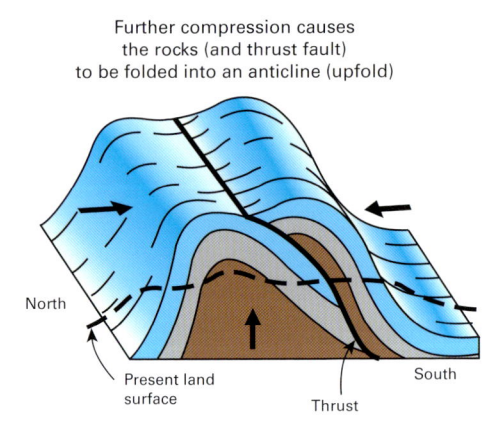

Thrust faulting and folding in the Mendips.

Rock types seen in the western Mendips

Devonian rocks

Portishead Formation (Old Red Sandstone)
The Portishead Formation comprises reddish brown sandstone with some conglomerate (pebble beds). The sandstones were deposited by seasonal rivers as channel fills in a desert environment. Cross-bedding and ripple marks can be seen. The Portishead Formation outcrops on Blackdown, North Hill, Pen Hill and Beacon Hill.

Carboniferous rocks

Avon Group (Lower Limestone Shale)
This group consists of interbedded mudstones and thin fossiliferous limestones, which mark the transgression of the sea at the start of the Carboniferous Period. Some of the thin limestone beds are crowded with fragments of crinoids and other fossils that indicate a marine setting. They are well exposed in the East Twin and West Twin valleys at Burrington.

Black Rock Limestone Subgroup
This is a very dark grey, fine-grained fossiliferous limestone. It contains many broken fragments of crinoids (sea lilies) and brachiopods. Black chert nodules are common, as are silicified *Spirifer* brachiopods. The Black Rock Limestone is particularly well exposed in Burrington Combe.

Burrington Oolite Subgroup
This rock is a light grey oolitic limestone. The rock is composed of many small spherical grains of carbonate known as ooliths. They formed by the deposition of carbonate in concentric layers around a nucleus, rather like a pearl. Oolites form today in warm, supersaturated, shallow, highly agitated marine water, often in areas with strong tidal currents. In eastern Mendip, the Burrington Oolite is locally replaced by the Vallis Limestone Formation, a crinoid-rich oolitic limestone.

Clifton Down Limestone Formation
The Clifton Down Limestone consists of dark-grey and black fine-grained muddy limestone, part of which known locally as 'Chinastone' because of its resemblance to porcelain. It contains *Lithostrotion* corals and large *Productus* brachiopods. It is best seen in Cheddar Gorge. Locally around Cheddar, two separate 'members' (the Cheddar Oolite and Cheddar Limestone) can be mapped.

Oxwich Head Limestone Formation
The Oxwich Head Limestone is the youngest part of the Carboniferous Limestone sequence. It consists of grey bioclastic limestone with much crinoid debris and some chert nodules, interbedded with oolitic limestone. This contrasts markedly with the fine-grained limestone of the Clifton Down Formation, which lies beneath it. It is best seen in the crags high above Cheddar Caves.

Rocks of Mendip

Quartzitic Sandstone and Coal Measures

Overlying the Carboniferous Limestone are coarse red sandstone and grey mudstones with thin coal seams. This marks a change from open marine to terrestrial conditions. The sandstones were deposited in a river delta as it built out into the sea. In western Mendip, these rocks are mostly buried beneath younger strata, but a small patch can be found in Ebbor Gorge. The Coal Measures outcrop more widely around Radstock where the thin coal seams were mined in the North Somerset Coalfield.

Triassic rocks

Dolomitic Conglomerate

This is a coarse-grained rock consisting of a mix of boulders and smaller fragments of Carboniferous Limestone and, less commonly, Portishead Formation, bound together with finer-grained sediment. It is found along the flanks of the Mendips and is often used as a building stone, known locally as 'Draycott Marble'.

Mercia Mudstone Group

This unit is mostly red mudstone with some siltstone and sandstone beds. The mudstone was deposited as wind-blown dust in a desert with periodic development of temporary lakes caused by flash floods from rain storms. Consequently, these sediments are thin or absent on the Mendip Hills, but are much thicker in the low-lying basins to the north and south. On the flanks of the Mendips, the mudstones either interfinger with the Dolomitic Conglomerate or overlie it. The top of the Mercia Mudstone is a green mudstone known as the Blue Anchor Formation.

Penarth Group

Above the Mercia Mudstone is the Penarth Group, which includes dark greyish-blue mudstone (Westbury Formation) and a distinctive pale fine-grained limestone (the Langport Member). These beds were deposited as the sea flooded over the Triassic desert landscape, and represent a variety of shallow marine, lagoonal and near-shore environments. They reflect the early stages of the rise in sea level that was maintained during the Early Jurassic. The Penarth Group is exposed in the Milton Lane section near Wells.

Jurassic rocks

Lias Group

The Lias Group is made up of two formations, the Blue Lias and the Charmouth Mudstone. The Blue Lias (shown on the map with the Langport Member) comprises an alternating succession of thin, hard limestones and dark mudstones The limestones usually weather out as pale resistant ribs giving the outcrops a very distinctive banded appearance. The Charmouth Mudstone is a dark grey fossiliferous mudstone. Both contain ammonites and bivalves. These rocks are exposed around Wells and the Chew Valley.

Harptree Beds

Over much of central Mendip the Lower Jurassic rocks have been silicified, and instead of a sequence of limestones and mudstones, the rock has been replaced by chert, a hard flint-like rock. This was caused by silica-rich fluids permeating through the rock after deposition and is related to the lead and zinc mineralisation. The Harptree Beds outcrop around Smitham Hill where they can be seen in several of the sinkholes in the area.

The Ice Age

The 'Ice Age', which began about 2.6 million years ago, actually comprises a series of very cold 'glacial' periods alternating with shorter, warmer periods known as 'interglacials'. We are currently in an interglacial which began about 10 000 years ago. During the most severe glaciation, about 450 000 years ago, an ice sheet extended as far south as the River Thames. Although the Mendips lay south of the maximum glacial advance, the climate at the time would have been very cold.

Under this periglacial climate the Mendips would have been much like northern Canada or Siberia, with long very cold winters, and brief warmer summers. The ground would have been permanently frozen (a condition known as permafrost) with snow cover for much of the year.

During the short warm summers, melting of the snow-pack generated brief meltwater floods. The spectacular limestone gorges and dry valleys that are such a feature of the Mendip landscape were carved by these torrents of water. When the climate warmed in the following interglacial period, underground drainage though the limestone was renewed, leaving the valleys and gorges high and dry. Each successive periglacial episode caused renewed incision. The wildlife at the time was adapted to the cold conditions, and animal remains found at several cave sites across the area include cave bear, bison, reindeer, wolf, brown bear, wolverine and arctic fox.

Material washed out from the gorges was deposited on the adjacent lowlands. Large spreads, or 'fans', of poorly

Limits of glaciation

sorted gravel, sand and silt occur in the dry valleys and at the outlets of the major gorges: these are shown as 'head' on the geological map. The best developed fan is at the mouth of Burrington Combe, but much of Cheddar is also developed on head.

Extensive scree deposits in Cheddar Gorge, Burrington Combe and Ebbor Gorge were formed by repeated frost shattering of the rock, splintering it into fragments that accumulated at the bottom of the cliffs.

Cave bear.

Much of the Mendip plateau is covered with a thin layer of fine-grained yellow-brown wind-blown silt. This loess is derived from glacial rock-flour, which has been blown here during the last glaciation. It masks the underlying limestone and gives rise to more acidic soils on which plants, such as gorse, that do not tolerate lime can thrive. Since the end of the last glacial, 10 000 years ago, extensive deposits of alluvium and peat have built up on the Somerset Levels.

A diorama of ice-age life in the Mendips.

Geology and man

The Mendip landscape has been shaped through time by both physical and human influences. Much of the character and sense of place is dictated by the underlying geology, and its influence on soils, land use, agriculture and settlement patterns. The landscape draws many visitors to the gorges and caves, and to the area as a whole for recreation.

As well as being important for tourism, the Mendips have provided a valuable mineral resource that has been exploited for centuries. A wide variety of minerals occur on Mendip, but only iron, lead, zinc and silver were really exploited by miners. Manganese, strontium and barium were mined on a small scale locally. By far the most valuable commodity was lead, mostly in the form of galena (PbS). It has been estimated that more than 100 000 tonnes of lead metal have been obtained from Mendip. The lead was associated with small amounts of silver. The largest orefields occur in central Mendip, around Charterhouse, Yoxter, Smitham Hill and the Chewton Warren to Stock Hill area. Smaller orefields occur on Sandford Hill, near Tynings Farm, Burrington Ham and Eaker Hill.

Around Shipham and Rowberrow, the miners prospected for zinc ore, present mostly as smithsonite and calamine but also present as sphalerite (ZnS). This was used with copper in the Bristol brass industry. Iron ore, mostly hematite and red and yellow ochre were mined at many places on Axbridge Hill and around Bleadon, Banwell, and Compton Martin.

A galena vein, Star Mine, Shipham.
© Chris Binding.

An example of galena.

Dumper truck, Whatley Quarry.

All of these mines have long since closed, but many of the old workings now form important wildlife habitats and nature reserves.

Today, quarrying is the major extractive industry and has had a significant impact on the Mendip Hills. Until the beginning of the 20th century, most quarries were small local concerns producing agricultural lime and building stone. The Carboniferous Limestone, Quartzitic Sandstone, Dolomitic Conglomerate and the Lower Jurassic limestones have all been quarried for building stone, examples of which can be seen in Wells Cathedral. Many of these old quarries are now important wildlife habitats and provide good exposures of the underlying geology.

By far the most valuable product is the Carboniferous Limestone. It is an important raw material that is used in a wide variety of processes, due to its physical properties and its chemical composition. It is used primary as crushed rock aggregate for the construction industry, as an essential raw material for cement manufacture and as a source of building stone. It is also used in steel and glass making, sugar refining, the chemical industry, and for reducing emissions of sulphur dioxide from coal-fired power stations.

Quarrying is a sensitive and complex issue. On the one hand, quarries supply raw materials to meet many of society's needs, create employment and contribute to the local economy, but on the other hand they can have a significant impact upon the environment and local communities. More information about quarrying can be found at www.mendiphills.com.

Cheddar Gorge

Batts Coombe Quarry

Black Rock Gate

Cheddar Gorge

Cheddar

Ample parking is available at the foot of the gorge, with limited parking at Black Rock Gate. Refreshments are available in Cheddar.

Cheddar Gorge [1] is perhaps the single best-known limestone karst feature in Britain. The superb scenery coupled with two show caves [2 and 3] make it a popular tourist destination. It is an excellent place to understand the local geology and contains many first-rate exposures of the Carboniferous Limestone. The cliffs also support a complex mosaic of valuable semi-natural habitats, home to a wide range of plant species, many of them rare. Please beware of falling rocks in the gorge!

As Cheddar Gorge and Caves are a major tourist attraction, it can be very busy in the summer months. There are public toilets, a tourist information centre and plenty of places for refreshment at the bottom end of the gorge. Parking is available in the lower part of Cheddar Gorge and at Black Rock Gate [4]. A good way to explore the area is to undertake the 5 km circular Gorge Walk from Cheddar to Black Rock Gate, returning on the other side of the gorge. On a clear day, there are superb views across the Somerset Levels to Glastonbury, the Quantock Hills and Exmoor.

Throughout the gorge the Carboniferous Limestone dips at about 20° to the south-west. As you travel down the gorge from Black Rock Gate, the dip causes successively younger rocks to descend to road level. The effect of the dip on the appearance of the gorge is readily apparent. The cliffs on the south side are dominantly vertical, cut along major fractures known as joints. The northern slopes are less steep, because the southerly dip of the rock allows loose blocks to slip down the bedding planes. This is particularly well seen in the old quarry opposite High Rock, just below Horseshoe Bend [5]; undercutting by the quarry here has caused a large landslide. In contrast, the southern side, towering to a height of 120 m, is relatively stable because the beds dip into the cliffs.

From Cox's Cave [3] up to Horseshoe Bend [5] the Clifton Down Limestone is exposed at road level while the overlying Oxwich Head Limestone forms the crags along the cliff-tops. The Clifton Down Limestone is mostly a fine-grained, dark, splintery limestone with chert nodules and *Lithostrotion* corals. Between Horseshoe Bend and the reservoirs, the underlying Cheddar Oolite can be seen at the base of the cliffs. This is typically a massively bedded, pale grey oolite with some fossiliferous bands.

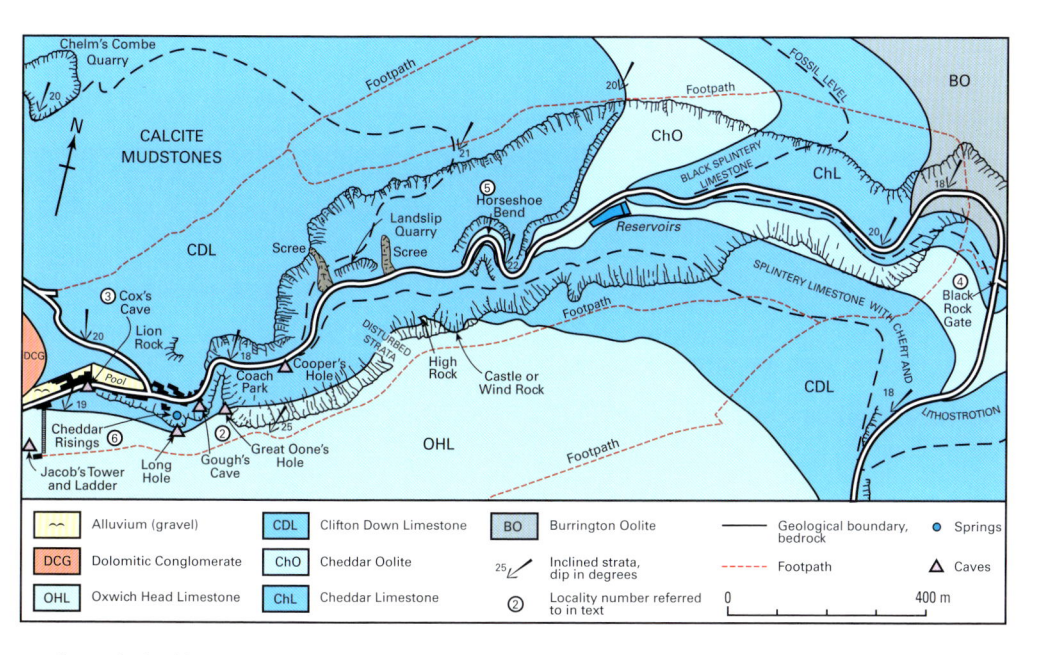

Geology of Cheddar Gorge.

Farther up the gorge from the reservoirs, the black, splintery, fine-grained Cheddar Limestone can be seen in the roadside crags, crowded with fossil brachiopods in some places. The pale grey Burrington Oolite dips down to road level at the bend just down from Black Rock Gate [4].

The origins of Cheddar Gorge have been the subject of much discussion since the early 1800s. Contrary to popular belief, Cheddar Gorge is not a collapsed cavern, but a fine example of a gorge cut by a surface river, and since left high and dry as drainage went underground.

Cheddar Gorge

North South

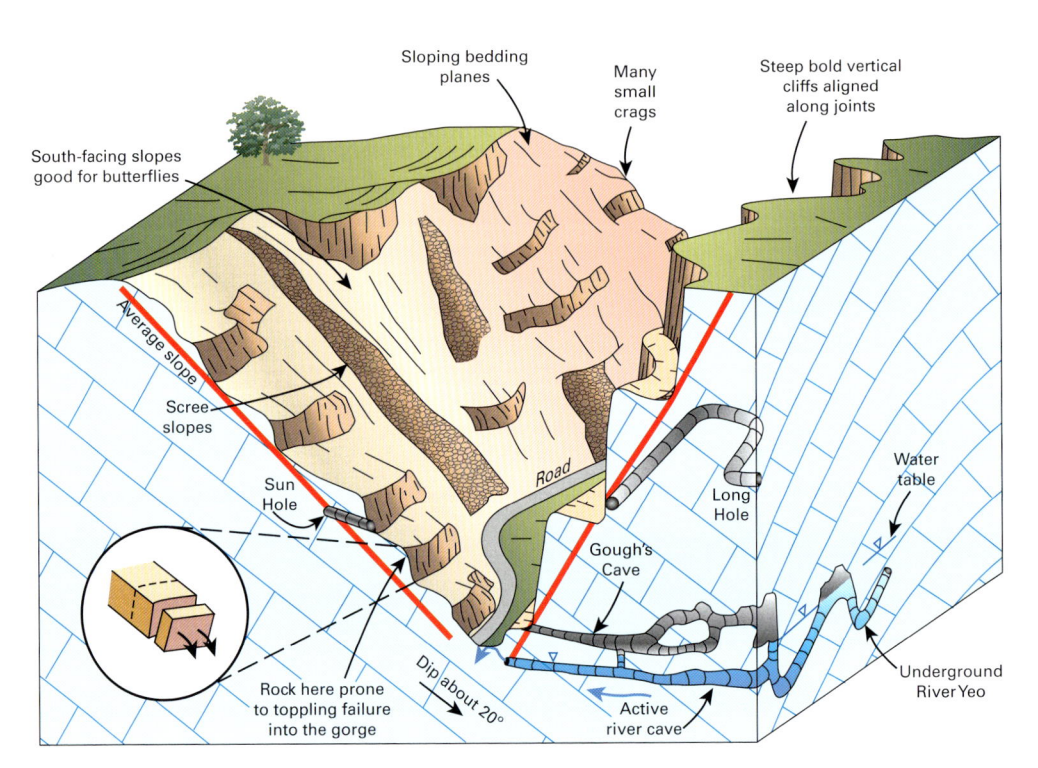

Cross-section of the gorge and cave systems.

Today the gorge is dry, but surface drainage has occurred in the past, particularly during the many cold periglacial periods over the last 1.2 million years (see p.10).

During these Arctic episodes, the development of permafrost blocked the caves with ice and frozen mud. Meltwater floods during the brief summers were forced to flow on the surface, carving out the gorge in the process. Each successive periglacial episode caused further erosion. During the interglacial periods underground drainage was renewed, creating the caves and leaving the gorge dry. Occasionally, extremely heavy rainfall such as that of July 1968 once again causes the gorge to become a torrent.

The caves that were formed during the earlier interglacials are now perched high and dry above the modern resurgence. Two of these are now show caves. The largest is Gough's Cave [2], a superb and easily accessible example of a phreatic cave, originally formed beneath the

Formation of caves

Caves form by the dissolution of limestone. Rainwater picks up carbon dioxide from the air and as it percolates through the soil, it turns into a weak acid. This slowly dissolves out the soluble limestone along the joints, bedding planes and fractures, some of which become enlarged enough to form caves.

The largest explored caves occur where water flowing off the impermeable Portishead Formation sandstone onto the Carboniferous Limestone sinks underground into holes known locally as 'swallets', some of which can be entered by cavers. The water reappears at the base of the limestone outcrop at large springs.

Over time, the water finds new lower routes leaving some caves high and dry. Some of these have been dug out by cavers.

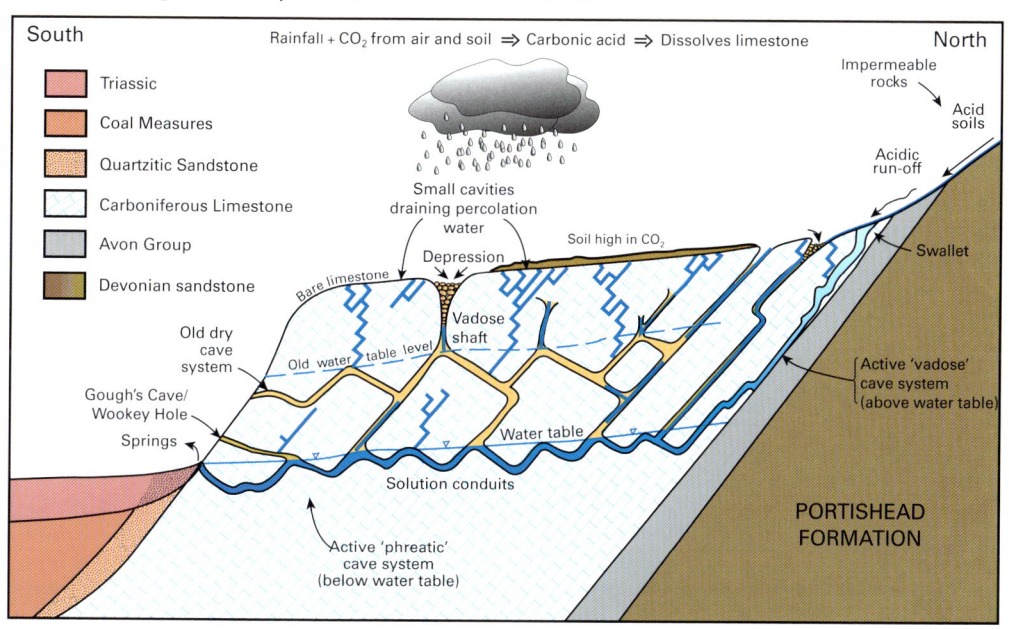

Schematic diagram showing cave development in the Mendips.

water table. Over 120 000 years ago, the ancestral River Yeo flowed through the cave but it has now found a lower route, except in times of flood when water may pour out through the turnstiles. The cave was choked with sediment until 1890 when Richard Gough began excavating the entrance. After eight years of work the cave was opened to the public in 1898.

Just inside the entrance, remains of several human skeletons, including the 9000-year-old Cheddar Man, were found. DNA extracted from the teeth of this skeleton proves that a local school teacher

Cheddar Gorge

Hibernating horseshoe bats. © Tessa Knight.

is a direct maternal descendant. Other archaeological remains found here include flint arrowheads, human bones with cut marks (suggesting cannibalism), and possible inscriptions of mammoths on the walls. This makes Gough's Cave one of the most important Palaeolithic sites in Europe.

Most of the show cave is aligned on the southern side of a small upfold, or anticline, which can be seen at the top of the steps just beyond the 'Ring of Bells'. A 'Neptunian dyke' can be seen where the show cave passes through a blasted section, just before St Paul's Chamber. This is a rift within the limestone infilled with much younger red Triassic sandstone. Diamond Chamber marks the farthest point in the show cave, although it is possible to enter a further series of phreatic passages and chambers on one of the 'adventure caving' trips. In 1985, cave divers discovered the underground River Yeo and have followed it upstream through deep underwater sections known as sumps, 58 m deep, to a point near Horseshoe Bend in the gorge. Exploration continues. Some of the stalagmites within the cave have been dated at around 250 000 years old.

The water emerges to daylight at Cheddar Risings [6], the largest resurgence in the Mendip Hills. Water emerges from two springs (the higher one is often dry in summer) and from about 16 points in the large pond downstream. The combined mean flow is about one cubic metre per second, and once powered 15 watermills. The catchment area includes most of the caves along the southern flank of Blackdown and some farther east including Tor Hole [574 520] about 11 kilometres away.

Farther downstream is Cox's Cave [3], the smaller of the two show caves. Discovered by George Cox in 1837 following widening of the road, it represents another short segment of abandoned phreatic passage. Several other short caves exist in the cliffs above Gough's Cave; these are the remnants of earlier courses of the underground River

Cheddar Gorge as it is today.

Yeo, long since abandoned by down-cutting of the gorge.

Many of the caves within Cheddar Gorge are important archaeological sites and also sites for roosting and hibernating bat species, including significant numbers of the greater horseshoe bat.

The limestone crags, rocky outcrops and cliff faces of the gorge are home to a wide range of plant species, including slender bedstraw and lesser meadow-rue, and the rare and protected Cheddar pink. Mixed scrub characterised by ash, yew, hazel and hawthorn is common on the steeper slopes, which also support whitebeam. The thin dry limestone soils on south-facing slopes are rich in lime-loving plants, including sheep's-fescue, salad burnet, wild thyme and common rock-rose. These grasslands are of outstanding importance for insects and other invertebrates, and in summer many different species of butterfly are abundant on open sunny slopes.

Cheddar pink. © Sharon Pilkington.

Scree slopes are common below the cliffs and in places support good populations of ferns, including maidenhair, spleenwort, rusty-back and the uncommon limestone fern. Peregrine falcons, ravens and feral rock doves can sometimes be seen soaring through the gorge.

To the north of Cheddar is Batts Coombe Quarry [7]. This quarry is developed in the Burrington Oolite, a very pure limestone (over 98 per cent $CaCO_3$) used for making quicklime, an essential material for the steel industry. It is one of only five sites producing the substance nationwide.

Cheddar village is located on a fan of 'head', which is a Pleistocene gravel washed out from the valleys north of the village. The soils here, coupled with the southerly aspect, favour market gardening, especially the production of strawberries.

Maerz lime kiln at Batts Coombe Quarry, 1974. © National Stone Centre.

The Charterhouse

Limited parking is available at Charterhouse and Black Rock Gate. No shops or refreshments are available.

Located on the contact between the sandstone uplands and the surrounding limestone plateau, the Charterhouse area has a wealth of interesting geology and evidence of a formerly extensive lead mining industry. This varied geology gives rise to a variety of special habitats, and much of the area has been designated as a Site of Special Scientific Interest because of the intricate juxtaposition of acidic, lime-loving and lead-tolerant vegetation, and for the cave systems beneath.

The name Charterhouse is a corruption of Chartreuse, the French town that was home to the Carthusian monks who set up an estate here in about 1180.

The hamlet of Charterhouse [8] sits on the narrow outcrop of Avon Group mudstone which separates the limestone plateau to the south from the acidic sandstone heath of Blackdown. To the south-east the remains of old lead workings can be seen. The mineral veins occur as open worked grooves or rakes cutting across the landscape. Blackmoor Valley and Ubley Warren [9] are covered with 'gruffy' ground, a local name for uneven mined ground, including worked-out rakes, black glassy slag heaps, round stone-lined 'buddle' pits used for washing the ore, smelting plants, old flues and a complex network of dams and leats. The miners were seeking lead ore, mostly galena (PbS), a heavy, grey, shiny, metallic mineral. The ore was a small component of the many calcite veins running south-east from Charterhouse towards Yoxter.

Worked-out lead rakes, Ubley Warren.

area

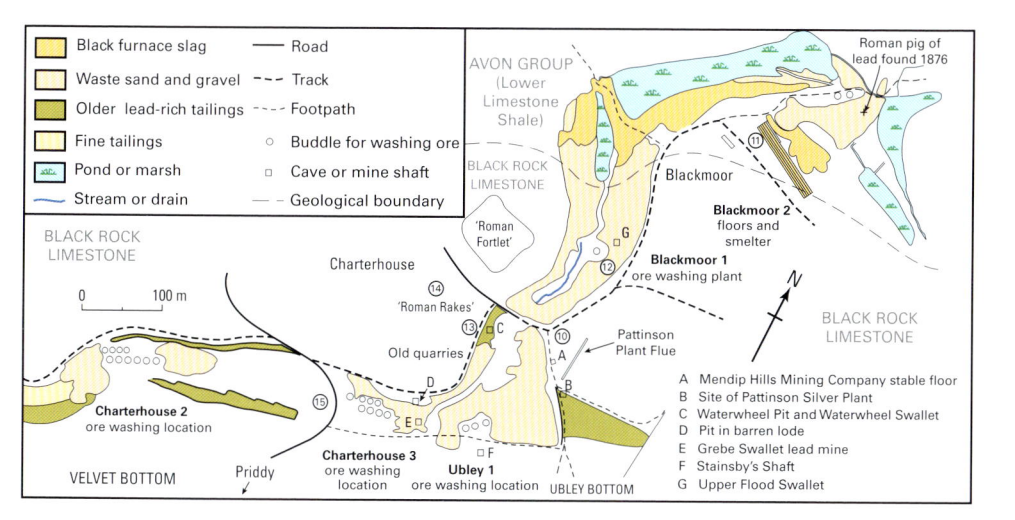

Legend:
- Black furnace slag
- Waste sand and gravel
- Older lead-rich tailings
- Fine tailings
- Pond or marsh
- Stream or drain
- Road
- Track
- Footpath
- Buddle for washing ore
- Cave or mine shaft
- Geological boundary

Map labels:
- Roman pig of lead found 1876
- AVON GROUP (Lower Limestone Shale)
- BLACK ROCK LIMESTONE
- Blackmoor
- Blackmoor 2 floors and smelter
- Blackmoor 1 ore washing plant
- Pattinson Plant Flue
- 'Roman Fortlet'
- Charterhouse
- 'Roman Rakes'
- Old quarries
- Charterhouse 2 ore washing location
- Charterhouse 3 ore washing location
- Ubley 1 ore washing location
- VELVET BOTTOM
- Priddy
- UBLEY BOTTOM
- BLACK ROCK LIMESTONE

A – Mendip Hills Mining Company stable floor
B – Site of Pattinson Silver Plant
C – Waterwheel Pit and Waterwheel Swallet
D – Pit in barren lode
E – Grebe Swallet lead mine
F – Stainsby's Shaft
G – Upper Flood Swallet

Charterhouse mine workings (after University of Bristol Spelaeological Society Proceedings, 1986).

The lead was probably first worked during the late Iron Age but it was in Roman times that the first serious mining took place. The Romans were mining in the Charterhouse area by AD49, within six years of arriving in Britain. Dated lead ingots and other Roman artefacts have been found in the area, some of which are now in the Wells and Mendip Museum. The heyday of mining was in the 17th and 18th centuries when local farmers, who took up mining in the winter months, dug many small shallow mines. Little surface evidence remains from this time.

In 1844 Cornish miners began work in the Charterhouse area, trying to exploit the deeper ore. However, unlike the large mineral veins of Derbyshire, most of the Mendip lead veins thin out rapidly with depth and the venture was unsuccessful. The rich residual deposits of lead ore near the surface had been largely worked out. Instead, they resmelted the lead-rich waste or slag from earlier mining operations, creating the landscape seen today.

Blackmoor's long history of lead mining has created a rich mosaic of valuable wildlife habitats. The rakes support important communities of mosses, liverworts, lichens and ferns, some of them nationally rare. The bare and sparsely vegetated slag heaps contain very low levels of plant nutrients and high levels of toxic heavy metals, especially lead, zinc and cadmium. A specialised community of metal-tolerant plants has colonised the slag heaps, which are covered in a low-growing mat of lichens, mosses, and tolerant vascular

Gruffy ground, Velvet Bottom.

The Charterhouse

plants. These include alpine penny-cress, a rare plant which, in Britain, is almost confined to sites rich in lead or zinc, sea campion, herb Robert and the tiny white-flowered common whitlow-grass. The slag heaps also support a diverse lichen community, which includes small lichens of the *Cladonia* genus and several species that are normally found on siliceous rocks in upland areas.

Alpine penny-cress.
© Sharon Pilkington.

The car park [505 556] is a good place to start exploring the area [10]. At the base of the rocky crag next to the car park are the remains of the Pattinson Plant. This extracted silver from lead ore by allowing molten lead to crystallise while pouring off the still molten silver-rich lead into separate containers.

A walk up the valley leads to the remains of an old smelting plant and flues which were in use until 1878 [11]. Here, a stream-driven fan forced hot air over the lead-rich slag and slime from earlier mining operations. The vapourised lead condensed in the flues and was removed by hand, a particularly unpleasant and dangerous job.

Nearby are several ponds that fed the leats supplying water to the buddles where the ore was washed and sorted. These ponds, and their associated wetlands are developed on the Avon Group mudstones, and support distinctive flora and fauna including a number of aquatic plants, such as mare's-tail, amphibious bistort, water-starwort and marsh marigold. The pools are also important for dragonflies and damselflies and a wide range of other invertebrate fauna.

The water from the ponds sinks underground at the contact with the Black Rock Limestone near the car park. This cannot be followed, but two gated caves occur nearby. Upper Flood Swallet [12] is a major cave system with a stream. Waterwheel Swallet [13], on the west side of the valley was used to dispose of lead tailings. The remains of a water wheel, fed by a leat from the pools upstream, were discovered during excavation of the cave entrance. The water from both of these caves emerges at Cheddar Risings.

On the hillside above [14] good exposures of gently dipping Black Rock Limestone can be seen where it has been quarried for lime. Remains of small *Spirifer* brachiopods, crinoids and corals can be found.

Upper Flood Swallet
© Peter Glanvill.

area

Farther down valley, the Cheddar to Charterhouse road crosses the valley. Beneath the embankment is a rather large, incongruous pipe [15]. This was installed after severe floods in 1968 washed the road away. Good buddles can be seen just up valley from the road. The manhole cover in one of the depressions nearby is the entrance to an 18th century lead mine. To the south-east are the spectacular worked out rakes of Ubley Warren [9]. Take care here as there are old mineshafts! The area is of special interest as acid-loving plants growing on loessic soils lie adjacent to lime-loving plants growing on the limestone rich spoil heaps and crags. A rich, varied, flora has developed, including the common spotted orchid, bee orchid, *Hutchinsia* and brittle bladder-fern. There are also many rare plants here, including the nationally scarce soft-leaved sedge which often grows in association with early purple orchid. Where lead-rich soil is present, the nationally scarce spring sandwort can be found. Ubley Warren is also an important site for reptiles, with slow worms, adders and common lizards all present.

Slag left from the 19th century resmelting operations, Blackmoor.

Continuing down towards Cheddar via Velvet Bottom, the remains of a smelting plant can be seen [496 553] [16]. Water was fed here along a leat from Long Wood. Good exposures of the black glassy slag occur in many places. Examination of the spoil tips reveals abundant calcite as well as crinoid fragments and other fossils from the Black Rock Limestone. Many of the tips are now covered in short, rabbit-cropped limestone turf and a wide diversity of typical herbs, grasses and wildflowers are present including carline thistle, common spotted orchid and devil's-bit scabious. These attract many insects especially butterflies and grasshoppers. In addition, the dry grassland supports large populations of adders and common lizard which may often be seen basking early or late in the day.

The curious steps farther down this valley are the former tailing dams and settlement ponds [17]. Much of the valley has been backfilled with spoil from the mining operations. During the heyday of mining, this valley must have looked very different from today.

At the junction with the Long Wood Valley, outcrops of the red Triassic Dolomitic Conglomerate can be seen [18]. This rock infills an ancient Triassic valley which can be traced from here to Harptree. The contact between this Triassic rock and the underlying

Examples of complete crinoids, Black Rock Limestone.

The Charterhouse

Black Rock Quarry. Close up of ooliths in the Burrington Oolite.

Carboniferous Limestone is clearly seen in a small roadside quarry on the Yoxter–Cheddar road [502 535] **[19]**.

Towards Cheddar, an old quarry [486 546] **[20]** on the north side of the valley is cut into the Burrington Oolite, here dipping to the south. If you look carefully you can see that the rock is made up of lots of small rounded grains of calcium carbonate known as ooliths. These formed in a shallow tropical sea about 340 million years ago. This particular rock is chemically very pure and was often quarried for lime. A superb restored lime kiln, which was operational in the 1930s, can be seen here. Black Rock Gate and the upper part of Cheddar Gorge is a short walk down the valley.

The steep, south-facing slopes here have very thin soils which support a diminutive herb-rich limestone grassland that includes sheep's-fescue, wild thyme and quaking-grass. Spring cinquefoil can be seen flowering in the spring. Typical semi-natural ash–hazel woodland clothes the steep and rocky valley slopes close to the top of Cheddar Gorge. Many ferns, mosses and liverworts thrive in the shady and humid conditions.

Heading back northwards up the tributary valley, Long Wood **[21]** has been woodland since possibly as early as the 13th century. It now supports many plants and animals that are usually restricted to ancient woodland sites, including toothwort and the common dormouse. Much of the wood was traditionally managed as coppice. Ramsons form dense white garlic-scented carpets near the stream, while higher ground favours bluebells, wood anemone and less commonly, herb Paris. Water occasionally flows down the dry valley during severe floods.

Long Wood Swallet.

area

Up a small side valley is the gated entrance to Rhino Rift [22] a predominantly vertical cave system. Beyond the gate, five deep shafts descend to a depth of 145 m. The name derives from rhino and hyena teeth found near the entrance.

At the top end of the wood is Long Wood Swallet [23]. The stream here disappears underground at the contact between the Avon Group and the Black Rock Limestone. The cave, accessible only to experienced cavers, follows the typical Mendip swallet cave pattern with a series of small inlet passages descending steeply down dip to unite in a streamway ending in a sump. Cavers have explored more than 1600 m of passage extending to a depth of 175 m. The water has been dye traced to Cheddar.

Grimmia donniana *growing on glassy lead-rich slag.* © Sharon Pilkington.

Blackdown

Parking is available at Charterhouse [505 556], Burrington Ham [489 581], Burrington Combe [476 587] and Tyning's Farm [470 564].

The summit of Blackdown, 325 m above sea level.

Blackdown is the highest point in the Mendips, rising to 325 m [**24**]. Formed of sandstone, this upland area is distinct from the surrounding limestone plateau. From the summit on a clear day you will have superb views across the Somerset Levels to the Quantocks and Exmoor, the Bristol Channel and south Wales, as well as Blagdon, Chew Valley and Broadfield Down. To the east, the other sandstone summits of North Hill and Pen Hill (with its distinctive TV mast) can be seen rising above the flat Mendip plateau.

The Portishead Formation forms the higher ground because the hard, red-purple sandstone, conglomerate and quartzite are immune from dissolution and resistant to erosion. Lumps of the sandstone can be found scattered all over Blackdown, in which it is still possible to find evidence of ripple marks and cross-bedding formed by the ancient river system that deposited them 360 million years ago.

The sandstone gives rise to acidic, wet soils, with peat developed on the summit ridge. Either side of the summit, the soil is slightly deeper and contains wind-blown silt known as loess *(see Ice Age)*. The change in soil type is easily seen in the distinct change from heathland vegetation to bracken.

These acidic soils support one of the largest stands of dwarf-shrub heath on the Mendips. Land higher than 300 m is dominated by mature heather and typical heathland grasses. Grassland forms a fringing mosaic in places, and on the acidic soil is characterised by common bent, western gorse, pill sedge, green-ribbed sedge and foxglove among other typical plants. The summit of Blackdown is also a good place to pick bilberries in summer. A few small mires are also present, providing suitably wet and acidic conditions for sphagnum mosses and a host of other interesting wetland plants, including the creeping, pink-flowered bog pimpernel and star sedge. Dense bracken has become established on the northern side of the hill, a consequence of occasional wildfires and reduced grazing pressure. Bracken produces a thick litter and excludes most other species.

Blackdown supports many heathland insects and birds, many of them nationally rare and/or declining. Sharp-eyed visitors may see meadow pipits, stonechats and skylarks. Barn owls can also sometimes be glimpsed hunting over the site at dusk.

The curious hummocks, tumps and straight lines on the summit are the remains of a World War II bombing decoy. They were designed to draw enemy bombs from the intended points of attack by mimicking potential targets in Bristol such as railway stations and marshalling yards.

Several small streams drain off the sandstone on the south side of the hill, and across the mudstone outcrop before disappearing underground on reaching the Black Rock Limestone. The outcrop of the Avon Group is marked by a band of marshy damp ground, which forms a marked contrast to the well drained limestone to the south. Occasional exposures can sometimes be seen in roadside ditches, but it is generally poorly exposed. Just south of the road, 700 m east of Tyning's Farm, is the Somerset Wildlife Trust's GB Gruffy Field Nature Reserve [ST 476 562] **[25]**.

Heathland developed on the impermeable Portishead Formation sandstone.

These two fields contain a selection of nationally important karst landforms developed at the contact between the Avon Group and the Black Rock Limestone. They include stream sinks, spectacular sinkholes and several caves, plus a wide variety of plant species and evidence of former lead mining. The area is a SSSI for its caves and karst landforms, as well as for its wildlife.

The main stream sinks at the end of a blind valley. The water can be seen again in GB Cave, whose entrance lies at the western side of the field. This is one of the most studied caves in Britain. Accessible only to cavers, it is almost 2 km long

View from the top of Blackdown towards Dolebury Warren.

Blackdown

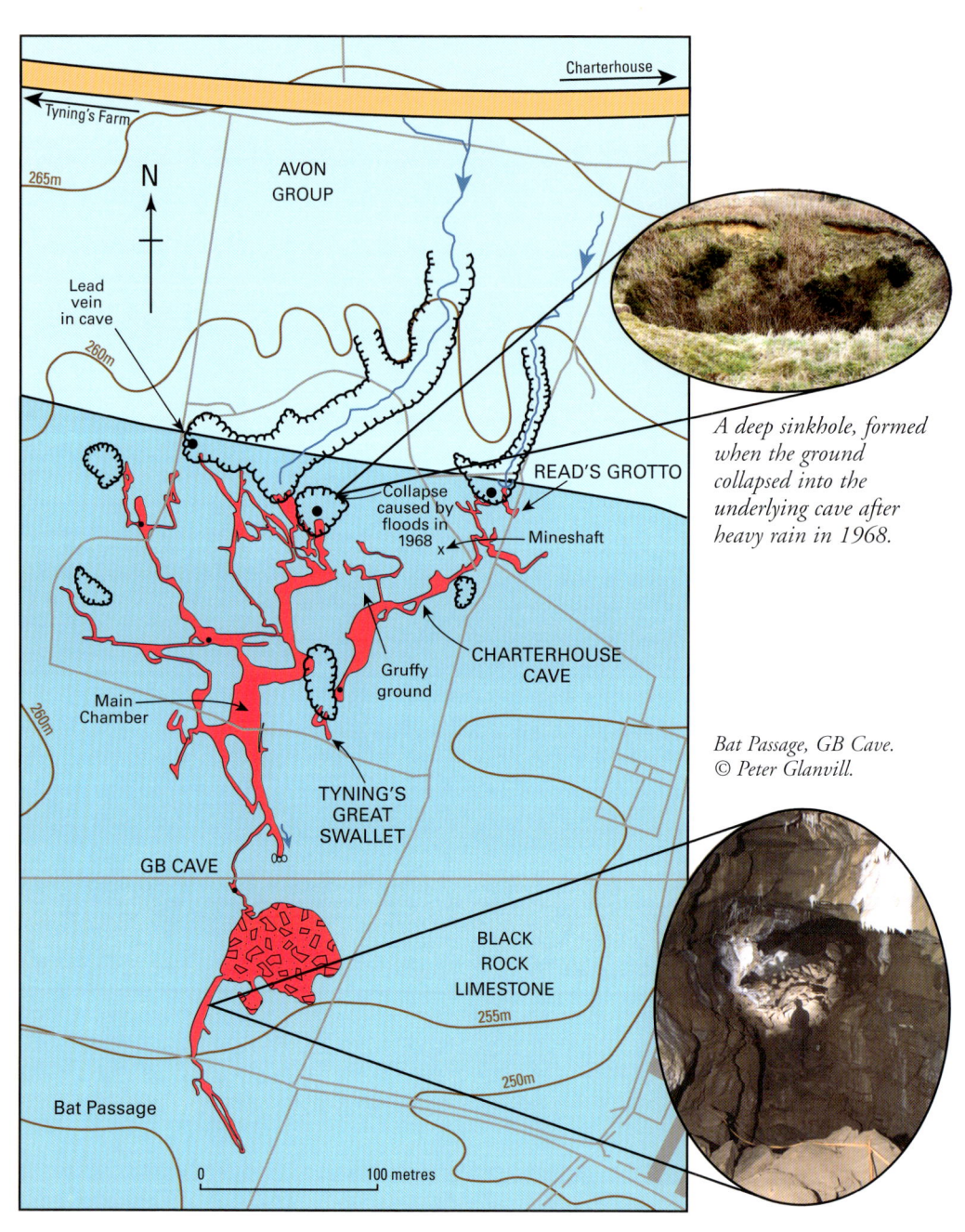

A deep sinkhole, formed when the ground collapsed into the underlying cave after heavy rain in 1968.

Bat Passage, GB Cave. © Peter Glanvill.

Plan of GB Cave and Charterhouse Cave, after University of Bristol Spelaeological Society.

and descends to a depth of 135 m. It follows the typical Mendip pattern of several inlets uniting to form a single streamway. The main passage includes one of the largest chambers in any Mendip cave. Comprehensive dating of the wealth of superb stalagmite formations has provided much information about cave development and the climatic oscillations during the Pleistocene. It is thought that cave development here may have begun more than 700 000 years ago.

The large, fenced depression on the hilltop just to the south of the stream sink marks the site of a major collapse into the cave directly below [25], which was caused by torrential rainstorms in 1968. The sides of the depression are formed of the fine-grained wind-blown loess, which covers much of the reserve. Another stream sink lies 150 m to the east; this water flows into Charterhouse Cave [27]. Discovered in 1984, this 430 m-long cave is similar to, but not connected with, the neighbouring GB Cave.

Mineshaft, GB Gruffy Field Nature Reserve.

Evidence of lead mining during the 16th to 18th centuries is still very apparent in the southern field. The miners were seeking galena occurring in veins within the underlying limestone. Pits, spoil heaps and old mine shafts create a hummocky terrain known as gruffy ground, now rare due to agricultural improvement. Lead-tolerant plant species including the nationally scarce alpine penny-cress, and spring sandwort occur here, as does the limestone-loving hairy rock-cress and the nationally scarce dwarf mouse-ear. Well-developed ant hills made by the yellow meadow-ant occur on the unimproved limestone pasture. The caves and larger sinkholes provide humid and sheltered conditions ideal for a wide range of ferns, including soft shield-fern, brittle bladder-fern and broad buckler-fern. Badgers have excavated extensive setts in the soft loessic soil.

Black Rock Limestone with abundant fossil crinoid fragments.

The dry-stone walls here are good places to examine the fossiliferous Black Rock Limestone. Examples of crinoids, brachiopods and corals can be seen here, but please take care not to damage the stone walls!

Loessic soils over mudstone in the northern half of the site support damp, species-rich neutral to acidic pasture, with bracken and rushes. Neutral to acid, species-rich grassland also occurs with plants such as devil's-bit scabious, meadow thistle and lousewort. Dormice are present in the hazel copse and hedges, while lesser horseshoe bats are known to roost in the caves.

The northern side of Blackdown is described in the Burrington Combe section. To the west, footpaths lead through Rowberrow Warren to Shipham and south to Charterhouse and Cheddar. The summit is on common land and can be reached by numerous footpaths.

Burrington Combe

Ample car parking is available at the top of the combe at Burrington Ham [489 581] and at the Burrington Combe Cafe [476 587].

Burrington Combe is a fine example of a typical Mendip gorge, cutting across the narrow steeply dipping limestone outcrop. In many ways it is very similar to Cheddar Gorge, but with smaller cliff sections. The combe provides a well exposed section through the Carboniferous Limestone sequence. Much of the sequence is easily accessible next to the road and many footpaths lead up onto Blackdown and Burrington Ham, and west to Dolebury and Rowberrow.

The youngest part of the Carboniferous Limestone can be seen in the small quarries behind the garden centre [28]. Here, good exposures of steeply dipping dark grey, fine-grained Clifton Down Limestone occur. The prominent bedding plane on the northern side of the quarry is the contact with the overlying Oxwich Head Limestone. The rest of the Clifton Down Limestone, with some colonies of *Lithostrotion* coral and large brachiopods, can be seen in the many small crags on the east side of the combe above the cafe [29].

The 'Rock of Ages', a crag of Burrington Oolite. The story of the Rev. Toplady sheltering here, prompting his famous hymn, is probably not true.

Continuing up the combe, the Rock of Ages towers over the road [30]. This prominent crag of Burrington Oolite is where the Reverend Augustus Toplady supposedly sought shelter during a storm, inspiring the hymn of the same name.

The quarry opposite provides a nice exposure of the massive pale grey oolitic limestone [31]. The prominent honey-coloured rock-rib running down the face is a bed of dolomite. In the small crag behind the public toilets, and by the road opposite the Burrington Combe Cafe, the Triassic Dolomitic Conglomerate can be seen. This infills a valley or wadi, which was cut into the northern flank of Mendip more than 200 million years ago.

Just up the valley from the Rock of Ages is Aveline's Hole [32]. Discovered in 1797 by two men digging for rabbits, this gaping hole is a fine example of a phreatic cave formed below the water table; it once acted as a spring, but is now abandoned by the river. The main passage extends for a short distance and can be explored with a good torch, appropriate footwear and some care. The cave was largely excavated by archaeologists, including William Boyd Dawkins, who named the site after his friend, William Aveline.

Mesolithic cave art in Aveline's Hole. A series of inscribed crosses can be seen scratched into the rock. Photo © University of Bristol Spelaeological Society.

Several human skeletons and a rich late Palaeolithic (about 10 000 years ago) fauna were found. The cave is also the site of the earliest dated human cemetery in Britain, with interments around 8400 years ago during the Mesolithic period. At the back of the cave, and gated for protection, is a series of Mesolithic inscribed crosses, one of the few known examples of cave art in the UK.

The upper part of Burrington Combe provides an excellent section through the Black Rock Limestone. The scree here is a good place to examine loose blocks of the fossiliferous, dark grey, muddy limestone [33]. Close inspection shows that the limestone is bioclastic with fragments of crinoids, *Spirifer* brachiopods and corals. Fragments of chert occur within the rock. This black, very hard material is similar to flint and is made of silica.

The thin soils developed on the steep slopes here provide a very species-rich limestone grassland habitat. Overall vegetation cover is very sparse, but supports many different lime-loving plants. Perennial herbs and shrubs help to stabilise the loose stony soil, including salad burnet, small scabious, common rock-rose and ploughman's-spikenard. The warm, south-facing slopes of

The main scarp in Burrington Combe, formed of the Black Rock Limestone.

Burrington Combe

The East Twin Brook, flowing off the sandstone uplands of Blackdown.

the combe are particularly important for butterflies and other invertebrates. The combe was virtually devoid of trees and scrub before myxomatosis wiped out much of the rabbit population in the 1950s.

Opposite are the East and West Twin valleys, two parallel tributaries which descend from the northern slopes of Blackdown. A walk up either of these valleys (take care; the stream bed is often overgrown, wet and slippery) will show the transition from the marine Carboniferous Black Rock Limestone through older shallow-water muddy limestones and mudstones (the Avon Group) to the Devonian continental river-deposited Portishead Formation. The sections through the Portishead Formation show beds that range from mudstone and fine-grained sandstone to coarse-grained quartz-dominated conglomerate. The conglomerates are resistant to erosion and form small waterfalls. Occasional thin seams of coal are found in these rocks.

The streams flowing down these valleys sink on reaching the limestone. In the West Twin valley the stream sinks a short distance up from the road [34]. Just upstream, on the west side, is the entrance to Sidcot Swallet [35]. Developed in the Black Rock Limestone, this cave can be explored by cavers for around 250 m through a series of small passages. Another popular cave, Goatchurch Cavern, lies a short distance up the east bank. It is an abandoned former stream sink [36]. Here, two entrances lead into a complex three-dimensional maze descending steeply with the dip of 60° to a depth of 60 m. Several other small phreatic caves formed below the water table can be found nearby. In the valley floor just upstream is a curious stone trough beside the path. This is the outfall for the West Twin Brook Adit. The adit was driven to tap the sandstone aquifer. However, the water yield was much less than hoped and the scheme was a failure. Much of the rock excavated from this adit has been tipped downstream. The East Twin Brook also disappears underground a short distance up from the road, into a prominent cave entrance at East Twin Swallet [37].

Many ferns, mosses and liverworts flourish in the humid sheltered East and West Twin valleys. Here, lady fern, intermediate polypody and hard fern, hairy woodrush and bitter vetch can be found alongside *Dicranum majus* and other

Young caver in Goatchurch Cavern.
© Peter Glanvill.

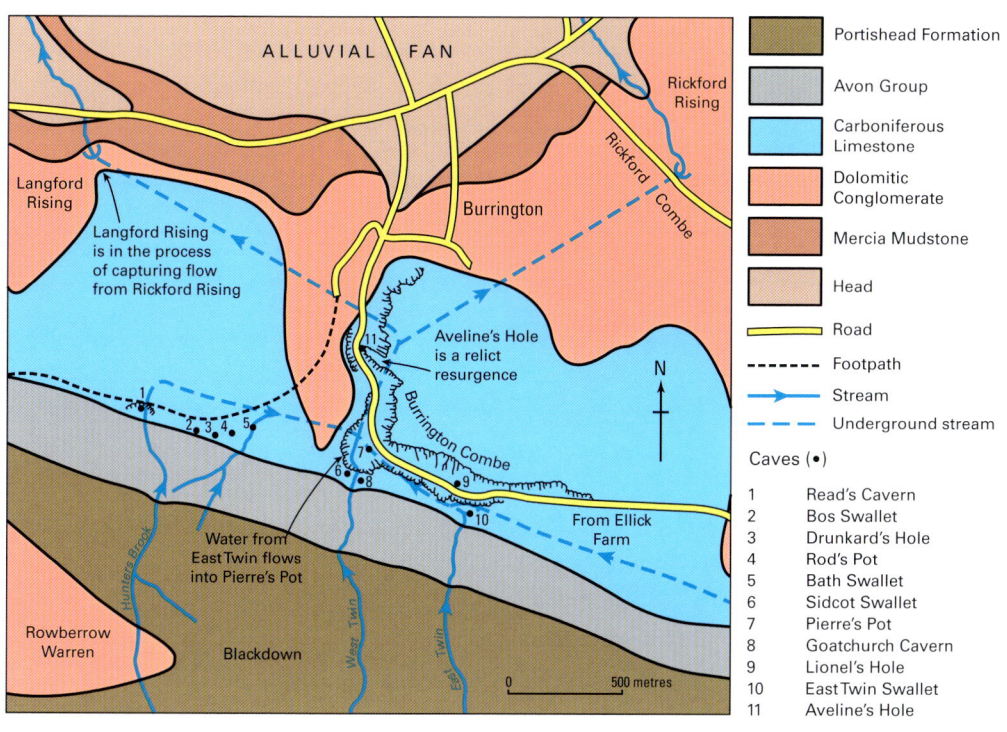

Geological map of the Burrington area showing the caves, springs and postulated underground drainage routes. Adapted from University of Bristol Spelaeological Society Proceedings, 1992.

mosses and liverworts. Many of the caves within the combe support populations of hibernating bats, including both species of horseshoe bat.

To the north of Burrington Combe is Burrington Ham [38]. Here lime-loving plants such as common rock-rose, dogwood and wild privet are abundant and many insects such as grasshoppers inhabit the warmer south-facing slopes. Thin strips of limestone heath are present on leached soils close to the top of the combe. Here, limestone grassland gives way to heath vegetation dominated by western gorse, with bell heather and occasional heather. To the north of the prominent Long Rock [39], which is an outcrop of the

The steep south-facing slope of Burrington Combe, a haven for lime-loving plants.

Burrington Combe

The Clifton Down Limestone locally contains fossil corals such as this example of Lithostrotion, *a colonial coral now extinct.*

Burrington Oolite, there are the remains of Burrington Camp, a small hill fort. The upper slopes of Burrington Ham form a good viewpoint across to Wales and north to the Bristol area, Broadfield Down and the intervening lowlands formed by the softer Mercia Mudstone.

The deep valley north of Burrington Ham is Blagdon Combe [40]. This large sinuous dry valley is incised over 60 m into the hard Triassic Dolomitic Conglomerate, but ends somewhat anomalously — its upper end 'hanging' above Blagdon Lake. Previously thought to be an overflow channel for an ice dammed lake, it is more likely that it was cut by the Congresbury Yeo, which once flowed at a much higher level through here. The river now has eroded a course through the softer rocks in the Vale of Wrington to the north, leaving Blagdon Combe high and dry. At the lower end of the valley is Rickford Rising [41], a large spring issuing from an impenetrable rift in the Dolomitic Conglomerate. This spring, along with that at Langford, drains all the Burrington caves.

The Dolomitic Conglomerate is well exposed in a series of small roadside crags and old quarries on the hillside south of Blagdon, near Street End [42].

At the foot of Burrington Combe extending out into the vale is a large well-developed alluvial fan, clearly marked by the contours and shown as head on the map [43]. This developed at the foot of the gorge, where material washed down the valley was deposited. The fan is made up of Portishead Formation and Carboniferous Limestone debris mixed in with wind-blown sand and slope wash (colluvium). Mapping of the fan surface revealed traces of former channels and lobes associated with deposition during the last glaciation.

Fossil brachiopod Syringothyris, *common in the Black Rock Limestone.*

Lower Carboniferous coral (Palaeosmilia murchisoni).

To the west of Burrington, a track known as The Link leads from the foot of the combe up past Mendip Lodge Wood and towards Dolebury and Rowberrow. The first part of this track is up the axis of an infilled Triassic valley and exposures of the Dolomitic Conglomerate can be seen in places. On reaching the open moorland [44] much of the Black Rock Limestone and Avon Group outcrop is completely masked by material washed down from the slopes of Blackdown. However, the contrast between the sandstone heath and limestone woodland is very distinct. Adjacent to the track lies a series of deep sinkholes, some of which take small streams. Four of these contain small caves. The largest, Rod's Pot [45] is popular with cavers. All the caves descend steeply down the dip before ending in chokes. In one of the depressions, Beaker age pottery (2500–600 BC) and earlier Neolithic implements were found.

At the edge of Rowberrow Forest the Hunter's Brook sinks into Read's Cavern along the contact between the Black Rock Limestone and the Avon Group [46]. Above the sink is a cliff of Black Rock Limestone. This short cave, accessible to cavers, was once used by early Iron Age occupants, and their remains were found during an archaeological dig. As with all the Burrington caves, the water reappears at springs in Rickford and Langford.

View of Burrington Combe from Blackdown, overlooking the Vale of Wrington to the limestone uplands of Broadfield Down.

Shipham and Rowberrow

Aerial view labelled: Dolebury, Rowberrow, Shipham

Nestling in the eroded core of the Blackdown Pericline, Shipham [47] and the neighbouring hamlet of Rowberrow [48] are situated in an area of great scenic and geological diversity within easy distance of much of western Mendip.

The discovery of zinc ore in the 16th century turned the small settlement at Shipham, noted in the Domesday Book, into a major mining centre. Calamine and smithsonite have been worked from the Triassic Dolomitic Conglomerate. These two common ores of zinc occur as thin veins, and galena (lead ore) may also be present.

The calamine mining industry started in England in the 16th century in the reign of Elizabeth I. The main use of calamine was as an alloy, mixed with copper to form brass, but it was also sold to pharmacists for its medicinal properties. Today calamine lotion is still available as a soothing and mild antiseptic lotion for use on irritating skin conditions.

At first calamine was mainly exported, but by the end of the 16th century the brass industry was well established in Britain. By the 18th century the calamine industry was at its height and Mendip calamine was considered to be the best in England. The biggest brass foundries were in nearby Bristol, but Mendip calamine was also transported to others at Birmingham. The ore was now also used to produce metallic zinc (spelter), with William Champion of Bristol being the first to patent the process in 1738. However, by the early 19th century the mining had

A stone wall in Rowberrow made up of grey Carboniferous Limestone, dark red sandstones of the Portishead Formation, and thin slabs of pinkish Triassic Dolomitic Conglomerate.

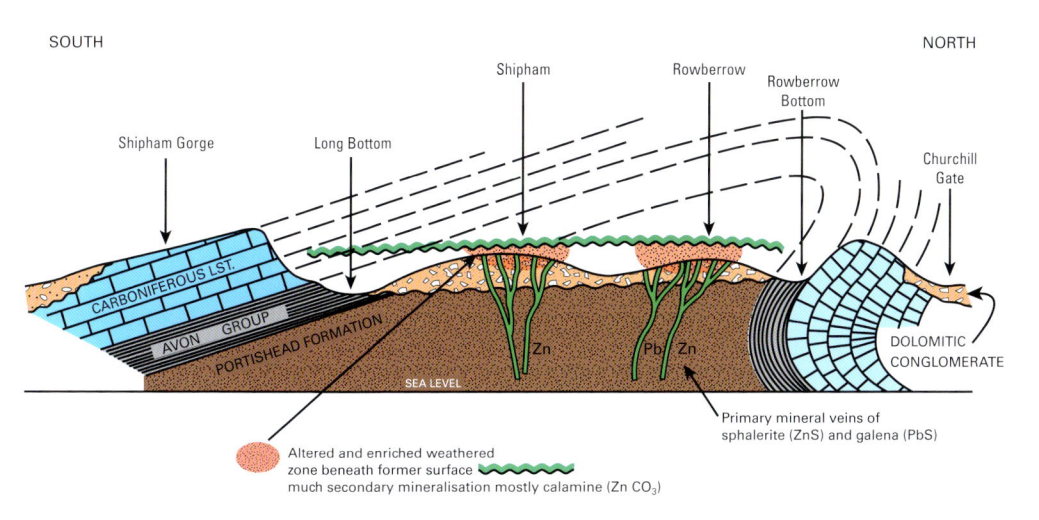

North–south cross-section from Shipham Gorge to Churchill Gate. Mineral veins bearing lead and zinc ore penetrate up though the Portishead Formation and into the Dolomitic Conglomerate. Near-surface weathering has altered and enriched the primary ores into the workable ore deposits exploited by miners in the 17th and 18th centuries.

almost ceased and in 1839 Sir Henry de la Beche (the first director of the British Geological Survey) noted that calamine working on Mendip had been largely discontinued for some time.

Mining gave employment to a large number of people in Shipham and Rowberrow. There were reported to be more than 100 mines around the Shipham area and four calamine ovens were built where the calamine was baked before being powdered and sold on. The last of these remained standing behind Court House until the 1980s. Many buildings sprang up on the common land to the east of the centre of Shipham where the miners laid their claims.

Although mining targeted calamine, galena was also commonly found and extracted for sale. The mines were mainly shallow as the ore formed within small veins in the Dolomitic Conglomerate. This lay close to the surface and extraction took place in numerous small mines and pits. The mines were generally only 30–40 m deep and were usually worked by hand with only the aid of a hand-turned windlass and a bucket. Some Cornish beam engines were employed later on in the deeper workings. The last mine to remain open in

An area of 'gruffy ground', a local name for areas of old mine workings, trial pits, spoil heaps and mine shafts on the south-east side of Shipham.

Shipham and Rowberrow

Rowberrow Bottom.

Shipham was the deepest, and was situated in the centre of the village. When mining in the Shipham area ceased many miners were forced to walk over Blackdown for work in the then thriving Charterhouse mines.

Many people living in Shipham were reliant on mining for income and life could be tough and squalid. The miners of Shipham were notorious for being rough, and it was reported that no constable would arrest them for fear of disappearing down one of the many mine shafts. Hannah More, the well-known philanthropic writer, was appalled by the poverty in the area and in 1790, with the help of William Wilberforce, the well-known social reformer, was instrumental in setting up both a Sunday school and a day school, as well as the first of the 'female clubs' on Mendip.

Shipham is a now a thriving community. However, around the village there is still plenty of evidence to bear testament to its mining history with street names such as Hind Pits, the Miners' Arms Public House and a Miners' Cottage listed along Hollow Road. To the south-east of the village the West Mendip Way passes through an area of gruffy ground [49], a local name which refers to hummocky ground formed by the remains of old mine workings and waste. Hollows where the numerous shafts entered the ground can still be clearly seen here. From this area of gruffy ground on a clear day there is a good view over to Weston-super-Mare and the coast.

Several mines are still accessible to cavers, notably Singing River Mine and Star Mine. The legacy of mining also remains in the form of heavy metal contamination of the soil. Shipham has the highest levels of cadmium in the soil anywhere in the UK. Cadmium is a toxic metal associated with old zinc mine workings. These have been disturbed by recent development and agriculture. Many houses and gardens are on the old mine workings. The health of Shipham residents was extensively investigated in 1979*. Even though the cadmium content of the soil was high, the dietary intake of cadmium by the villagers had no

Rowberrow Bottom. The stream here is flowing on the impermeable sandstones of the Portishead Formation.

*See for details: www.mod.uk/publications/zinc_cadmium/summary.htm

measurable effect on health. As the cadmium in the soil is tightly bound up in minerals, it is not readily available for uptake by plants and hence does not enter the food chain.

To the north of Shipham in Rowberrow [48] the numerous cottages built during the influx of miners have mostly disappeared, although the influence of the miners is still apparent in the hummocky nature of much of the land in the area. The majority of the miners' dwellings were located along what is now School Lane and in the valley known as Rowberrow Bottom.

The upper reaches of this delightful valley [50] are excavated in the relatively impermeable Portishead Formation sandstone. A small stream flows down here, but disappears underground at several points into the Dolomitic Conglomerate near Rowberrow, to emerge at Banwell Risings several days later. From the area around Shipham and Rowberrow a large number of footpaths and cycle ways can be accessed, which lead through Rowberrow Forest and over the sandstone heath of Blackdown to the east, towards Shute Shelve to the south-west and towards Dolebury Warren and Churchill in the north.

South of Shipham is Long Bottom [51]. This straight valley is a good example of differential erosion. Here the softer Avon Group mudstone has been preferentially eroded, leaving the harder Carboniferous Limestone forming a craggy scarp to the south.

Old limekiln, Rowberrow Bottom.

South flank: Crook Peak

Aerial view labelled: Sidcot, Callow Rock Quarry, Shute Shelve, Axbridge.

Parking is available along the road at the foot of Crook Peak, at King's Wood [421 560], in Cross and at the foot of Shute Shelve Hill [423 548]. Public toilets and refreshments are available in Winscombe and Axbridge.

This area comprises the southern flank of the Mendips from Crook Peak [52] in the west to Shipham Perch in the east. Wavering Down [53] and Axbridge Hill [54] form one of two ridges that encompass the Lox Yeo Valley, which occupies the eroded sandstone core of the Blackdown Pericline. Both ridges are made of Carboniferous Limestone that forms the limbs of the pericline. Wavering Down and Axbridge Hill are on the southern limb, and the limestone can be seen dipping gently to the south at many localities. The northern side of the ridge forms a steep scarp. To the north, Winscombe Drove and Barton Drove run along the outcrop of the softer Avon Group mudstone, which forms a small col or bench. Winterhead Hill and Church Knoll are small hills developed in the underlying Portishead Formation.

Outcrops of Mercia Mudstone and Dolomitic Conglomerate in the Lox Yeo valley (for example the roadside section on Church Road in Winscombe [55]) show that the core of the Blackdown Pericline was already eroded by Triassic times, and then subsequently infilled. The southern side of the limestone ridge is indented by several small valleys, many of which follow the lines of earlier Triassic valleys. Modern erosion has preferentially removed the softer Triassic rocks effectively recreating the Triassic landscape.

View from Crook Peak, looking east. The peak is a crag of dipping Burrington Oolite limestone.

and Axbridge

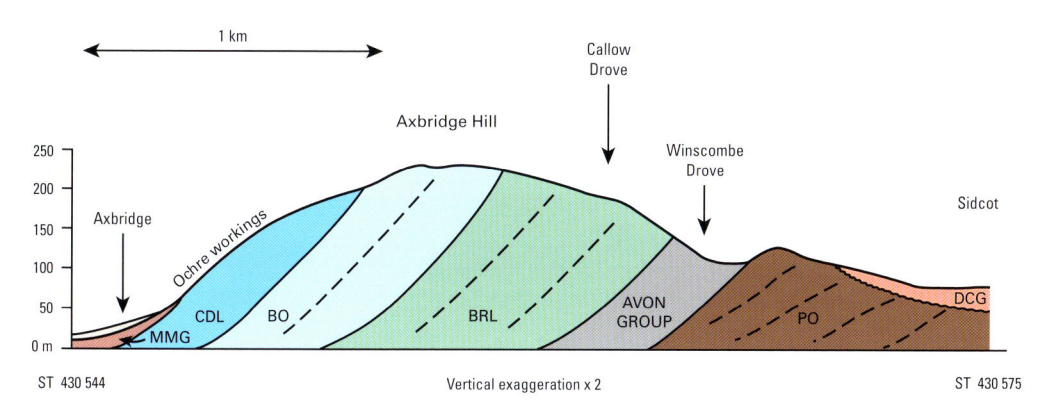

Cross-section across Axbridge Hill. For abbreviations see map key.

Much of the area is owned by the National Trust and is open access. The ridge is covered in limestone grassland with excellent views across the Somerset Levels and along the southern flank of the Mendips. In contrast, King's Wood, Rose Wood and Cheddar Wood are superb woodland habitats developed on the Carboniferous Limestone. There are several localities where the underlying bedrock can be seen in more detail. On the north side of Crook Peak is a small disused quarry [56] that admirably displays the southerly dipping, fossiliferous Black Rock Limestone. The vertical western face is aligned along a major joint or fracture.

Good exposures of the lower part of the Black Rock Limestone can also be seen in the southern approach cutting to the Shute Shelve railway tunnel [57], part of the Winscombe–Cheddar Railway Walk. The tunnel was on the line from Yatton to Cheddar, which opened in 1869. The northern half of the tunnel is in the older, softer Avon Group mudstone, which has necessitated lining part of the tunnel. The northern cutting is in red Triassic rocks overlying the mudstone. The line was finally closed on 10th June 1963 and the track lifted in October 1964.

Shute Shelve railway tunnel, a good exposure of the Black Rock Limestone on the cycle track between Axbridge and Winscombe.

The crags at the top of Crook Peak [52] are formed in the younger, gently dipping, pale grey Burrington Oolite, here with some crinoid debris. The same strata can be seen in the small disused quarries at the foot of the ridge south of Compton Bishop.

At Cross, a disused quarry [58] provides an excellent place to examine the lower part of the Clifton Down Limestone. The oolitic limestone is clearly exposed on a series of south-dipping bedding planes, and is fossiliferous in places.

South flank: Crook Peak

Fragments of yellow and red ochre, once dug from many small pits and mines on Axbridge Hill.

The cutting at the western end of the Axbridge bypass **[59]** also shows part of the Clifton Down Limestone. The hillside above is dotted with numerous ochre pits, which were worked as late as the 1920s. When the mines were active, a tramway was constructed from Axbridge railway station up to an ochre pit **[60]** [427 555], which is still accessible. Here, the ochre infilled a large water-worn rift, possibly of Triassic age, cut into the Burrington Oolite. The walls are pockmarked by dissolution. Fragments of yellow and red ochre, which consists of various iron oxide minerals including limonite, goethite and hematite can be found scattered around the area. Other ochre workings exist along the south flank of Axbridge Hill and in Cheddar Wood, one of which had a steel cableway linking it to the station.

One of the many small pits hidden within Rose Wood is the entrance to Shute Shelve Cavern **[61]** [424 554]. Discovered in 1994 by local cavers, the small entrance opens up into a large relict phreatic passage up to 20 m wide. Part of the cave had been entered by the miners and it could be the 'Lost Cave of Axbridge' rumoured to exist on the hill. Close by are the remains of an old miners' hut, and the entrance shaft of Carcass Cave. The nationally rare greater and lesser horseshoe bats roost within the caves and old mines in the area.

The south-facing slopes of Axbridge Hill and Wavering Down are superb wildlife habitats. Immature calcareous soils are dominant on many of the steeper slopes, and a rich limestone flora has developed. On parts of Crook Peak and Shute Shelve Hill, sparse, low-growing vegetation is exceptionally rich in places, and supports a number of rarities including honewort, Somerset hair-grass, Cheddar pink and several rare lichens.

Many small ferns and plants such as these love the thin rocky calcareous soils developed on the Carboniferous Limestone. © Sharon Pilkington.

Rock bluffs and limestone screes support a distinctive assemblage of species, including slender bedstraw, sea stork's-bill which is rare so far inland, dwarf mouse-ear and rusty-back, wall rue and maidenhair spleenwort ferns. Saxicolous (rock-dwelling) lichens, particularly *Cladonia* and bryophytes are very diverse on the bare rock and the thin soils associated with rock outcrops. The combination of rich vegetation and warm, south-facing aspect is highly attractive to butterflies.

and Axbridge

In some areas, for example near the summit of Crook Peak and on the upper parts of Wavering Down, acidic loessic soils occur, which support dwarf-shrub heath with bracken, western gorse, heather and bell heather. Locally, a good mixture of scrub is present with gorse, hawthorn, blackthorn, roses, elder and hazel.

King's Wood [62] is an ancient woodland with a documented history reaching back to the 13th century. It is mostly semi-natural in character, and supports a very rich flora and fauna. Ash standards dominate, along with pedunculate oak, and small-leaved lime, the latter being especially abundant as standards and pollards near the old boundary banks. Limestone boulder scree is also common in the upper parts of the wood, and this is covered by dense growths of mosses. King's Wood also supports a number of notable epiphytic lichens and fungi.

Large vertical kilns at Callow Rock, Cheddar. © National Stone Centre.

Farther east, the summit of Callow Hill is dominated by Callow Rock Quarry. [63]. Named after the prominent crags of limestone on the skyline, this active quarry, covering 43 hectares is excavated in the chemically pure Burrington Oolite. This is used in the adjacent concrete block works, which supplies mainly a local market.

During construction of the block-works plant [64] the remnants of a sediment-filled cave were found. The sediment contained many rounded fragments of an unusual yellow-brown fossiliferous limestone. Ammonites from this rock indicate an Early Jurassic age. The nearest outcrop of rocks this age occur 4 km to the south-west at a much lower elevation and is unlikely to be the source area. Instead, the limestone probably came from outcrops which once infilled the Lox Yeo valley. This limestone has now been completely eroded away and no trace remains. The gravel was probably washed into the cave by a stream which once drained the Shipham area.

Several old quarries occur in Shipham Gorge. Although inaccessible, the lower of these at The Perch can be viewed from the road [65]. It shows a section through the Burrington Oolite. The prominent red gash at the top of the quarry is a rift that was eroded along a small fault and infilled with a red breccia of angular limestone blocks. At the foot of the hill, Axbridge [66] is sited on a broad spread of stony clay known as 'head', washed off the slopes north of the village.

Shipham Perch Quarry. A small quarry in the Burrington Oolite, with a prominent red-stained fault breccia exposed at the top of the quarry.

North flank: Banwell

Limited parking is available at Dolebury [446 587].

'Bristol Diamonds', quartz crystals lining a geode or 'potato stone'.

The northern flank of Mendip between Banwell [67] and Dolebury [68] is dominated by the narrow broken ridge of Carboniferous Limestone running the length of Banwell and Sandford Hill. This forms the steeply dipping northern limb of the Blackdown Pericline. The southern limb, formed by the Wavering Down ridge, can be seen two kilometres away on the other side of the Lox Yeo Valley.

This ridge is actually an exhumed Triassic feature. During the Triassic period, the Mendips were a steep rugged mountain range. A deep valley was excavated from Rowberrow Warren westwards through Winscombe and out to Loxton, leaving the western end of the Blackdown Pericline looking rather like a hollow tooth. This valley was subsequently infilled with scree and material washed down from the higher ground. This was then cemented to form the Dolomitic Conglomerate. Over time, the ridge was buried under the Mercia Mudstone. Only in the last couple of million years has erosion stripped away the softer Triassic rocks to reveal the hard limestone beneath, in effect exhuming the former Triassic landscape.

The climate during the Triassic was very arid. Salt lakes were present in places and these dried out to leave halite and gypsum nodules behind. Over time these nodules were dissolved away, and replaced with quartz to create geodes known locally as potato stones. These are present in the Mercia Mudstone around Sandford. Pockets of iron ore and ochre are also found in the Triassic rocks and the underlying Carboniferous Limestone. Evidence for old ochre workings can be seen on the northern flank of Sandford Hill [69]. The footpath here passes many small pits, spoil heaps, old trenches and adits. Specimens of ochre and quartz crystals, or 'Bristol Diamonds' can be found on the old spoil heaps.

Near the dry-ski slope is the entrance to Sandford Levvy [70]. This 600 m-long adit was driven in 1830 by miners seeking lead but failed to find any significant ore. Higher up the hillside is the entrance to Mangle Hole, a series of shafts which intercepts the underground river feeding the springs in Banwell.

At the western end of Banwell Hill, located in the grounds of a large private house are two caves, Banwell Bone Cave and Banwell Stalactite Cave [71], which have a fascinating history stretching back to the last glacial period. Miners broke into Banwell Stalactite Cave in 1757, but the entrance collapsed and the cave was largely forgotten about. In an attempt to reopen the Stalactite Cave to visitors, the local vicar, the Rev. Francis Randolph, employed two miners to find the cave. This they did but, in September 1824, they also inadvertently broke into the Bone Cave. There they found a large chamber almost filled with sediment and containing many thousands of bones. The fauna, dating from the early part of the last glaciation about 80 000 years ago, includes many cold-climate species such as bison, reindeer, wolf, brown bear, wolverine and

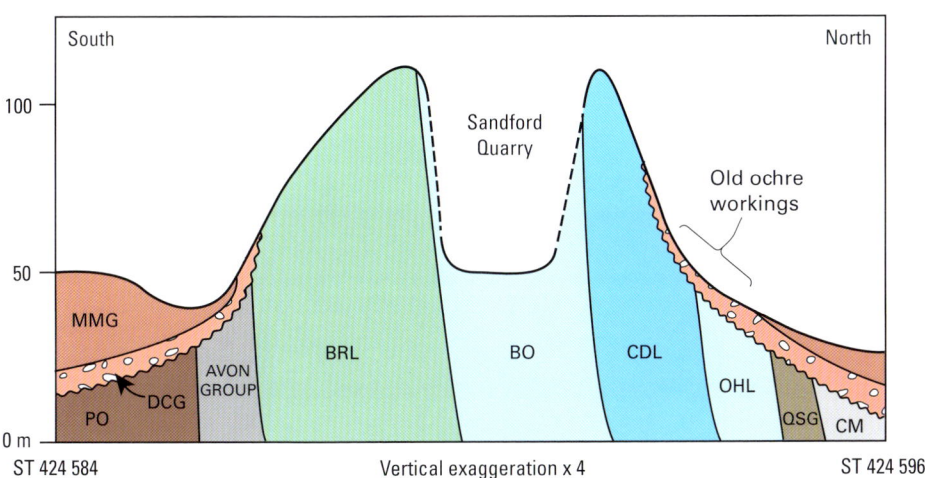

Stacked bones in Banwell Bone Cave. © John Chapman.

Cross-section of Sandford Hill. For abbreviations see map key.

North flank: Banwell

Steeply dipping limestone, Sandford Quarry.

arctic fox. The caves quickly became famous as a tourist attraction. The Bishop of Bath and Wells, George Henry Law, who owned the land, took the bones as wonderful evidence for Noah's Flood. With the help of William Beard who managed the caves, he subsequently built the Banwell Tower to remind visitors of the follies of the pagan world! Both caves are on private land but are occasionally open to the public.

At the eastern end of Sandford Hill is the disused Sandford Quarry [72]. In 1884, the quarry was a few small pits on the south side of the hill. By 1931, the quarry had expanded considerably into the western side of the hill and was connected to the Cheddar Valley Railway. The quarry was closed in the 1990s as part of an arrangement to extend Whatley Quarry near Frome and parts of the site are now used for climbing and abseiling. Like many other quarries on Mendip, it is developed primarily in the Burrington Oolite, a very pure limestone. The rock here dips to the north at over 70°, giving rise to very steeply sloping bedding plane slabs on the south side of the quarry.

At the east end of Sandford Hill, the Carboniferous Limestone is well exposed in an old quarry adjacent to the A38 at Churchill Rocks [73]. The graffiti-covered slabs of thickly bedded limestone belong to the Burrington Oolite Formation. On closer inspection, it will be apparent

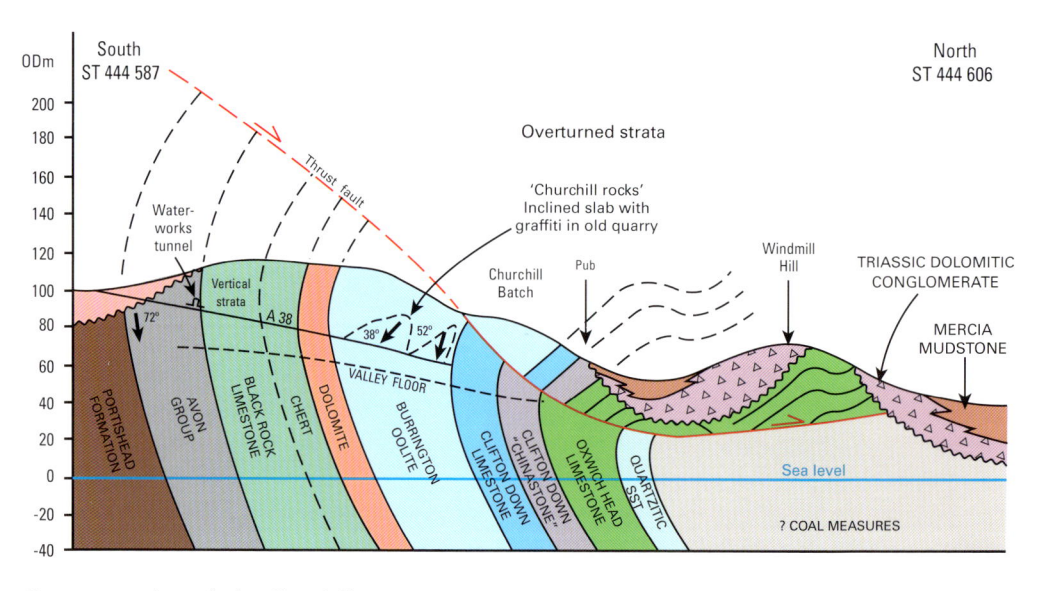

Cross-section through the Churchill nappe.

that the rock appears to dip to the south at about 50°, while elsewhere along the northern side of Mendip, the limestone dips steeply to the north. The reason for this anomaly is that here the limestone has been so severely folded that it has been overturned, and the bedding plane slab visible is actually the underside of a bed of rock. A fold in which one side is overturned is known as a nappe.

The transition from overturned rock to vertically bedded and then upright, northerly dipping strata can be seen in the cliffs along the A38 between here and the Shipham turnoff. At the mouth of Bristol Water's tunnel opposite the Rowberrow turning, the bedding is vertical, while on the bend it dips about 70° to the north.

To the east of Churchill lies Dolebury Warren [68], which is dominated by the Iron Age hill fort and has also been used as a medieval rabbit warren, from which it takes its name. The ridge is formed from steeply north-dipping Carboniferous Limestone of the Black Rock Limestone and the Burrington Oolite formations. Fragments of the fossiliferous Black Rock Limestone Formation can be seen in the scree on the steep southern slopes, whilst good specimens of the pale grey Burrington Oolite can be seen in the northern ramparts of Dolebury Fort.

Overturned strata, Churchill rocks.

The nature reserve at Dolebury Warren is owned by the National Trust and managed by the Avon Wildlife Trust. This is an area of contrasting flower-rich limestone grassland and heathland. Early purple, bee and pyramidal orchids thrive in the grassland. The heathland is developed on loess, a sandy silty soil derived from wind-blown glacial silt that was probably deposited here during the last glaciation. This creates an acid soil, favouring bell heather and bilberry. Butterflies and insects are plentiful, especially on south-facing slopes where the conditions tend to be warmer.

There is easy access to Dolebury Warren via footpaths from all directions. From the top there are clear views over the Bristol Channel, and it was probably the good vantage point that influenced the building of the hill fort here.

View across Dolebury Warren, towards Blackdown.

The Priddy area

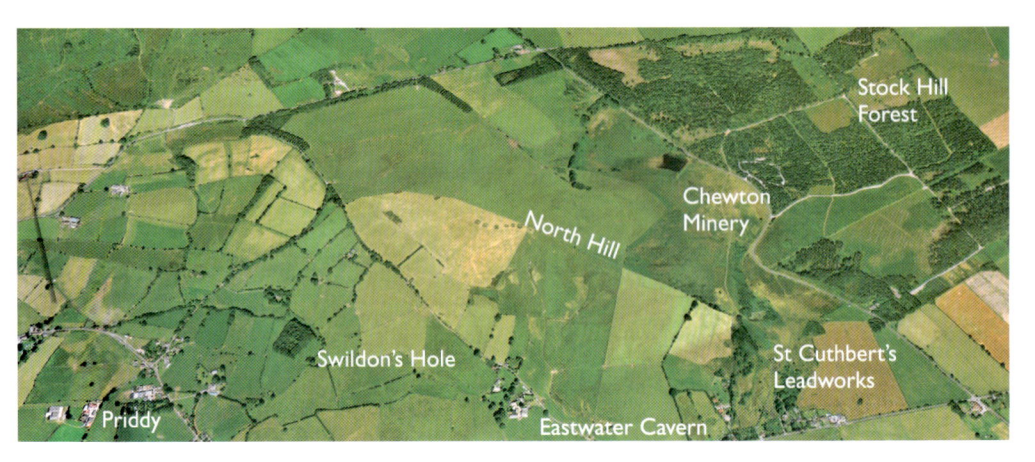

Parking is available on Priddy Green and at Stock Hill Forest [549 513].

Priddy [74] is located in the heart of the Mendip Plateau and is a good base for exploring the central part of the Mendips. Several major cave systems occur here, and the area is very popular with cavers. The village is focused around the green, the site of the famous Priddy Sheep Fair which has been held here every year since 1348. Legend has it that the Priddy Fair will return each year so long as the symbolic thatched hurdle stack remains standing on the village green.

Much of Priddy village is on the Black Rock Limestone, which has been used in many of the buildings and drystone walls in the area. The rocks dip gently to the south here at about 25°. The overlying Burrington Oolite occurs just south of the village, but it is poorly

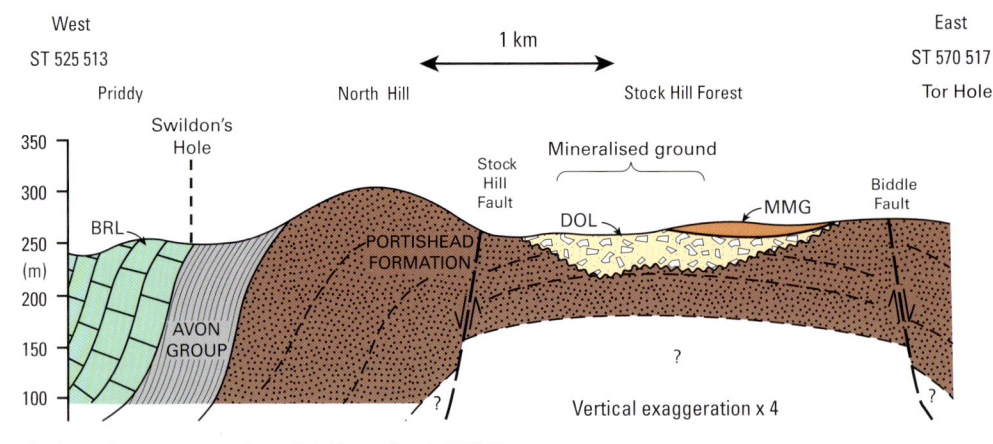

Geological cross-section from Priddy to Stock Hill Forest.

exposed. The Avon Group mudstone outcrops between the village and North Hill [76]. There are very few exposures, but the outcrop is generally marked by a shallow valley or damp marshy ground.

North-east of Priddy is North Hill, at 305 m, one of the highest points on Mendip. On a clear day, most of central Mendip can be seen from this point. Like Blackdown and Pen Hill, this hill is formed from the more resistant Portishead Formation exposed in the core of the North Hill Pericline, rising above the generally flat Mendip plateau. Fragments of the coarse sandstone can be seen scattered over the summit. The sandstone is drained by surface streams, but these sink underground on reaching the surrounding limestone. The largest stream sinks into Swildon's Hole [77]. At 9.4 km in length, it is the longest cave on Mendip. First descended in 1901, it is also one of the earliest systematically explored caves in Britain.

Folding in the Black Rock Limestone, Swildon's Hole.

From the entrance, experienced cavers can follow the stream down to a water-filled section, Sump One, almost under Priddy church. This sump was the location in 1934 for a pioneering diving attempt using a home-made respirator (now on display in the Wells and Mendip Museum). From here the stream turns along the strike through eleven more sumps, passing under Priddy Green. The farthest point yet reached lies 170 m below the Queen Victoria pub, east of Priddy Green. Above the streamway lies a complex series of interconnected passages now abandoned by the stream. The water reappears at Wookey Hole.

To the east are two other swallet caves, Eastwater Swallet is located at the end of a classic small blind valley [78]. St Cuthbert's Swallet [79] is the second longest cave on Mendip at nearly 7 km, and certainly the most complex. Below the entrance, several streams enter a series of chambers and passages, before entering a sump 140 m lower.

The Priddy area was an important lead mining area from Roman times right up to the beginning of the 20th century. The ore, principally galena, was won from veins in the Triassic Dolomitic Conglomerate in what is now Stock Hill Forest [75]. The Dolomitic Conglomerate infills a deep valley that was cut into the Portishead Formation during Triassic times. Good examples of the red conglomerate can be seen in the dry-stone walls alongside the road between the Miners' Arms and the Hunters' Lodge Inn. Numerous closed depressions pock-mark the area. Many of these are pits related to lead mining in the area, but some are natural, and formed where the ground has subsided into dissolution cavities in the limestone-rich conglomerate.

The remains of the lead workings with spoil heaps, pits, leats and reservoirs are still clearly visible in the valley between North Hill [76] and Stock Hill Forest [75]. The orefield in this area was divided

The Priddy area

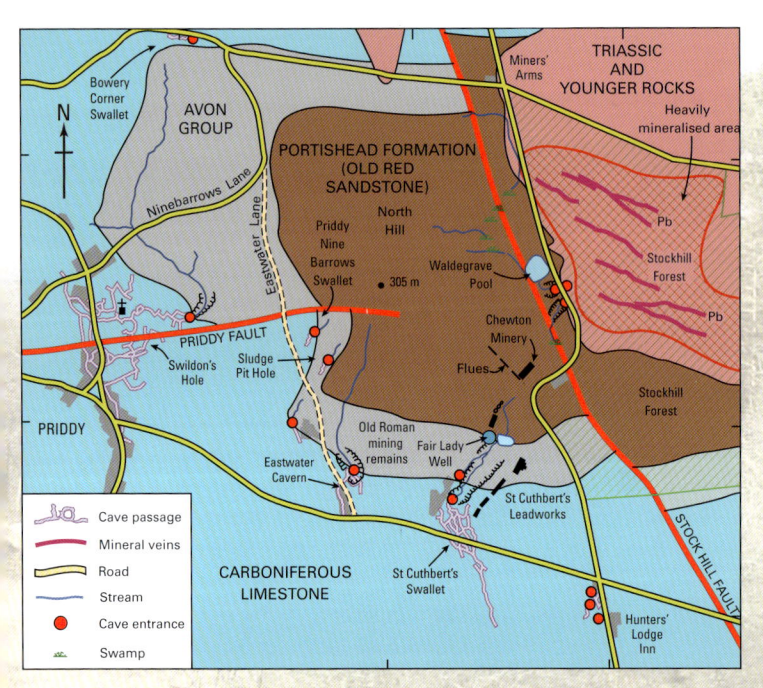

Map of cave systems, mines and veins.

between two of the four mining ownerships known as 'liberties', either side of the parish boundary. The St Cuthbert's Lead Works (part of the Priddy Minery) operated by the Bishop of Bath and Wells, lies at the southern end of the valley **[80]** close to the Priddy to Hunters' Lodge Inn road. Farther north, the remains of the Waldegrave Lead Works (part of the Chewton Minery) **[81]**, owned by the Waldegrave Family, can be seen near Waldegrave Pool.

In 1860, the owners of Wookey Hole Paper Mill, concerned about pollution of their water supply, traced the water from St Cuthbert's Swallet to Wookey Hole using 'Vanadium Red' dye, having first had several unsuccessful attempts using chaff and even ink. This provided the basis for a successful lawsuit in 1863 against the St Cuthbert's Leadworks for polluting the stream. This has since been confirmed by dye tracing, the water flowing to Wookey Hole in about eight hours.

In 1862, five furnaces, employing about 40 men, were erected at the St Cuthbert's Lead Works to smelt the old lead-rich slag left over from earlier mining. The plant closed in 1869, but reopened in 1875 when it became more profitable to 'dress' the slag and sell it to lead smelters in Bristol. The site was bought by Mr Theobold in 1890 but, despite investment by him and a new syndicate in 1897, fluctuations in the price of lead caused the works to shut on several occasions, finally closing in May 1908. The Chewton mines are first mentioned in 1541 though they had probably been in existence before then. The medieval works were never really profitable until Cornish miners, notably Nicholas Ennor, introduced new technology in the mid 18th century and started resmelting the old lead-rich spoil, known locally as 'slimes'. However, the requirement for water led to disputes with the owners of the neighbouring Priddy Minery. The works were never very successful and, in 1881, the smelter was abandoned and the lead-rich slimes sold to a smelter in Bristol. However, by 1883 this venture failed and the works were finally abandoned.

Much of the remains visible today are the legacy of Victorian miners resmelting the lead-rich waste from previous mining operations. Remnants of the smelting plants, with their distinctive stone flues can be seen.

The Priddy and Chewton Mineries are now a Nature Reserve, known as 'Priddy Mineries', managed by the Somerset Wildlife Trust. The biodiversity and habitats of the mineries reflects the past history of lead mining in the area. Valley

Waldegrave Pool.

mire, open water, wetland habitats and lead-rich spoil heaps are all present, and the site supports a very wide range of flora and fauna. Valley mire is a very uncommon habitat in the Mendip Hills and here it is especially important for its rich wetland flora, supporting good populations of all three British newts, many different species of dragonfly, as well as frogs and toads. Common lizard and adder are often seen. Greater tussock sedge, purple moor-grass, bog asphodel, cross-leaved heath, hare's-tail cotton-grass, which is rare on Mendip, and several species of sphagnum moss occur here.

Bare mining spoil and dams are high in lead and other heavy metals, and this generally deters vegetation growth. The rare alpine penny-cress and spring sandwort, another regionally rare plant that thrives on lead-rich soil, are early pioneers of bare slag, occurring alongside sea campion, which is rare so far inland in Somerset. Elsewhere the loose slag is stabilised by rafts of mosses and lichens, including the diminutive and very rare moss *Ditrichum plumbicola*, which is restricted to lead mine spoil. Other spoil heaps in the valley bottom have been colonised by a neutral grassland that is moderately diverse. Cowslip, yellow-rattle and lady's bedstraw can all be found. Lady fern, with its characteristic shuttlecock profile, also occurs, one of only a few species of fern that can tolerate metalliferous soils.

Lead mining also took place north of Priddy, now part of the Yoxter Rifle Range [82]. The rectilinear pattern of the mineral veins, marked by small pits, can be clearly seen in air photographs, but public access is not permitted on the range.

St Cuthbert's Lead Works, in the Priddy Minery, c. 1903. Courtesy John Cornwell collection.

South flank: Draycott

Draycott Sleights

Rodney Stoke

Draycott

Parking is available at Deer Leap [519 492] and in many of the villages along the A371.

The southern flank of Mendip between Cheddar and Wells forms an imposing scarp when viewed from the south. Much of the southern facing slope is part of the wildlife rich 'Mendip Scarp Prime Biodiversity Area'.

The southern margin of the Mendip plateau comprises several stacked 'sheets' of Carboniferous Limestone which have been thrust up over each other like a pack of cards along two major thrust faults. These are the 'South-western Overthrust' and the 'Ebbor Thrust Fault'. Although the faults cannot be seen, their presence can be inferred from the juxtaposition of older rocks overlying younger rocks.

Syncline

Draycott Sleights reserve, with dipping Burrington Oolite. © Sharon Pilkington.

Much of the lower slopes between Cheddar and Wells are underlain by a drape of Triassic Dolomitic Conglomerate, which partially buries the Carboniferous Limestone. Known locally as 'Draycott Marble', the Dolomitic Conglomerate is composed of cemented fragments of Carboniferous Limestone deposited as scree and slope deposits on the flanks of a rugged mountain range more than 200 million years ago. To the south, away from the Mendips, the coarse conglomerates become finer and grade into the fine-grained Mercia Mudstone.

and Westbury

The Dolomitic Conglomerate was quarried for building stone at several places in Draycott and Westbury-sub-Mendip, where good exposures can be examined along Old Ditch Lane [83]. It can be seen to great effect in the many stone-built houses, walls and gateposts in the villages between Cheddar and Wells. Excellent examples of polished 'Draycott Marble' can be seen on the steps of St Peter's Church in Draycott [84]. Draycott stone was also used by Brunel in the construction of Temple Meads railway station in Bristol.

The hill above Draycott is known as Draycott Sleights [85]. On Mendip, 'sleight' means sheep-pasture, and this site has been managed by traditional sheep-grazing for centuries. Now a nature reserve, Draycott Sleights occupies a steep south-west-facing scarp slope overlooking the Somerset Levels. Its principal habitats are herb-rich limestone grassland with scattered scrub, rocky limestone crags, small cliffs and rock exposures.

Draycott Marble Quarry. Courtesy J Hanwell collection.

The Draycott Sleights Reserve offers a glimpse of the underlying geology. At the entrance to the reserve [86] outcrops of gently dipping, coarse-grained, red Dolomitic Conglomerate are well exposed in crags in the field to the east of the lane. Rounded fragments of limestone up to 30 cm across are set in a finer matrix of red silt. Some fragments have been dissolved out giving the rock a curious hollow appearance. On the west side of the road, a shallow quarry exposes the Carboniferous Burrington Oolite. Here, the bedding planes are well exposed and close inspection of the limestone will show the small round carbonate 'ooliths' from which the rock is composed. The rock here dips to the south at 20°–25°. In the reserve a short distance farther west, the same rock unit can be seen dipping east [87]. The rocks between the two outcrops have been folded into a small down-fold or syncline. Dolomitic Conglomerate underlies the southern, lower slopes of the reserve, and gives rise to very red soil. The calcareous soil supports a wide range of lime-loving herbs, sedges and grasses. On the slopes the most abundant grasses and sedges include upright brome, crested hair-grass, and glaucous sedge. The grassland is rich in herbs, supporting squinancywort, yellow-rattle, kidney vetch and many other typical species. Orchids that might be seen in summer include pyramidal orchid and greater butterfly orchid.

Bluebells in Stoke Wood.
© Sharon Pilkington.

The northern part of Draycott Sleights supports a slightly different calcareous grassland community, which is dominated

South flank: Draycott

Kidney vetch. © English Nature.

by sheep's-fescue and meadow oat-grass. Many different, low-growing herbs are also present, including the uncommon green-winged orchid in spring. In summer, many different herbs attract butterflies and other invertebrates. Blue butterflies are especially notable, and include the local adonis blue and silver-studded blue. The reserve also has a good snail fauna including the rock-boring dark-lipped banded snail *(Cepaea nemoralis)* and *Helicella itala.*

Farther south-east, the hillside above Rodney Stoke is composed mainly of Dolomitic Conglomerate with a few small patches of Carboniferous Limestone poking through. Rodney Stoke National Nature Reserve encompasses broad-leaved woodland, scrub and limestone grassland. Accessible only along the footpath, the woods here are a good example of a typical Mendip ash wood **[88]**. Originally managed as coppice the woods are mostly ancient in origin, but were almost entirely clear-felled in the 1914–18 war. Wild service-tree is locally distributed in the wood. Many typical ancient woodland species thrive here, while numerous ferns, bryophytes, fungi, mosses and liverworts flourish in the humid environment.

Hyena, which once roamed across Mendip.

and Westbury

Cave bear tooth from Westbury-sub-Mendip.

Farther south-east, there is a lovely view across the Somerset Levels from the top of the hill above Westbury-sub-Mendip. From here, the small Carboniferous Limestone inliers of Nyland Hill and Lodge Hill stand proud of the Somerset Levels. These represent eroded remnants of another thrust sheet of Carboniferous Limestone just appearing through the cover of younger Triassic and Jurassic rocks.

Just below the summit is Westbury Quarry [89]. Although quarrying has ceased, the site is still operational. In 1969, blasting here exposed a massive sediment-filled cave, at least 70 m long and 30 m high, developed in the Clifton Down Limestone. Within the sediment, well-preserved faunal remains were found, attributed to a Middle Pleistocene interglacial about 620 000 years ago. Between 1976 and 1984 the site was excavated by the Natural History Museum. The upper parts of the deposit yielded abundant small mammal bones and in places remains of the extinct cave bear *Ursus deningeri,* suggesting that the cave was used as a bear den and an owl roost at different times. The lower part of the sediment fill is thought to be at least 780 000 years old. Much of the deposit is now grassed over.

On the plateau behind Westbury Quarry the road crosses what appears to be a dry valley at Brimble Pit [90]. In fact, this is a large shallow closed basin formed by dissolution of the limestone. A belt of twelve such basins extends along

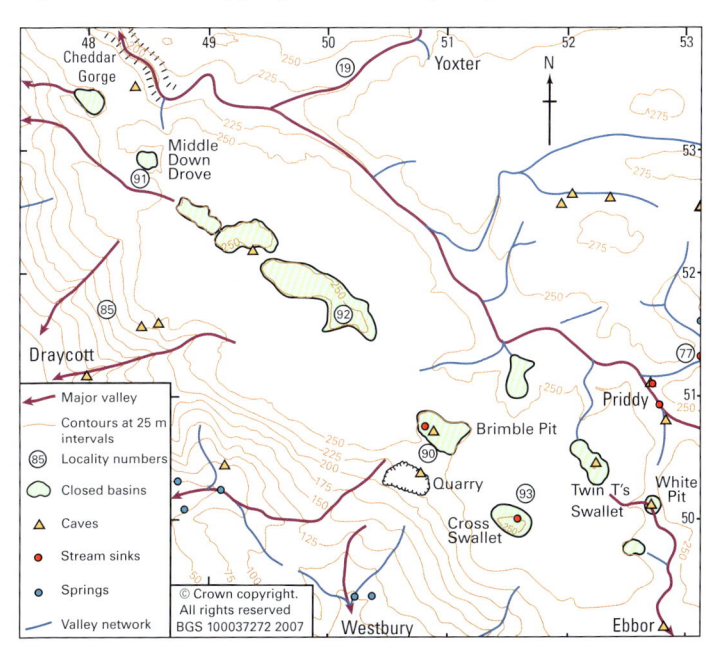

Topographical map of closed depressions.

South flank: Draycott

Cross Swallet, a large closed basin near Westbury-sub-Mendip.

the southern rim of the Mendip plateau from Cheddar Gorge to Ebbor Gorge. Brimble Pit is one of the largest of the chain. During the last glaciation underground drainage was impeded by permafrost and these depressions became lakes. Their floors are covered with a fine reddish-brown wind-blown silt, or loess, deposited here during the last glaciation. The floor of this particular basin is pockmarked by nine small sinkholes where the loess has subsided into cavities in the underlying limestone. Many of these had been infilled by farmers, but have since been cleaned out by the present landowner.

Three kilometres to the north-west the Somerset Wildlife Trust's Middledown Reserve [91] is centered on another of these closed basins. The former lake bed is floored with loess, up to 10 m thick and pockmarked by two very large sinkholes. The loessic silt supports an old hay meadow, while the thin limestone soils around the basin sustain a flower-rich grassland with wild thyme, salad burnet and fairy flax. Two other closed basins can be seen: the road from Draycott to Cheddar Head crosses one at Bristol Plain Farm [92], the other, Cross Swallet, can be seen from the Priddy–Westbury footpath [93].

Two kilometres south-east of Brimble Pit are the Deer Leap and Ramspit nature reserves [94]. The car park here provides some of the best views across Somerset stretching east from the Cretaceous Upper Greensand scarp on the Wiltshire border across the low Jurassic Polden Hills to the Blackdown Hills, and west across to the Devonian uplands of Exmoor and Quantock. Glastonbury Tor, formed of Middle Jurassic limestone and sandstone, can be seen rising ethereally from the Somerset Levels.

The geology here is quite unusual, being one of the few places on western Mendip where upper Carboniferous rocks are found. The Carboniferous Limestone, which dips to the south at about 25°–30°, is overlain by the upper Carboniferous Quartzitic Sandstone Formation and the Coal Measures (mostly sandstone and shale). A small sliver of wet boggy ground 200 m south-west of the car park marks the outcrop.

and Westbury

However, most of the Coal Measures is cut out by the Ebbor Thrust, which runs through the reserve. Along this fault, the Black Rock Limestone has been thrust over the top of the younger sandstone. Here, the small stream sinks underground into the limestone where it crosses the thrust fault [95]. The unimproved calcareous and neutral grassland and semi-natural woodland is a rich wildlife habitat. The West Mendip Way runs through the area linking Ebbor Gorge, a short distance to the west, to Cheddar via Priddy and Draycott.

Mendip archaeology

The Mendip Hills are host to many archaeological sites, many of which are underground in caves. The earliest at Westbury-sub-Mendip, was once a cave-bear lair and dates back over 600 000 years. It was later used as an owl roost whose droppings contained small mammal bones. At Banwell, the Bone Cave acted as a pitfall trap into which many ice age animals fell including mammoth, woolly rhino and bison around 75 000 years ago.

Some caves were occupied by humans during the late Upper Palaeolithic (10 000–8500 BC), including Gough's Cave in Cheddar, while during the Mesolithic (9000–4000 BC) Aveline's Hole in Burrington was used as a cemetery. Caves were also used during Neolithic (4000–2000 BC) and Bronze Age (2000–650 BC) times. There are even examples of cave art in Gough's Cave and Aveline's Hole.

As well as its caves, other archaeological sites including long barrows, henges, standing stones, round barrows and Iron-Age hill forts can be found. The Priddy Circles are good examples of Neolithic henges, while over 300 Bronze Age round barrows (or *tumuli*) can be found scattered throughout the region. These were used for burials and were often arranged in linear cemeteries such as Priddy Nine Barrows on North Hill.

Iron Age (650 BC–60 AD) settlements and hill forts occur at Dolebury, Burrington and Maesbury near Shepton Mallet. The Romans left their mark with roads, villas and forts, especially around the former lead mining areas. More recent archaeological sites include a Saxon palace at Cheddar, King John's Hunting Lodge in Axbridge, the extensive 18th and 19th century mining remains at Shipham, Charterhouse, Priddy and elsewhere, and a Second World War bombing decoy on Blackdown.

Remains at Banwell Bone Cave. © J Chapman.

Wookey Hole and

Parking is available at both Wookey Hole and Ebbor Gorge.

The River Axe emerges from its journey underground at the mouth of Wookey Hole.

Wookey Hole and Ebbor Gorge are two geological gems nestling under the southern flank of the Mendip Hills, three kilometres north-west of Wells. Wookey Hole, **[96]** now a show cave, has inspired visitors for centuries. The cave is the source of the River Axe and the legend of the 'Witch of Wookey'. Visitors enter the cave by a passage now abandoned by the river and descend to meet the underground Axe in the 'Witch's Kitchen' containing the stalagmite effigy of the 'Witch of Wookey'. Her actual bones are on display in the Wells and Mendip Museum. Beyond, the show cave enters a splendid series of rift chambers developed along prominent joints, to enter Cathedral Chamber (Chamber Nine). The subterranean Axe can be followed upstream by cave-divers through a series of sumps to the current limit of exploration at Wookey 25. Here the water rises up from a deep sump which has been pushed to a British depth record of 90 m (about 30 m below sea level!). Exploration continues.

The cave is unusual in that it is developed mostly in the Triassic Dolomitic Conglomerate, unlike most caves which are developed in the Carboniferous Limestone. The conglomerate is particularly well exposed in the exit tunnel.

The gorge downstream of the cave is unlike many other gorges on Mendip in that there are no feeder valleys. Instead the ravine is probably a product of cliff retreat and cavern collapse. Several small caves here have yielded important archaeological finds, which can be seen in Wookey Hole Caves Museum. Hyena Den has been used

Ebbor Gorge

Wookey Chamber Nine. This large chamber is the furthest point in the show cave. The lake is the underground River Axe.

both by Palaeolithic man and as a hyena den. The caves also support an important roost of greater horseshoe bats.

The River Axe drains much of central Mendip, including most of the caves in the Priddy area. The connection was proven in 1860 when the owners of Wookey Hole Paper Mill successfully traced the water from St Cuthbert's Swallet *(see Priddy Chapter)* to Wookey Hole, using 'Vanadium Red' dye, after several unsuccessful attempts using chaff and even ink!

A short distance to the north-west is Ebbor Gorge, a National Nature Reserve with both geological and wildlife importance. The car park [ST 520 484] **[97]** offers a superb view across the Somerset Levels to Glastonbury Tor, a prominent 'outlier' of Jurassic rocks.

From the car park a footpath descends down into the valley. The prominent line of cliffs here marks the line of the Ebbor Thrust Fault. Here a slice of the Burrington Oolite has been thrust up over the younger Quartzitic Sandstone and the Coal Measures. The impermeable upper Carboniferous sandstone and shale crop out in the valley floor, **[98]** which explains why there is a small stream flowing here.

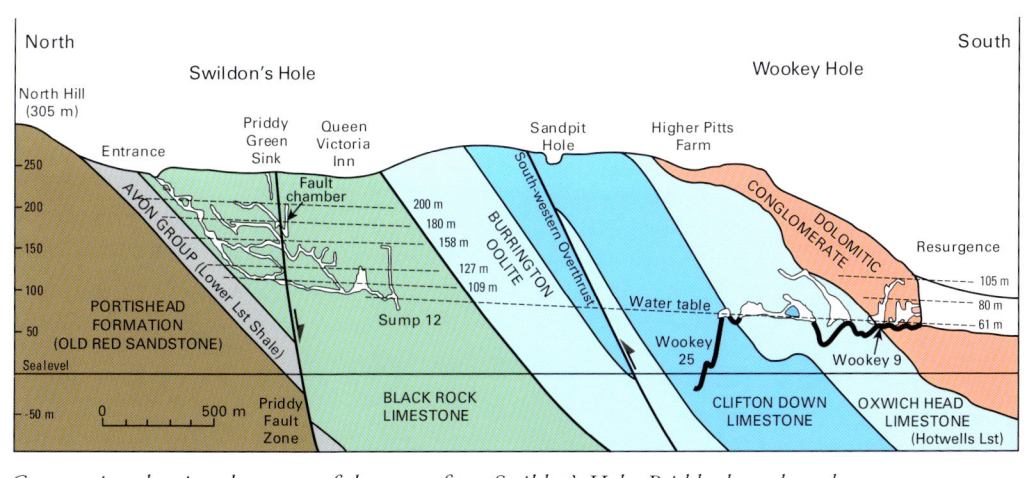

Cross-section showing the course of the water from Swildon's Hole, Priddy through to the resurgence at Wookey Hole, with former water tables shown.

Wookey Hole and

Ebbor Gorge. This rocky ravine is a National Nature Reserve owned by the National Trust. The reserve supports a wide variety of flora and fauna.

Ebbor Gorge itself **[99]** is incised into the Carboniferous Clifton Down Limestone. This spectacular ravine was formed by summer melt water run-off during cold phases in the Quaternary, when underground drainage was prevented by permafrost. The narrowest part of the gorge (known as 'The Narrows') forms a prominent 'knick point'; the remnants of a well-preserved former waterfall and plunge pool are evident here. This waterfall is a consequence of valley rejuvenation during the Quaternary cold periods. Each successive phase of valley incision is graded to a new lower base level as a consequence of regional lowering to the south. This creates a series of knick points, which gradually migrate up the valley as erosion proceeds. The steep scree slopes are relics from frost shattering during the last cold period which ended 10 000 years ago.

Ebbor Gorge is a largely wooded nature reserve with way-marked footpaths. Ancient ash woodland, now regenerated after clear-felling during the First World War, dominates the steep rocky limestone slopes. The ground flora is very rich, with many ancient woodland species, and includes yellow archangel, dog's-mercury, wild anemone and bluebell. On the wetter sandstone at the bottom of the gorge, opposite-leaved golden saxifrage is abundant, with enchanter's-nightshade, moschatel and wood sedge.

Butterflies are abundant at Ebbor Gorge, and the site supports some rare species, including white-letter hairstreak and high brown fritillary. Many others are found on the rich limestone grassland.

Cliffs, scree and bluffs in the gorge itself are home to many ferns, lower plants, lichens and fungi, which are favoured by the sheltered, very humid microclimate. More than 150 lichen species have been recorded, in rich communities on the limestone outcrops and older trees, and the gorge also supports more than 100 species of moss and liverwort, including several rarities. Greater horseshoe bats use the gorge as a roosting site.

At the top of Ebbor Gorge is Higher Pitts Farm, the site of an old iron mine in the 1890s **[100]**. The iron ore was mined from the Dolomitic

Ebbor Gorge

Conglomerate. The iron is associated with a unique assemblage of rare secondary lead, copper and manganese minerals. These minerals, mendipite, chloroxiphite and diaboleite, are rare or unknown outside the Mendip area. Little is left to see on the surface, most of the pits having being filled in and the former spoil tips leveled.

The area between Wookey Hole and Wells has some fascinating geology. Here, the Triassic and Jurassic rocks lap onto the southern flank of the Mendip Hills, forming a distinctive bench around Milton. The best place to see these rocks is Milton Lane, just off the Old Bristol Road at [548 472] **[101]**. This track provides the best section through the top Triassic and basal Jurassic rocks in the area, from the terrestrial red Triassic Mercia Mudstone and Dolomitic Conglomerate, up into the interbedded creamy limestone and mudstone of the Penarth Group and the basal Jurassic. At the lower end of the cutting, a small fault juxtaposes the red marl with the limestone beds. Fossils including bivalves, crinoids and the ammonite *Caloceras* can be found in the limestone bands. This transition can also be identified in a couple of other tracks around Milton and Walcombe.

Further up the track is a small stream sink **[102]**. Here, a stream draining off the Lower Jurassic Charmouth Mudstone sinks into the underlying limestone. However, the water must flow into and through the Carboniferous Limestone at depth to reach the resurgence at St Andrew's Risings in Wells.

To the south, Milton Hill is bisected by the aptly named Split Rock Quarry. **[103]**. Popular with abseilers, the western side of this quarry is cut along a major joint-face, stained red with the iron mineral haematite. The larger quarry nearby is no longer active, but quarrying in 1935 intercepted a vertical fissure which was destroyed by 1938. This fissure contained remains of hippopotamus and straight-tusked elephant dating back to the Ipswichian interglacial 120 000 years ago. The remains are in the Wells and Mendip Museum.

Toothwort forming a tall flowering spike rising above the woodland floor.
© *Sharon Pilkington.*

The Milton Lane section. The track here exposes a section of the basal Jurassic strata, here consisting of interbedded limestone and mudstone.

Wells

The area is well served by public transport and ample parking is available in Wells.

The city of Wells nestles at the foot of Pen Hill, one of the four periclines that form the backbone of Mendip. The area has a good range of geological interest and a superb cathedral that acts as a showcase for local building stone.

Wells is named after the springs that rise here. It is the smallest city in England, and is dominated by its cathedral [104]. The building of the present-day cathedral was started in the 12th century using mostly local stone and is an excellent place to examine the local geology!

The west front is composed of the beautiful yellow 'Doulting Stone'. This rock, part of the Middle Jurassic Inferior Oolite, was quarried from Doulting Quarry about 10 km to the east, near Shepton Mallet *(see eastern Mendip guide)*. Close inspection shows that it is a shelly oolitic limestone, with crinoid ossicles and trace fossils of burrows. When first quarried, it is a brownish colour, but this gradually develops to a cream colour. Much of the cathedral, including the nave, has been built with this stone, although tufa was used for the vaults because of its lightweight porous nature. Tufa is a very light rock formed of calcium carbonate deposited by lime-rich springs and streams, and probably came from Chilton Polden.

Later in the 12th century, local Chilcote Stone was used as a replacement when the Doulting quarries were under the control of Glastonbury Abbey and unavailable. This calcareous conglomerate, from the littoral (near-shore) Lower Jurassic Lias Group sediments, was obtained from small quarries between West Horrington and Shepton Mallet, and can be seen in walls around Horrington [105]. The Chilcote Stone forms a prominent topographic bench, best viewed from the A39 [106], between here and Shepton Mallet where it is known as the Downside Stone

South of the west front, the west wall of the west cloister is formed of rubble blocks of the Triassic Dolomitic Conglomerate. On close examination these can be seen to be composed of angular limestone chips in a red sand matrix. Known locally as Draycott Marble, this rock has often been used as a building stone locally and can be seen in many of the houses and churches in the area. This rock underlies part of the city and can be seen outcropping in Milton Lane, just north of the A39 relief road [107].

The Jurassic Blue Lias Formation has been used extensively for paving and tombstones. This greyish blue rock, which contains scattered bivalve shells can be split easily and is often used for flagstones, but suffers from frost heaving. Dark reddish brown Carboniferous Pennant Sandstone slabs have also been used for paving and in some of the gravestones.

Wells Cathedral from the east side. The large ponds in the foreground are the St Andrews Risings, a large karst spring draining the hills to the east of Wells.

The grey columns, on the west front are of 'Kilkenny Marble'. Marble is a term used by quarrymen for any rock that can be worked and takes a polish. This 'marble' is actually a fine-grained Carboniferous limestone, which can easily be worked to produce the columns. These columns, shipped in from Ireland in 1872, replaced earlier columns made from the local Jurassic Blue Lias limestone, which weathers easily and had to be replaced.

Inside the cathedral, the Jurassic Great Oolite Limestone, a golden-yellow oolitic limestone, was used for fine carved work such as the font and the pulpit. This oolite is better known as Bath Stone, and was also used during the Anglo-Saxon period. The tombstones have been made from a variety of materials including local red Dolomitic Conglomerate and fine-grained grey Purbeck Marble that is crowded with freshwater bivalve shells.

One of the well-loved features of Wells is the conduit on the corner of the Market Place [108] from which water flows down the High Street in stone gutters made from the Blue Lias Formation limestone. This conduit dates from 1799 and is fed from the Scotland Spring,

View of the cathedral and Glastonbury Tor.

Wells

The Wells and Mendip Museum, which houses many exhibits showing the geology, archaeology and natural history of the Mendip Hills.

one of the group of springs that form St Andrews Risings in the Bishop's Palace gardens [109]. Four other springs rise up in the floor of the ornamental lake. Dye tracing proves that all these springs are fed by a single underground conduit in the underlying Carboniferous Limestone, which bursts up through the overlying Triassic strata. These springs are fed by stream sinks on the slopes of Beacon Hill to the north-east of Wells.

Adjacent to the cathedral on Cathedral Green is the Wells and Mendip Museum [110]. Founded in 1893, it houses a fine collection of local rocks, fossils and minerals and even an Elizabethan mining map of Mendip. It is a good starting point to learn about the geology of the region. The museum's founder, Herbert Balch (1869–1958), held a lifelong interest in the geomorphology and history of Mendip. He was a pioneering caver and amateur archaeologist, and was responsible for opening up two of the largest cave systems on Mendip, Eastwater Cavern and Swildon's Hole. In his honour, the museum hosts the Balch Room, which displays some of the many bones found by him in the caves and also artifacts from early human inhabitation of the Mendips. The museum also includes a history of cave diving and has many other local displays.

To the north of Wells, a small outcrop of Carboniferous Limestone at Stoberry Park is entirely surrounded by Triassic strata. The unconformity between these two rock units can be seen in a field just west of the A39 [111]. Close by, hidden behind undergrowth is the entrance to Stoberry Tunnel, where the Clifton Down Limestone can be seen. The same rock outcrops in a series of small quarries 300 m to the south-east. The largest quarry is now a private garden [112] — an unusual use for an old quarry.

The Clifton Down Limestone on Tor Hill contains fossil stromatolites, a type of algal structure today only found in hypersaline lagoons.

A short distance east of Wells is Tor Hill. This elongate promontory of Carboniferous Clifton Down Limestone is flanked on each side by Triassic Dolomitic Conglomerate. Many small pits on the northern side [113] expose these rocks. A small quarry on top of the hill [114] provides a small but significant outcrop of the fossiliferous Clifton Down Limestone. Examination of the loose blocks here will yield large *Productus* brachiopods and *Lithostrotion* corals. Algal stromatolites can

Dulcote Quarry, [117] near Wells. Here the Carboniferous Limestone strata have been so severely folded the rocks are vertical or even overturned.

also be found in the area. The rocks dip to the north here, but just a short distance away to the south, outcrops of limestone in the track [115] dip to the south. This marks the axis of the Tor Hill Anticline, which can be seen in the adjacent quarry (now a privately owned concrete works). The contact between the Carboniferous and Triassic strata can be seen in the cutting at the entrance to the concrete works [116].

South-east of Wells at Dulcote [117], a working quarry exposes the lower part of the Carboniferous Clifton Down Limestone Formation in a steeply dipping sequence overlain by the Burrington Oolite Subgroup. The limestones are locally fossiliferous and include *Lithostrotion* corals and crinoid debris. Here, the rocks are vertical or even overturned; spectacular testament to the enormous geological forces operating at the end of the Carboniferous. The same formation outcrops in the cutting on the A371, 150 m to the north-west.

The quarry has been operational for about 100 years and supplies aggregate for the local construction market. Around the quarry and unconformably overlying the Carboniferous Limestone are beds of the Triassic Mercia Mudstone and Dolomitic Conglomerate. Now mostly worked out, concretionary nodules and geodes known locally as 'potato stones' or 'Bristol Diamonds' occurred within the mudstones. These are composed mainly of quartz with secondary calcite and dolomite filling; other iron and manganese oxide minerals also occur.

Dulcote Quarry used to be the source of Dulcote geodes, formed by the replacement of anhydrite nodules by quartz. © David Roche Geoconsulting.

North flank: Harptree

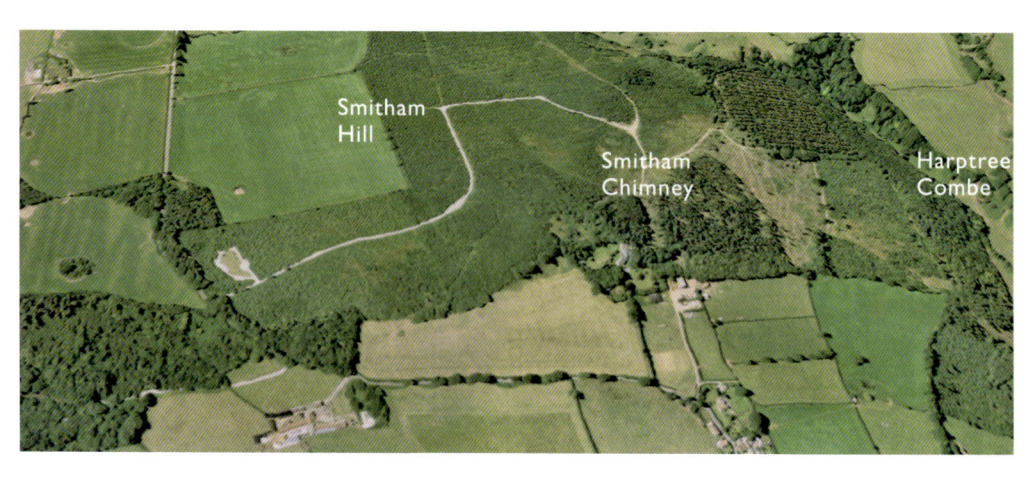

Parking is available at Harptree Woods [557 541].

The picturesque villages of East and West Harptree are located at the base of the northern side of Mendip. Between the two villages lies Harptree Combe, a narrow gorge designated a Site of Special Scientific Interest (SSSI), which is easily accessible along footpaths from either village. Harptree Combe [**118**] is incised into the Triassic Dolomitic Conglomerate. This rock, made up of cobbles of Carboniferous limestone and sandstone, was deposited at the mouth of a deep Triassic valley, which can be traced back westwards to Long Wood near Charterhouse. There are many good exposures where the rock can be examined. The rounded nature of the cobbles show that they had been transported some distance before they were incorporated within the conglomerate. To the north, the Dolomitic Conglomerate becomes thinner and passes laterally into the fine-grained Mercia Mudstone, deposited farther out into the basin to the north of the Mendips.

Locally, manganese and zinc were mined from veins in the conglomerate, and there are signs of the old mine workings within the gorge. The large metal pipe running across the combe is part of Bristol Water's 16 km long 'line of works'. Completed in 1847, this is a series of aqueducts and tunnels feeding water from springs around Chewton Mendip to the Barrow Gurney reservoirs.

Several distinct wildlife habitats occur within the gorge including old ash woodland, rough grassland, marshy grassland, and rocky crags. The ash woodland is very rich in woody species, and interesting ground flora plants include dog's-mercury, herb Paris, meadow saffron and yellow archangel. In the upper reaches of the combe, pedunculate oak

This aqueduct, part of the Bristol Water's 'line of works' takes water from springs around Chewton Mendip to the water treatment plants at Barrow Gurney.

and Smitham Hill

The drystone walls on Smitham Hill contain large blocks of silicified Harptree Beds chert, with many lichens and small ferns thriving on the lime mortar.

replaces ash as the dominant tree, with old hazel coppice and drifts of bluebells in the spring. The walls of the aqueduct and bare rock faces are home to many different mosses and ferns, some of which are rare in southern England.

The top end of Harptree Combe leads up onto Smitham Hill [119] and East Harptree Woods. This is an area of Forestry Commission woodland, planted on an area of heathland. The heath is developed on the Harptree Beds. These rocks, of Triassic and Lower Jurassic age, are formed of chert (a rock similar to flint). The rock has been formed by replacement of the Lower Jurassic limestone and sandstone with silica (quartz). This rock is relatively impermeable and gives rise to a very boggy acidic soil.

Smitham Hill, as its name suggests, was also an important lead and zinc mining area. On top of the hill is the Smitham Chimney [120], the last old lead smelting chimney still standing on Mendip. The chimney was built in 1867 by a group of Cornish engineers, who, as at Charterhouse, came to revitalise the old worked out lead mines and to re-smelt the old slag heaps. They set up the East Harptree Lead Works Company in 1867, but the venture closed in 1875. The earthworks of the mine buildings, the furnace, flues and reservoirs can still be seen, but all the other buildings were demolished in 1876 except the chimney. This fell into disrepair but was restored by the Mendip Society in the early 1970s.

The most extensive lead workings were around Gibbets Brow [121] on the Compton Martin–Castle of Comfort road. The lead occurs mainly as veins of galena in the Carboniferous Limestone known as rakes. These were worked at the surface, creating the pockmarked gruffy ground. In about 1674 lead miners broke into Lamb Leer Cavern, containing one of the largest chambers on Mendip. Between here and the Miners' Arms, several large sinkholes occur. These have been formed by the dissolution of Carboniferous Limestone at depth, followed by collapse and subsidence of the cover rocks. Several fine examples occur south of Eaker Hill and can be seen from the road between the Castle of Comfort and Lamb Leer. The largest is the Devil's Punch-Bowl, south of Swallet Farm [122], an impressive depression over 50 m in diameter and almost 20 m deep.

Smitham Chimney, the last remaining lead-smelting chimney on Mendip, restored in the 1970s by the Mendip Society.

Geological glossary

Alluvial fan — A fan-shaped deposit of material deposited at the mouth of a gorge or valley where it emerges onto less steeply sloping terrain.

Anticline — A type of fold, where the rocks are folded upwards into an arch.

Bed — A layer of sedimentary rock. Beds can vary in thickness from a few millimetres to many metres.

Breccia — A sedimentary rock made up of angular fragments of rock in a finer-grained matrix. Similar to cemented scree.

Calcite (calcium carbonate) — A mineral made of calcium, carbon and oxygen — $CaCO_3$; the main component of limestone and marble.

Conglomerate — A sedimentary rock made up of rounded cobbles and boulders of rock in a finer-grained matrix.

Crinoid — A fossil sea lily made up of small ossicles or plates of calcium carbonate. These plates are the major constituent of crinoidal limestone.

Cross-bedding — A feature of sedimentary rocks deposited by flowing water or strong tidal currents, where the sediment is lain down in sloping laminae.

Cryoturbation — Disturbance to the soil caused by repeated freezing and thawing, typically under periglacial conditions.

Diagenesis — A term used to describe the process of how sediment is transformed into rock.

Dolomite — A mineral made of calcium, magnesium, carbon and oxygen — $CaMg(CO_3)_2$; also the name given to a rock made up of dolomite.

Galena — Lead sulphide — PbS. A heavy, grey shiny mineral with cubic cleavage. Principal lead ore mined on Mendip.

Gruffy ground — A local term used to describe the uneven ground produced by mining, possibly derived from 'groovy ground'.

Inlier — A term used to describe an area of older rocks surrounded by younger rocks.

Karst — A term used to describe a limestone landscape. Karst features include caves, sinking streams, closed depressions and dry valleys.

Limestone — A sedimentary rock consisting mainly of calcium carbonate grains such as ooliths, shell and coral fragments and lime mud. Often fossiliferous.

Loess	A fine-grained, wind-blown silty soil, often derived from rock flour produced by glaciers.
Oolith/ oolite	A grain of calcium carbonate formed by precipitation of calcium carbonate around a nucleus, much like a pearl. A limestone made of ooliths is known as an oolite.
Outlier	A term used to describe an area of younger rocks surrounded by older rocks.
Pericline	A type of fold, similar to anticline where the rocks are folded upwards, but plunging at each end, forming an elongate structure like an upturned boat.
Periglacial	A term used to describe very cold conditions. Often used to denote the climate or environment close to the edge of an ice sheet.
Phreatic	A term used to describe caves which were formed below the water table.
Rake	A miner's term for a mineral vein.
Scree	A deposit of angular rock fragments at the base of a cliff, often formed by frost shattering during periglacial climates.
Smithsonite	Zinc ore. Zinc carbonate — $ZnCO_3$, also known as calamine.
Sump	Water-filled cave passage, sometimes passable by cave divers.
Swallet	A local term for a stream sink, commonly developed at the contact between the Avon Group and the Black Rock Limestone.
Syncline	A type of fold, where the rocks are folded downwards into a U-shape.
Thrust fault	A fault that is near horizontal or gently dipping, and along which older rocks have been forced over younger rocks.
Unconformity	A term used to describe the surface between two sets of rocks where there is a time gap or a layer of rocks missing. Where the younger rocks are folded at a different angle to those above, this is termed an angular unconformity.
Vadose	A term used to describe caves which were formed above the water table.
Wadi	An Arabic term used to describe an ephemeral water course, only active after storms or during the rainy season.

Useful information

Dipping Burrington Oolite exposed at Black Rock, near Cheddar.

Water conduit, made from the Blue Lias limestone, Wells.

How to get to Mendip

Car: The Mendips are about 25 km southwest of Bristol, approximately an hour's drive via the A38, or the A39. From the M5, take junction 20 and follow the A371 to Banwell, Winscombe, Cheddar and Wells, or the A368 to Churchill, Blagdon and the northern flank of Mendip. The B3134, B3135, and B3371 cross the central Mendip plateau via Burrington Combe and Cheddar Gorge.

Rail: Yatton and Weston-super-Mare are both on the national rail network.

Bus: Wells is a hub for local bus services, with National Express coach services from Newcastle, York, Birmingham, London, London Heathrow Airport and Weymouth. Local buses link Weston-super-Mare and Wells via Cheddar and Winscombe, Wells and Bath, Wells and Bristol, Wells and Wookey Hole. There is also the Chew Valley Explorer Bus between Bristol and Cheddar via Burrington Combe and Charterhouse.

Cycle: The National Cycleway Route 3 crosses the Mendip Hills and links the Bath–Bristol Cycle path to Wells.

Tourist information

The Mendips are a popular tourist destination and there are many facilities for visitors. A huge amount of information is available from the Tourist Information Centres located at:

Cheddar Gorge: The Cliffs, Cheddar, Somerset, BS27 3QE. E-mail: cheddar.tic@sedgemoor.gov.uk Tel: 01934 744071. Fax: 01934 744614.

Frome: The Round Tower, 2 Bridge Street, Frome, Somerset, BA11 1BB. Tel: 01373 467271. Fax: 01373 451733. E-mail: frome.tic@ukonline.co.uk. www.frometouristinfo.co.uk/

Shepton Mallet: 70 High Street, Shepton Mallet, Somerset, BA4 5AS. Tel: 01749 345258. E-mail: sheptonmallet.tic@ukonline.co.uk. www.sheptonmallet-touristinfocentre.co.uk

Wells: Town Hall, Market Place, Wells, Somerset, BA5 2RB. Tel: 01749 672552. E-mail: wells.tic@ukonline.co.uk

Sedgemoor Services: M5 (southbound) (Closed Sat & Sun in the winter months). Tel: 01934 750833, Fax: 01934 750646. E-mail: somersetvisitorcentre@somerset.gov.uk

The Mendip Hills AONB office can provide information on activities within the Mendip Hills AONB. Their office is located in the heart of the Mendips at the Charterhouse Centre, near Blagdon, BS40 7XR, Tel. 01761 462338. Their website has much useful information on the Mendip Hills http://www.mendiphills.org.uk/

Accommodation

Most of the local towns have a variety of hotel, bed and breakfast, hostel and self-catering accommodation. There are also a large number of campsites and caravan sites within easy reach of the Mendip Hills. There is a Youth Hostel in Cheddar. Some local caving clubs also have huts with bunkhouse accommodation.

Details can be obtained from the tourist information sites listed above.

Yellow archangel from the Ebbor Gorge area of west Mendip. © Sharon Pilkington.

Further reading

General

Atthill, R. 1984. *Old Mendip.* Bran's Head Books. ISBN 0 905220 55 2.

Firth, H. 2007. *Mendip from the air. A changing landscape.* The Lavenham Press. ISBN 978 0861 833900.

Hanwell, J D, and Newson, M D. 1970. The great storms and floods of July 1968 on Mendip. *Occasional Publications of the Wessex Cave Club,* 1 (2). ISBN 0 950043 31 1.

Geology and geomorphology

Andrews, P. 1990. *Owls, Caves and Fossils.* Natural History Museum, London. ISBN 978 022602 0372.

Duff, K L, McKirdy, A P, and Harley, M J. 1985. *New sites for old. A students guide to the geology of the East Mendips.* Nature Conservancy Council. ISBN 0 86139 319 8.

Farrant A R, and Smart, P L. 1997. The geomorphic evolution of the Mendip Hills. Chapter in *Proceedings of the Bristol Naturalists' Society,* 55, Special Issue: The Mendips. p. 135–155.

Findlay, D C. 1965. *The soils of the Mendip District of Somerset.* Agricultural Research Council, Memoir of the Soil Survey of Great Britain, England and Wales, Harpenden.

Ford, D C, and Stanton, W I. 1968. The geomorphology of the south-central Mendip Hills. *Proceedings of the Geologists' Association,* Vol. 79, 26–427.

Green, G W, and Welch, F B A. 1965. Geology of the country around Wells and Cheddar. *Memoir of the British Geological Survey.*

Hardy, P. 2002. *The Geology of Somerset.* Ex Libris Press. ISBN 0 948578 42 4.

Savage, R J S (editor). 1977. *Geological Excursions in the Bristol District.* University of Bristol, Bristol. ISBN 0 901239 22 4.

Simms, M J. 1997. The geological history of The Mendip Hills and, their margins. Chapter in *Proceedings of the Bristol Naturalists' Society,* 55, Special Issue: The Mendips. p. 113–114.

Priddy Mineries.

Humps mark the line of a World War II bombing decoy leading up to the summit of Blackdown.

Natural history

Bristol Naturalists' Society. 1997. The Mendips. *Proceedings of the Bristol Naturalists' Society.* Vol. 55.

Green, P R, Green, I P, and Crouch, G A. 1997. *The Atlas Flora of Somerset.* ISBN 0 953132 404.

Lousley, J E. 1969. *Wild flowers of Chalk and Limestone.* Collins. ISBN 1870630548.

Caving

Barrington, N, and Stanton, W I. 1977. *Mendip. The complete caves and a view of the hills.* Cheddar Valley Press, Cheddar. ISBN 0 9501459 2 0.

Farrant, A R. 1999. *Walks around the caves and karst of the Mendip Hills.* Cave Studies Series, British Cave Research Association, London. ISBN 0 900265 21 3.

Irwin, D J, and Jarrett, A R. 1999. *Mendip Underground. A Caver's Guide.* 4th Edition. Castle Cary, Mendip Publishing. ISBN 0 95361 0 303.

Smith, D I (editor). 1975. *Limestones and Caves of the Mendip Hills.* David and Charles, Newton Abbott. ISBN 0 71536 572X.

Waltham, A C, Simms, M J, Farrant, A R, and Goldie, H. 1997. *Karst and Caves of Great Britain: Geological Conservation Review.* Chapman and Hall. ISBN 0 0412 7888608.

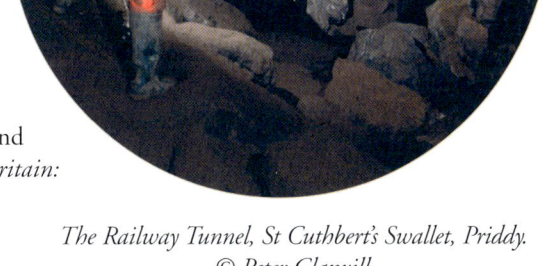

The Railway Tunnel, St Cuthbert's Swallet, Priddy.
© *Peter Glanvill.*

Quarrying and mining

Alabastor, C. 1982. The Minerals of Mendip. *Somerset Mines Research Group,* Vol. 1, No 4.

Gough, J W. 1967. *The Mines of Mendip.* David and Charles.

Raymond, F (editor). 1994. *Mendip Limestone Quarrying — A Conflict of Interest.* Somerset Books. ISBN 0 86183 266 3.

Further reading

Common vetch.
© *Sharon Pilkington.*

Useful websites

The website to accompany this guidebook can be found at: www.mendiphills.com/

British Geological Survey	www.bgs.ac.uk/
Mendip Hills AONB	www.mendiphills.org.uk/
Somerset County Council	www.somerset.gov.uk/
Sedgemoor District Council	www.sedgemoor.gov.uk/
Bath and NE Somerset Council	www.bathnes.gov.uk/
Mendip District Council	www.mendip.gov.uk/
Mendip Society	www.mendipsociety.org.uk/
Wells and Mendip Museum	www.wellsmuseum.org.uk/
Cheddar Caves	www.cheddarcaves.co.uk/
Wookey Hole	www.wookey.co.uk/
Mineral Industry Research Organisation	www.miro.co.uk/
Aggregate Industries	www.aggregate-uk.com/
Somerset Wildlife Trust	www.somersetwildlife.org/
Natural England	www.naturalengland.org.uk
The Mendip Times	www.mendiptimes.co.uk/
Active Mendip	www.activemendip.co.uk/
British Caving Association	www.british-caving.org.uk/

Bee orchid.
© *Sharon Pilkington.*

Acknowledgements

This book and map have been produced by the British Geological Survey (BGS) with funding from the Aggregate Levy Sustainability Fund (ALSF). The authors, designers and cartographers are based at BGS, Keyworth, Nottingham.

We would like to thank those who have contributed text and photographs. Sharon Pilkington and John Knight *(both from Nicholas Pearson Associates)* provided information on the wildlife and biodiversity of Mendip, while Ian Thomas (National Stone Centre) provided data on the aggregates industry. Thanks are due to members of the Mendip Society, the Somerset Geology Group, the local Wildlife Trusts and the Mendip Hills AONB office including Jim Hanwell, Jim Hardcastle, Hugh Prudden, Richard Bull, Sharon Pilkington, Mike Simms, John Chapman and Lin Carter, who kindly read proofs of the book or provided useful comments. Thanks are also due to the late John Cornwell, who provided much information on the industrial archaeology of the region, and who sadly passed away during the production of this guide. Paul Stevenson (Palaeoscene) produced the artwork, and the figures were drawn by Paul Lappage (BGS). The University of Bristol Spelaeological Society is thanked for permission to reproduce figures from their Proceedings.

The book was edited by Audrey Jackson and Joanna Thomas, and designed by Adrian Minks. Photographs were taken by Andy Farrant, Sharon Pilkington, Elaine Burt, Paul Witney, Adrian Minks, John Chapman, Mike Simms and Peter Glanvill. Photographs taken by BGS staff are all in the BGS collection. High quality prints can be obtained from BGS photographic services. BGS photographic materials are © NERC.

Photographs courtesy of the Somerset Geodiversity Audit, (funded by the GAAAQ Somerset MIST Project) were taken by Steve Parkhouse, Clive Nicolas, David Allen, David Roche and Peter Scott, are © David Roche GeoConsulting. The full audits are available from www.somerset.gov.uk/somerset/ete/countryside/geodiversity/

West front, Wells Cathedral.

Dulcote fountain, created in 1861, out of a block of tufa. © M Simms.

Green Lane, Axbridge Hill.

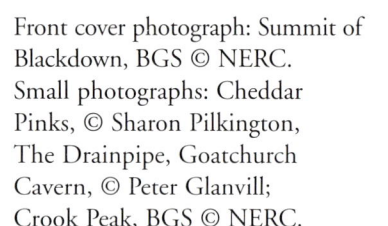

Front cover photograph: Summit of Blackdown, BGS © NERC. Small photographs: Cheddar Pinks, © Sharon Pilkington, The Drainpipe, Goatchurch Cavern, © Peter Glanvill; Crook Peak, BGS © NERC.

Printed in the UK for the British Geological Survey by Halstan & Co Ltd, Amersham, Buckinghamshire.

This guidebook and map has been prepared by the British Geological Survey with funding from the Sustainable Land-Won and Marine Dredged Aggregate Minerals Programme (SAMP) funded through the Department for Environment, Food and Rural Affairs as part of the Aggregate Levy Sustainability Fund (ALSF), administered by the Mineral Industry Research Organisation for The Department of Communities and Local Government.

This publication and references within it to any methodology, process, service, manufacturer, or company do not constitute its endorsement or recommendation by the Department for Environment, Food and Rural Affairs, The Department of Communities and Local Government or the Minerals Industry Research Organisation.

British Geological Survey offices:
Kingsley Dunham Centre, Keyworth,
Nottingham, NG12 5GG
Tel: 0115 936 3100
www.bgs.ac.uk

Murchison House, West Mains Road,
Edinburgh, EH9 3LA
Tel: 0131 667 1000

Maclean Building, Crowmarsh Gifford,
Wallingford, OX10 8BB
Tel: 01491 838800

London Information Office,
Natural History Museum,
Earth Galleries, Exhibition Road,
London, SW7 2DE
Tel: 020 7589 4090

Columbus House, Greenmeadow Spring
Tongwynlais, Cardiff, CF15 7NE
Tel: 029 2052 1962

Geological Survey of Northern Ireland
Colby House, Stranmillis Court,
Belfast, BT9 5BF
Tel: 028 9038 8462

Parent Body
Natural Environment Research Council
Polaris House, North Star Avenue,
Swindon, Wiltshire, SN2 1EU
Tel: 01793 411500